ANTHROPOLOGICAL PAPERS

MUSEUM OF ANTHROPOLOGY, UNIV

NO. 32

I0891797

CONTRIBUTIONS TO MICHIGAN ARCHAEOLOGY

BY

JAMES E. FITTING

JOHN R. HALSEY

H. MARTIN WOBST

ANN ARBOR

THE UNIVERSITY OF MICHIGAN, 1968

© 1968 by the Regents of the University of Michigan
The Museum of Anthropology
All rights reserved

ISBN (print): 978-1-949098-15-0
ISBN (ebook): 978-1-951519-37-7

Browse all of our books at
sites.lsa.umich.edu/archaeology-books.

Order our books from the University of Michigan
Press at www.press.umich.edu.

For permissions, questions, or manuscript queries,
contact Museum publications by email at umma-
pubs@umich.edu or visit the Museum website at
lsa.umich.edu/ummaa.

FOREWORD

THIS volume, as originally conceived, was to have been entitled "Contributions to the Archaeology of the Carolinian-Canadian Edge Area in Central Michigan." In order to simplify, the title was changed to *Contributions to Michigan Archaeology*. It presents several of the longer research reports prepared under a National Science Foundation Project *Archaeological Investigations of the Carolinian-Canadian Edge area in Michigan* (GS-666) under my direction and is complementary to the series of survey reports already published as *Edge Area Archaeology* in Volume 12, Number 4 of *The Michigan Archaeologist*. It is not intended to be a final report on the edge project. It is only a contribution toward that end.

The three papers in this volume were prepared in different ways and from different types of information. The first paper, by Fitting, is a report on the Spring Creek site in Muskegon County, excavated a decade ago by members of the Wright L. Coffinberry Chapter of the Michigan Archaeological Society. It is an attempt to analyze a large artifact sample with less than perfect provenience data. Most of the report is descriptive and only in a few instances can we deal with internal artifact distribution. Even though this material must be presented almost as a surface collection, it does add something to our understanding of a key area in western Michigan at a key time period.

John R. Halsey has prepared an analysis of the Springwells Mound group in southern Michigan for the second section of this volume. With the exception of materials uncovered during our own brief 1965 excavations, Halsey too has had to work with notes and maps prepared by other researchers. Much of his information had to be extracted from nineteenth century sources. He was fortunate in having the collections and notes from the Aboriginal Research Club of Detroit's excavation of the Fort Wayne Mound, which took place over twenty years ago. This more recently excavated comparative material was essential for his interpretation of earlier accounts.

The Springwells Mound group is located to the south of the transition region between the Carolinian and Canadian biotic provinces. It is also a burial site where we would expect to recover little environmental data, but is key to the edge project. In order to understand groups within the transition it is necessary to understand cultural types and adaptations on either site of the transition area.

Wobst was dealing only with his own excavations when he prepared the third report in this volume on the Butterfield site in eastern Michigan. While this was a part of the edge project, he was supported during actual excavation as a National Science Foundation Research Participant (GE-6226) and most of his paper was prepared during the academic year while he received support from that grant.

Wobst has been able to apply techniques of soils and lithic analysis to this site. He has not only prepared a report on a key site for the edge project but, in my opinion, has established a model site report for extracting maximum information from a small amount of excavation.

One of the main features of this volume is that it demonstrates the importance of work by nonprofessional archaeologists in Michigan. Without the dedicated efforts of men like George Davis, Edward Gillis, Carl Holmquist, and Walter Schmidt these papers could not have been written. These are men whose interest in expanding the horizons of Michigan prehistory far outweighs their interest in building bigger collections. We in Michigan are fortunate that they are not unique among the members of the Michigan Archaeological Society.

Most of the specific acknowledgments for this volume are to be found with the individual papers. I should like to make special mention of Mrs. Linda B. Halsey and Mrs. Clara Johnston who did the final editing of this volume. I should also like to express my thanks to Dr. James B. Griffin, Director of the Museum of Anthropology of the University of Michigan, for permitting its publication by that institution.

James E. Fitting

CONTENTS

PART I: THE SPRING CREEK SITE

James E. Fitting

PART II: THE SPRINGWELLS MOUND GROUP

John R. Halsey

PART III: THE BUTTERFIELD SITE

H. Martin Wobst

Part I

THE SPRING CREEK SITE, 20 MU 3, MUSKEGON COUNTY, MICHIGAN

James E. Fitting

I

PREFACE

SPRING CREEK is a site which has played an important part in the understanding of Michigan prehistory for over a decade. Unfortunately, it remained a type of esoteric knowledge, a site known only to those few who had seen the collections. Many people have referred to it but almost nothing has actually been published on it. When the edge program was initiated in 1964 it became evident that the Muskegon River Valley in general and the Spring Creek site in particular would play a key role in this project. Mr. Edward V. Gillis and Mr. George W. Davis of Grand Rapids, Michigan, graciously made their collections available to the Great Lakes Division of the University of Michigan Museum of Anthropology for intensive study. The results of this study are presented in the following pages.

We are heavily indebted to Edward V. Gillis and George W. Davis for lending us their collections, photographs and field notes. The Consumers Power Company deserves thanks for allowing excavation on their lands.

There are many people who have assisted in the laboratory work on this site over the past few years. Megan Biesele prepared the section on the faunal remains from the site as an NSF-USEP project under my direction. I was assisted in the analysis of ceramics by Douglas Bridges, Katherine Livingstone and Mary Hrones, all of whom put in more hours with this material than they care to remember. Gary A. Wright assisted in the analysis of chipped-stone materials and was to write part of the section on these objects. Field work in Israel prevented his writing but I have benefited much from an exchange of ideas over the past year. Plates I and II were prepared by George Davis. The rest of the plates were prepared by George Stuber. George Stuber, Jeanne Schilman, and Mehmet Nuri Turyan prepared the figures for publication.

I am indebted to Dr. Richard E. Flanders for his comments on the section on ceramics, which lead to extensive revision. Dr. Charles E. Cleland commented on earlier versions of the chapter on fauna and his own research lead to our understanding of the significance of this material. Dr. James V. Wright gave assistance on the sections on lithic material and social organization. I owe a great intellectual debt to Cleland, Flanders, and Alan McPherron and many of the ideas expressed herein, both acknowledged and unacknowledged, can be traced to them. This present study, like so many others to come out of the University of Michigan Museum of Anthropology in the past few years, was stimulated by Dr. James B. Griffin. We acknowledge his support and criticism.

Financial support for the preparation of this manuscript has come from National Science Foundation-Undergraduate Research Participation grant GE-6226 and from National Science Foundation Research grant GS-666, Archaeological Investigations of the Carolinian-Canadian Edge Area in Central Michigan.

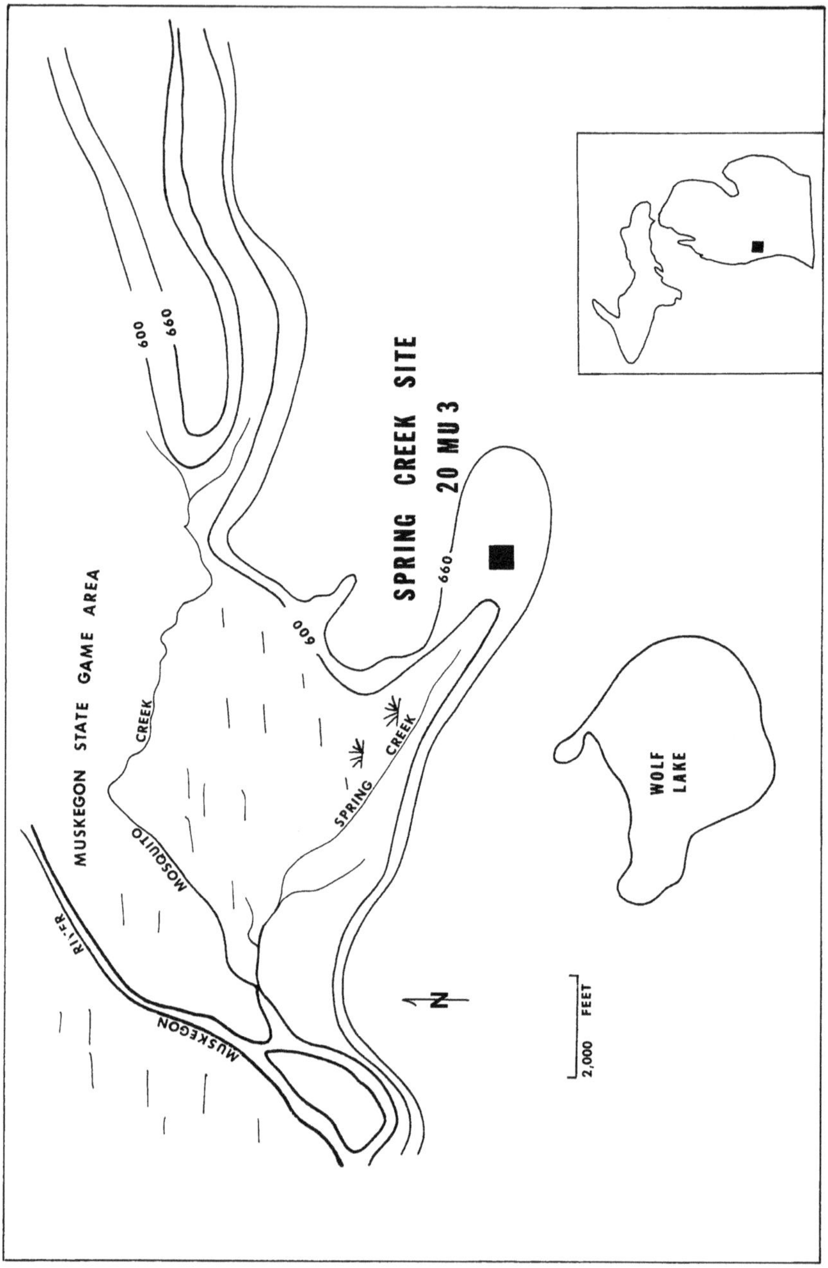

FIG. 1. Location of The Spring Creek Site.

II

INTRODUCTION

The Spring Creek site is the first major village site to be excavated in the important Muskegon River Valley. The Muskegon is one of the principal drainage systems in the state of Michigan. Its basin is 120 miles long and drains over 2600 square miles. This river runs through a series of moraines which break the valley into a series of distinct units. Along with variations in drainage and surface features there are distinct variations in soil type and forest potential (Leestma, 1951:10-41). Prahl (1966) has divided the valley into four major ecological and cultural divisions: an upland area near the headwaters of Houghton and Higgins lakes with poor soil and little prehistoric or historic occupation; a second area of intermediate occupation in Osceola and Mecosta counties; third area of higher cultural and ecological potential in Newaygo County (see Hinsdale, 1932:31 for further discussion of this area) and a final area, which he refers to as Zone 4, the delta region, in Muskegon County itself. The Spring Creek site is located in this delta region.

The Muskegon River for its last 10 miles is bordered by an extensive marshy area with a width of 2 to 4 miles. The river has several channels in this region and several smaller creeks run to the river from the surrounding uplands including Cedar Creek, Spring Creek (Plate I) Mosquito Creek, and the Maple River. The swampy area is below 600 feet above sea level. Bordering the marsh and starting at about the 600-foot contour there is a steep rise of the 680-foot elevation of the uplands.

Around the perimeters of the swamp are stands of cedar. On the higher uplands in places which have not been cleared for agriculture, there are stands of deciduous forest. The small creeks running into the swamp have cut deep ravines; between these ravines are the uplands. The site is located in a clearing on an intermediate terrace with an elevation slightly over 620 feet above sea level overlooking the creek itself (Figure 1).

The Spring Creek site, 20 MU 3, is located in section 9 of Eggleton Township of Muskegon County, Michigan (T 10N, R 15W). The site is owned by Consumers Power Company, a corporation

PLATE I

Spring Creek
(Photograph by George Davis.)

with an interest not only in the commercial and recreational importance of their lands, but in their prehistoric significance as well.

Consumers Power Company gave George W. Davis and Edward V. Gillis of Grand Rapids permission to dig the site. These excavations were carried out on weekends and holidays in 1955 and 1956. The present report deals with artifactual material and notes loaned to the Great Lakes Division of the University of Michigan Museum of Anthropology by Davis and Gillis. Carl Adams, Maxine Atwater, Bob Barrett, Jean Beltrone, Mary Edmonson, Dick Freye, Bertha Freye, Edmund P. Gibson, Verland Mcleod and other members of the Wright L. Coffinberry chapter of the Michigan Archaeological Society also worked at the site. Gillis and Davis alone spent twenty-four days working on the site, many from daylight to sunset, and excavated over 3,000 square feet of the living area.

The site had been known for many years. It was apparently known to W. B. Hinsdale as early as 1925. The site was visited by B. H. Bingham and C. E. Guthe in September of 1931. According to notes in the Great Lakes Division of the University of Michigan Museum of Anthropology they opened several test pits at that time. A number of Muskegon residents were listed as having collections from the site. In 1937 George I. Quimby opened several test pits on the site for the Muskegon Centennial Association (Quimby, 1965:168).

Gillis and Davis prepared a manuscript report on the extent of their excavations for the Consumers Power Company but, in 1959, Gillis (1959:30) noted that the publication of a more comprehensive report would depend upon a complete analysis of the prodigious quantity of specimens gathered and that neither he nor Davis had the time nor laboratory space for preparing such a report. In the fall of 1964, at the suggestion of Gillis and Davis, the collections from the site were brought to Ann Arbor for study by personnel of the Great Lakes Division of the University of Michigan Museum of Anthropology. We found ourselves faced with the same problems of time and space so it has taken three years to complete this report. Many people assisted in this analysis and the hours spent in the field were tripled in the laboratory before writing could begin.

Extensive excavation of the site was started in October of 1955. The site was mapped and a grid system was established (Figure 2). The site was excavated in 5- by 5-foot squares. These squares were designated by the distance to the north and east of the zero point in the grid system.

After removing the sod, the excavators troweled through the

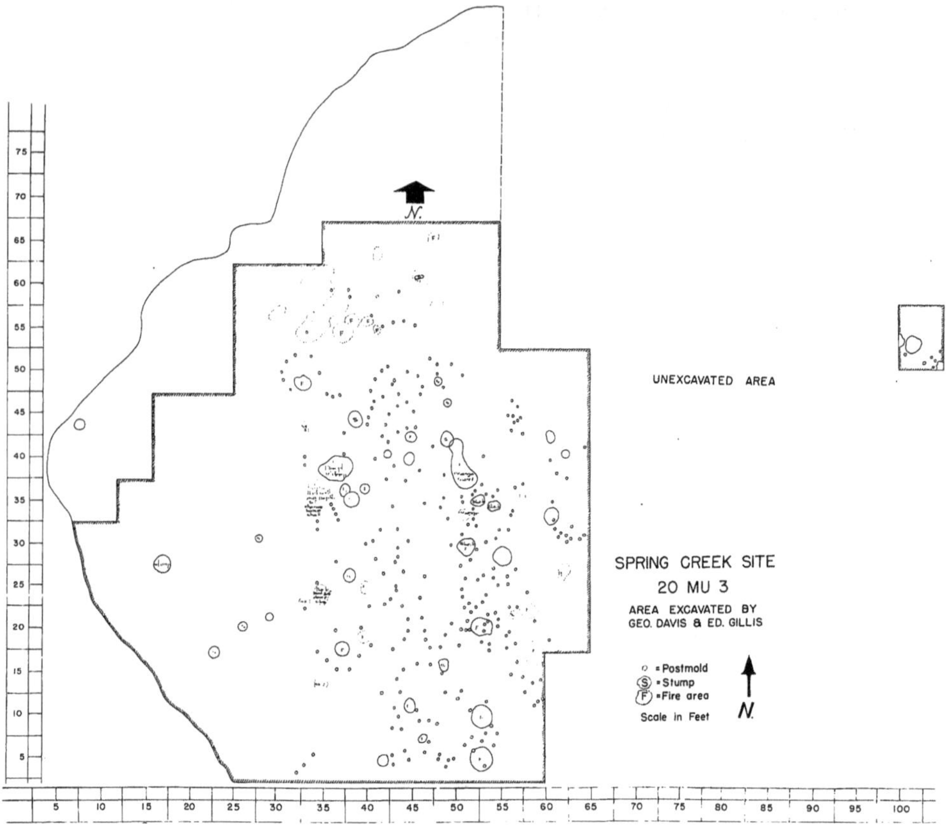

FIG. 2. Detailed map of site area.

midden deposit noting the exact location of complete projectile points, pipes and concentrations of cultural material (Plate II). They recorded and diagrammed fire pits, post molds, and other features. The back dirt from each square was sifted through a 1-1/2-inch screen and the cultural material was placed in 8- by 10- by 4-inch cardboard boxes. One of the first tasks of the laboratory workers was to sort the sherds, chert, bone, and shell in these boxes.

The stratigraphic sequence was rather uniform over the entire site. The deepest deposits excavated on the site were whitish sands near the water table approximately 4 feet below the surface. Overlying them were approximately 30 inches of yellow sand which graded to a light grey sand level 6 to 12 inches thick. This level seemed to contain a great deal of cultural material and is referred to in the notes as a "midden." Over much of the

PLATE II

Excavations at the Spring Creek site showing work on two five-foot squares.

site this zone graded into the modern sod but in the areas of densest concentrations of cultural material there was an additional dense black midden deposit up to 6 inches thick. The modern sod had formed on top of this midden but there were no indications of the development of a new soil profile. What seems to be suggested is the clearing of a forested area, an intensive short occupation followed by an abandonment of the site with no heavy re-occupation of the area.

Several types of features were encountered during the course of excavation. These included concentrations of sherds (marked "s" in Figure 2), fire pits containing ash and charcoal as well as midden debris (marked "f" in Figure 2), storage pits containing only midden debris and some large dark areas containing particularly dense concentrations of cultural material. Charcoal from one of the features on the site yielded a radiocarbon date of A.D. 960 ± 75 years (M-512, Crane and Griffin, 1958:1119).

For analytical purposes the site was divided into four areas. This was convenient because of the provenience data which we had on the northern and eastern parts of the site. Everything north of the N 50 line falling between E 25 and 50 was grouped into Area I. Everything between N 5 and N 50 to the east of E 50, with the exception of the East Unit, was designated as Area II. The East Unit was a 5- by 7-foot unit, originally opened as a 5- by 5-foot unit at N 50 E 100 in the site grid system. This eastern extension of the excavations proved to be important for the understanding of the site.

The excavated area west of, and including the E 50 line and south of N 50 was referred to as the "rest of site." This served as a residual category and all material of unknown provenience was assumed to have come from this area. It proved to be valid for most artifact categories. Where bias was noted, however, it is mentioned in the sections dealing with artifact analysis.

III

CERAMICS

Description of the Sample

Two things impress the observer upon seeing the ceramics from the Spring Creek site. The first is, for a site in Michigan at least, the quantity. Gillis and Davis, using a one-half inch screen, recovered over 18,000 sherds, amounting to over 200 pounds of ceramics. The second is the uniformity of the sample. There are, perhaps, a dozen deviant pots. The remainder of the material looks as though it could have been made by the same person.

The color of the sherds ranges from dark brown (Munsell 10YR 3/2) to brown (10YR 4/3, 5/3) and yellowish brown (10YR 3/4, 4/4, 5/4, 6/4). While no cooking encrustations were found on the sherds it is possible that some of the darker coloration was caused by cooking activities.

The temper is a crushed granitic material. John Speth of the University of Michigan Museum of Anthropology examined the tempering material of several sherds under a binocular microscope and reported that it consisted primarily of crushed quartz with varying amounts of ferromagnesium minerals (primarily hornbled and biotite mica). The tempering particles varied from .5 mm to 5.5 mm but the vast majority were between 1.5 mm and 3 mm. The larger tempering particles tended to be found near the interior of the sherds. A number of rounded, clear quartz sand grains were found in the paste which may have been in the original clay source. Microscopic examination also revealed manufacturing coils which were obliterated near the interior rim of the vessels by extensive smoothing.

Body Sherds

The majority of sherds from the site were body sherds and the majority of these were either cord-marked or smoothed-over cord-marked sherds. A number were classified as smooth but these were, no doubt, originally cord-marked. A very small percentage of the body sherds (and none from areas of known provenience) were textile-impressed with textiles similar to those from the Valley Sweets site (Brose, 1966:4). Many sherds were too small to accurately determine if they were cord-marked, textile-impressed or decorated in any fashion at all. These sherds were placed in an "Indeterminate" category. The counts, weights, and percentages for these body sherds are given in Table 1.

There is a great deal of uniformity between the provenience and the nonprovenience samples from the site. The major differences are in the smoothed cord-marked and smoothed categories which grade into each other. There are more small sherds with indeterminate surface treatment from the areas of known provenience which might reflect better sampling in these areas. The size of the sherds, as reflected by the average weight, was also less in areas of known provenience.

The average weight of the body sherd groups may reflect the part of the vessel from which the sherds were derived. The large size of the smoothed cord-marked sherd, as opposed to the smaller size of the cord-marked sherds, might indicate that they came from nearer the base of the vessel.

The larger size and weight of textile-impressed body sherds is misleading. As we shall see, most textile-impressed rims are from collared vessels which are, as a whole, larger with thicker walls.

The percentage of various types of surface treatment for the areas of known provenience on the site are given in Table 2. With the exception of the east unit, N 50 E 100, the percentages are very close, particularly if we combine the smoothed cord-marked and smoothed categories. Greater frequencies of cord-marked body sherds were recovered from the east unit than from any other unit. However, less than 100 body sherds were found in this unit as opposed to over 2,000 in each of the other areas.

Rim Sherds

The rim sherds from the site were analyzed with keysort cards. We were interested in whole vessels rather than sherds alone (see Plate III for restorable vessels from the site). Our initial sample of over 1,100 rims was sorted and matched in order to find the minimum number of vessels represented at the site. Most of the rims could not be matched and we ended with a suggested total of 966 vessels. This number would be even further reduced if both thickened and rounded lips occur on the same vessel as they did at Spoonville (Flanders, 1965:345). It would be impossible, however, to further group the rims in the Spring Creek sample if both variants did not occur on the same rim sherd.

TABLE 1

BODY SHERDS FROM THE SPRING CREEK SITE

Counts, Weights in Ounces, Percentages, and Average Weights for Cord-marked, Smoothed Cord-marked, Smooth, Textile-impressed and Indeterminate Body Sherds from the Spring Creek Site

	No Provenience					Provenience					Total				
	N	Per Cent N	Wt.	Per Cent Wt.	$\bar{x}$Wt.	N	Per Cent N	Wt.	Per Cent Wt.	$\bar{x}$Wt.	N	Per Cent N	Wt.	Per Cent Wt.	$\bar{x}$Wt.
Cord-marked	6984	66	1441	66	.20	4226	63	771	66	.18	11210	65	2212	66	.20
Smoothed Cord-marked	1591	15	465	21	.29	1294	19	279	24	.22	2885	17	744	22	.26
Smooth.........	254	2	60	3	.24	32	1	6	1	.19	286	2	66	2	.23
Textile-impressed .	154	2	48	2	.31	...	..	...	..	...	154	1	48	1	.31
Indeterminate	1574	15	158	7	.10	1148	17	113	10	.10	2722	16	271	8	.10
Total	10557	..	2172	..	...	6700	..	1169	..	...	17257	..	3341	..	...

TABLE 2

PROVENIENCE OF SPRING CREEK BODY SHERDS

Percentage of Sherds from Areas of Known Provenience at the Spring Creek Site and Total Number of Sherds from Each Area

	Area I	Area II	East Unit	Rest of Site (No Provenience)
	Per Cent	Per Cent	Per Cent	Per Cent
Cord-marked	77	74	87	78
Smoothed Cord-marked.	23	25	9	18
Smoothed	..	1	4	2
Textile-impressed	..	..	..	2
Sample size	3411	2044	99	8983

PLATE III

Restorable vessels from the site.

The following information was recorded on keysort cards for the minimal vessel sample: rim shape, rim profile, surface treatment, presence of rim decoration, lip decoration, and interior rim decoration, rim diameter, thickness below the rim and the coarseness of cord impressions on cord-marked vessels.

The vessels themselves had an average rim diameter of 16 centimeters but a very high standard deviation, 12 centimeters. This was a reflection of the very large rim diameters of a few vessels. Figure 3 shows the distribution of vessel rim diameters.

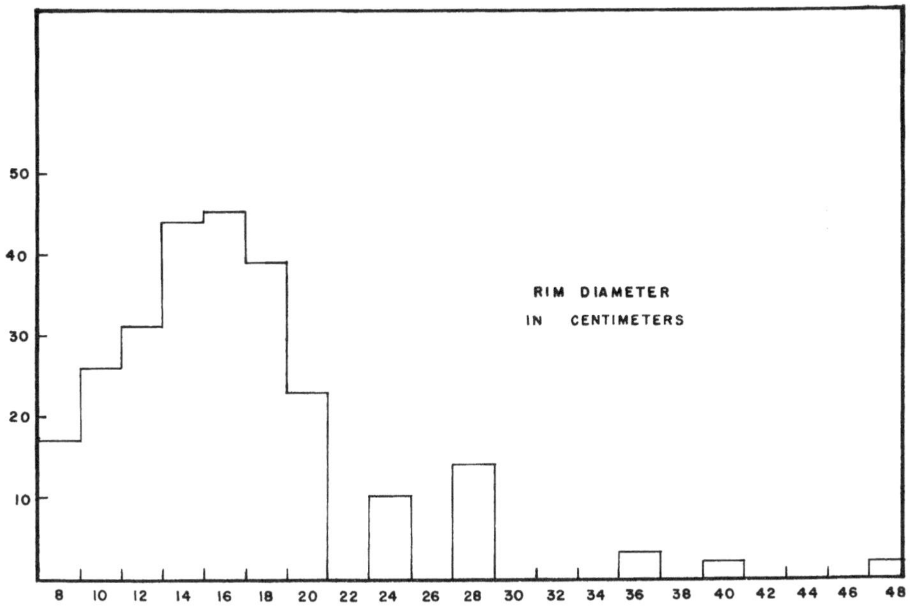

FIG. 3. Distribution of rim diameter in centimeters on Spring Creek vessels.

Fitting and Halsey (1966) have developed a formula relating rim diameter and vessel volume on Wayne ware from eastern Michigan. When this is applied to the Spring Creek sample we find an average vessel volume of about 5-1/2 liters. In establishing categories for tables of paired attributes, which were tested by chi-square, four categories were used; vessels with a rim diameter of 12 centimeters or less, 13 to 17 centimeters, 18 to 23 centimeters and vessels with a rim diameter of 24 centimeters or more.

The thickness of vessel walls was measured far enough below the rim to avoid including any thickening for a collar or thickened lip. Vessel thickness ranged from .2 to 1.1 centimeters.

The average thickness was .6 centimeters with a standard deviation of .3 centimeters. The distribution of vessel thickness is shown in Figure 4. Five categories were established for our quantitative comparisons: less than .4 centimeters, .41 to .5 centimeters, .51 to .6 centimeters, .61 to .7 centimeters, and over .7 centimeters.

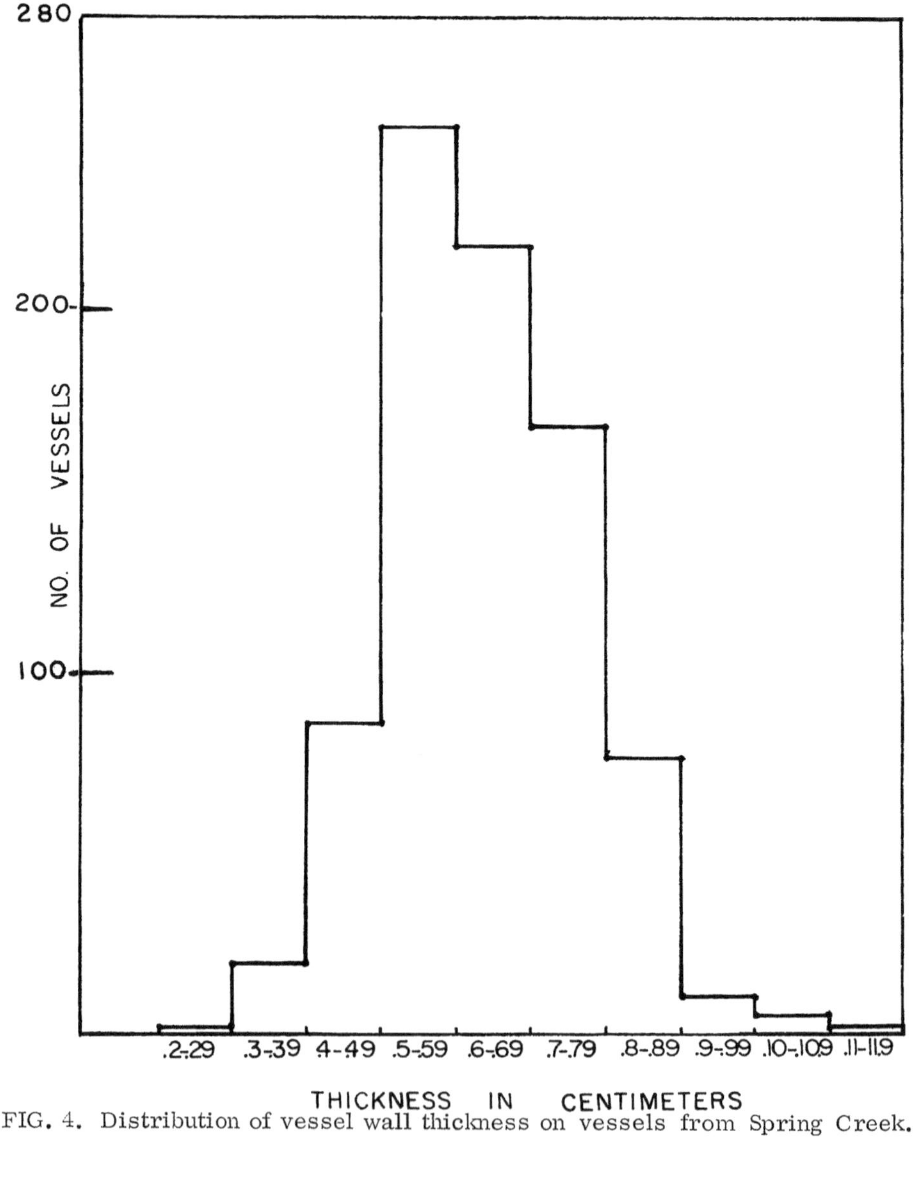

FIG. 4. Distribution of vessel wall thickness on vessels from Spring Creek.

All of the Spring Creek rim sherds could be sorted according to three basic rim profiles, each with many variants. These groupings are illustrated in Figure 5. The first group was collared with the wet clay having been folded back over the outer surface. After the manufacture of the collar there might be any number of additional alterations including notching of the collar and pinching or folding the lip out over the collar (Figure 5, Plate IV). The collars on the vessels from Spring Creek were all very small, nothing like the wide collars that are found on Riviere wares in eastern Michigan (Fitting, 1965: Plates XIII-XVII), the Juntunen wares in northern Michigan (McPherron, 1967:502-5) or on the Wisconsin type, Aztalan Collared (Baerreis and Freeman, 1958: Figures 1-4).

A second rim variant could be described as thickened (Figure 5). Here there was a pinching or flattening of the lip toward the outer surface of the vessel. Again, there are many variations. It still can be contrasted to the third rim variant on the site, the plain rim (Figure 5). Plain rims vary from squared to pointed with the majority being rounded. Rim profile variation was one of the most significant attributes of Spring Creek ceramics.

Four categories of surface treatment were recognized on rim sherds. Horizontal cord-marking, which was very rare; vertical cord-marking, the modal surface treatment technique accounting for 65 per cent of the vessels; smoothed-over cord-marking and textile impression, which was rare. Cord-marking ran from fine, with as many as 9 cord impressions per centimeter, to coarse, with as few as 2 cord impressions per centimeter. The 517 vessels on which the number of cord impressions per centimeter as recorded had a mean of 4 with a standard deviation of 1.1 impressions (see Figure 6 for distribution). Three categories were used for our comparisons: coarse, 3 or fewer cord impressions per centimeter; medium, between 3 and 5 cord impressions; and fine, 5 or more cord impressions per centimeter.

Only the presence or absence of rim decoration was noted on the keysort cards. If any complex decoration did occur, which was very rare, it was drawn on the card. Lip and interior rim decoration was limited to cord-wrapped stick or paddle edge and solid tool impressions.

A last attribute used for comparison was rim shape. Rims were separated into those which appeared to have a vertical orientation on a vessel and into those which appeared to flare outward. This last category was rare.

The attributes were paired and tested against an expected chance distribution by the chi-square technique. An association

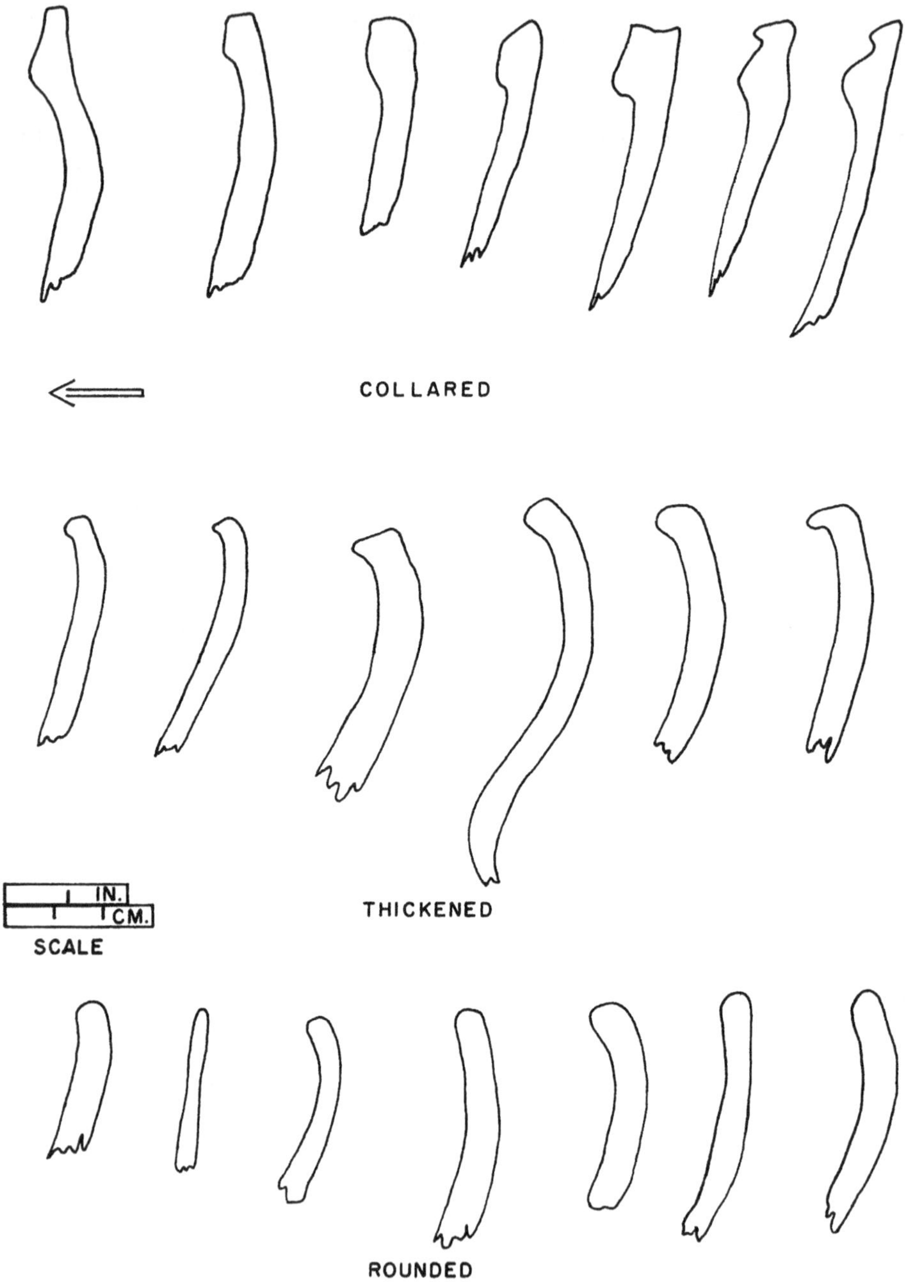

FIG. 5. Spring Creek rim profiles.

PLATE IV

Spring Creek collared rim sherds.

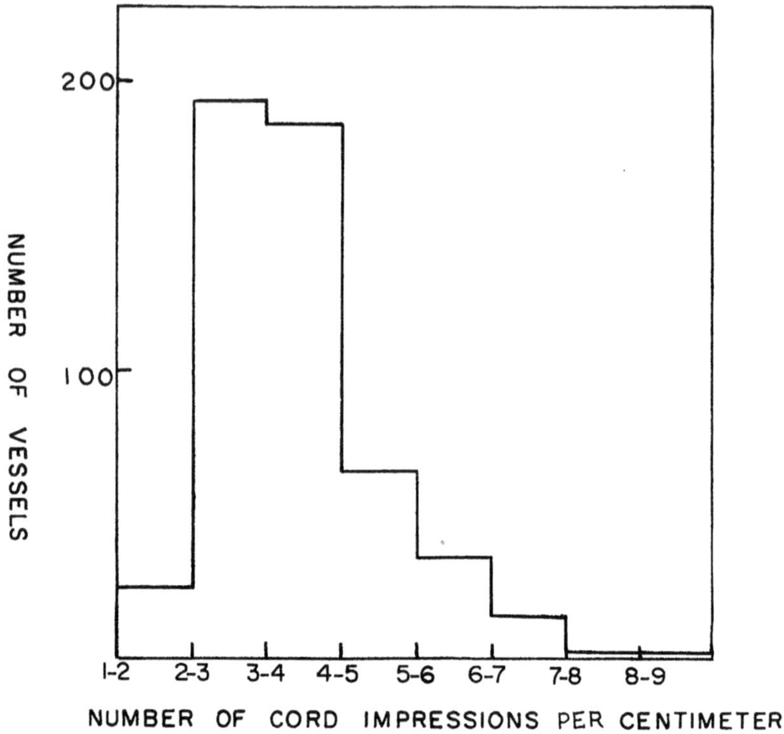

FIG. 6. Distribution of cord impressions per centimeter on vessels from Spring Creek.

was accepted as significant only if the probability factor was .01 or less. As visual inspection had indicated, there were few significant associations. The sample size, chi-square values, number of degrees of freedom and probability factors for those attributes with an apparently random association are given in Table 3. The same factors for those combinations with significant associations are given in Table 4.

Less than one-third of the associations showed significant clustering. Many of the associations in Table 4 were the results of mechanical factors rather than cultural differences. As an example, vessel thickness increases along with increased vessel size as measured by the rim diameter. Exterior rim decoration, lip decoration, and interior rim decoration tend to be associated with each other. If the potter bothered to alter one of these, she altered several.

TABLE 3

ATTRIBUTES WITHOUT SIGNIFICANT ASSOCIATIONS

Comparisons of Attributes on Spring Creek Ceramics which did not Show any Significant Clustering with Sample Size, Chi-square Values, Degrees of Freedom and Probability Factor

Test	N	x^2	df	p <
Rim shape/surface.	742	5.44	3	.20
Rim shape/decoration.	893	.46	1	.50
Rim shape/lip	913	1.27	1	.30
Rim shape/interior	914	.43	1	.70
Rim shape/cord-marking . . .	500	1.84	2	.50
Rim shape/rim type	864	.87	2	.70
Rim shape/diameter.	239	1.24	3	.90
Rim shape/thickness.	821	3.80	4	.50
Rim type/interior	881	1.84	2	.50
Rim type/lip	892	3.72	2	.20
Rim type/thickness	811	9.82	8	.30
Rim type/cord-marking.	546	12.24	4	.02
Surface/cord-marking.	517	.38	2	.90
Surface/thickness	749	14.06	8	.10
Surface/diameter.	244	4.15	6	.70
Surface/interior.	877	1.75	2	.50
Decoration/interior	966	3.80	1	.10
Decoration/diameter.	285	1.94	3	.70
Lip/diameter.	249	2.75	3	.50
Lip/cord-marking	517	4.46	2	.20
Interior/diameter	244	.53	3	.95
Interior/thickness	823	4.34	4	.50
Interior/cord-marking	517	2.59	2	.30
Rim type/decoration.	884	4.47	2	.20
Thickness/decoration	831	3.41	4	.50

Some of the associations, however, seem to have cultural significance. In the association between rim type and surface treatment we noted a strong tendency for smoothed cord-marked vessels to have plain rims and for vessels with thickened lips to have distinct cord-marking right up to the lip. There also was a tendency for more than expected numbers of collared rims to bear textile impressions. This was complicated by the confusing observation that we had a larger percentage of textile-impressed rim sherds than body sherds. This is a result of the difficulty one has in distinguishing coarse cord-marking and the textile impressions found on ceramics in western Michigan. As Quimby has stated (1961:428), ". . .I assume that fabric-impressing and cord-marking are closely related techniques and part of the same

TABLE 4

ATTRIBUTES WITH SIGNIFICANT ASSOCIATIONS

Comparisons of Attributes on Spring Creek Ceramics which showed Significant Clustering with Sample Size, Chi-square Values, Degrees of Freedom and Probability Factors

Test	N	x^2	df	p
Rim type/surface.	844	20.16	6	.01
Rim type/diameter.	245	32.18	6	.001
Surface/lip	897	11.36	2	.01
Surface/decoration.	891	111.96	2	.001
Decoration/lip.	966	18.38	1	.001
Decoration/cord-marking . . .	590	12.26	2	.01
Lip/interior	965	11.09	1	.001
Lip/thickness	858	32.37	4	.001
Diameter/thickness	274	52.90	4	.001
Diameter/cord-marking	136	14.78	4	.01
Thickness/cord-marking.	489	27.39	8	.001

cultural tradition. However, I can only conclude that I still cannot tell with certainty the difference between some kinds of cord-marking and some kinds of fabric impressing." I believe that one per cent textile impression found among the body sherds would be a conservative estimate for the rim sherds once all the small, and hence dubious, examples are eliminated.

The association between rim type and rim diameter was another important association. There was a strong tendency for vessels with collars to have the largest rim diameters, vessels with thickened lips to occupy an intermediate position and vessels with plain rims to have the smallest rim diameters. The average rim diameter of collared vessels was 17.9 centimeters, of vessels with thickened rims 15.9 centimeters and vessels with plain rims, 14.7 centimeters. When we apply the rim diameter-volume formula (Fitting and Halsey, 1966) we have an average capacity of 6.8 liters for vessels with collars, 5.3 liters for vessels with thickened rims and 4.4 liters for vessels with plain rims.

There is a tendency for vessels with vertical cord-marking to have decoration on the lip of the vessel. Lip decoration tends to be absent on vessels with smoothed cord-marking. The same thing is true for extensive rim decoration, punctations and cord-marked stick impressions. They tend to be more common on vessels with vertical cord-marking and less common on vessels with smoothed cord-marking.

There is a tendency for rim decoration to occur on vessels with coarser cord-marking. This is related to the association between diameter and cord-marking and thickness and cord-marking. The smaller, thinner vessels have finer cord-marking. Larger, thicker vessels tend to be coarsely cord-marked and rim decoration, primarily punctates, tends to occur on these larger vessels.

This leaves us with the association between lip decoration and vessel thickness. Vessels in the intermediate size range have greater than the expected frequencies of lip decoration. These are also the vessels that tend to have thickened lips, which would provide the best surface for such alterations. This alteration tends to be absent on the smaller plain-rimmed vessels and on the larger collared vessels.

In spite of the homogeneity of the ceramics from the Spring Creek site we can describe three significant clusters of attributes which furnish the basis for a more formal definition of types.

There are a group of larger, collared vessels, which tend to be more coarsely cord-marked, or occasionally textile-impressed. They are thick-walled and tend not to have lip or interior rim decorations. A second group consists of medium-sized vessels with vertical cord-marking, thickened lips and lip and interior rim decoration. The third group would consist of smaller vessels with finer cord-marking, plain rims and a relative lack of lip and interior rim decoration.

Spring Creek Collared (Plate IV) is the term which will be used to describe the large collared vessels from the site. These vessels have an average rim diameter of 17.9 centimeters and an average capacity of 6.8 liters. The majority are cord-marked but there is a variant with textile impressions which might eventually be classified as a separate type. At Spring Creek there are 230 vessels of this type representing 23.8 per cent of the total vessel sample.

Spring Creek Collared is representative of a widespread cord-marked collared horizon in the early Late Woodland period. In Michigan a few sherds have been reported from the Riviere au Vase site (Fitting, 1965:22) and Flanders illustrated (1965:348) a vessel of this type from Newaygo County.

Further to the south in Illinois, Maxwell (1951:279) has defined Dillinger Cord-marked, a crushed clay-clay grit-tempered cord-marked pottery which is occasionally collared. A related form, Korando Cord-marked, has been defined by Keslin in Missouri (1964:3809). One of the Canton ware sherds illustrated by Fowler (1952:139) from the Clear Lake site in Tazwell County, Illinois, has a thin cord-marked collar. Similar forms are also included in Winters' type, Albee Cord-marked, a Late Woodland type from the Wabash Valley (1963:105-6). In the Chicago area similar pottery has been reported along with such forms as Madison Cord-impressed (Fenner, 1961:41).

Baby and Potter (1965) have reported cord-impressed collared rims in a Late Woodland context from Ohio and Mayer-Oakes (1955:191-92) includes this form in his type "Mahoning Cord-marked."

One thing which should be noted is that all of the above types have both collared and uncollared variants. In my study of Wayne ware in southeastern Michigan I noted several collared cord-marked sherds from the Riviere au Vase site which I classed as Wayne Cord-marked. I now feel that a distinction between the collared and uncollared cord-marked forms should be made. Apart from obvious chronological implications, with uncollared forms appearing earlier, there are functional implications with the correlation between this rim form and increased vessel size. If different seasonal activities required different size vessels, different frequencies of these vessel types would occur. There are many other possible correlations. At Spring Creek, for example, vessel size appears to be related to distance from the water source.

There is a collared cord-marked Woodland pottery type from Wisconsin which I feel is not specifically related to Spring Creek Collared. This type is Aztalan Collared as described by Baerreis and Freeman (1958). The vessel shape, the thickness of the vessel walls, and the width and height of the collars set Aztalan Collared apart from Spring Creek Collared. Baerreis and Bryson (1965:209), in a recent evaluation of the dating of Aztalan, have suggested that, "a possible range of occupation from A.D. 1100 to A.D. 1300 seems reasonable on the basis of present evidence." Even though Aztalan Collared is not present at Spring Creek it is found at a site in the dunes between Hamlin Lake and Lake Michigan (Fitting, 1967) so we are not dealing with mutually exclusive distributions. I would tend to view Spring Creek Collared as an example of the generalized early Late Woodland base out of which Aztalan Collared, a later, more localized type, evolved.

Wayne Cord-marked is a type which was defined in southeastern Michigan (Fitting, 1965:158-59) but, it holds for Spring Creek ceramics as well. This is a type which is associated with a widespread late Middle Woodland and early Late Woodland horizon. A discussion of this distribution may be found with the original type description.

At Spring Creek two variants seemed to have significance. Wayne Cord-marked variant No. 1 consisted of those vessels with

PLATE V

Wayne Cord-marked variant No. 1.

lip alteration, usually paddle edge or cord-wrapped stick impressions (Plate V). There is a strong tendency for this type of vessel to have a thickened lip. They are in the medium size range. At the Riviere au Vase site 78 per cent and at the Fort Wayne Mound 80 per cent of the Wayne ware vessels had this type of lip alteration. At Spring Creek 509 vessels were of this cord-marked variant, No. 1 accounting for 52.7 per cent of the vessels from the site.

A second cord-marked variant consists of those vessels without lip alteration, usually with rounded rims and of a smaller size than the first cord-marked variant (Plate VI). At Spring Creek this cord-marked variant No. 2 is represented by 153 vessels, 15.8 per cent of the vessels from the site.

There is a group of 74 vessels from the site, 7.7 per cent of the sample, which were not typed. The majority of these were vessels too fragmentary to accurately determine surface or rim treatment. There were a number of distinctive variants. Several vessels had either horizontal cord-marking or horizontal cord-wrapped stick impressions (Plate VII, *e,i*). One vessel has an appliqué strip with notches along the edge and cord-wrapped stick impressions along the upper edge of the rim (Plate VII, *h*). A number of rims could be related to the small, usually temperless, miniature vessels so common on sites in the Great Lakes (Plate VII, *f,g*).

There was a final series of four vessels with incisions over cord-marking. On two of the series (Plate VII, *b,d*) the incising is a chevron pattern of oblique lines, for another (Plate VII, *c*) it is a series of rough horizontal lines. The fourth (Plate VII, *a*) is marked with oblique lines and some crosshatching on the exterior surface and crosshatching on the lip itself. I am hesitant even to illustrate much of this material. These variants are all insignificant. The incised vessels, for example, constitute less than one half of 1 per cent of the vessel sample from the site. These, and the other minority variants, should not in any way detract from the homogeneity of the rest of the collection.

Distribution of Vessel Types

Flanders (1965:353) has suggested that Spring Creek represents a site with multiple ceramic occupations. In light of the apparent consistency of paste, temper, and surface treatment this position needed further investigation. It was tested by examining vessel distribution throughout the site. If the site were occupied at several different times we would expect to find some area clusterings of types such as we noted at the Riviere au Vase site.

PLATE VI

Wayne Cord-marked variant No. 2.

PLATE VII

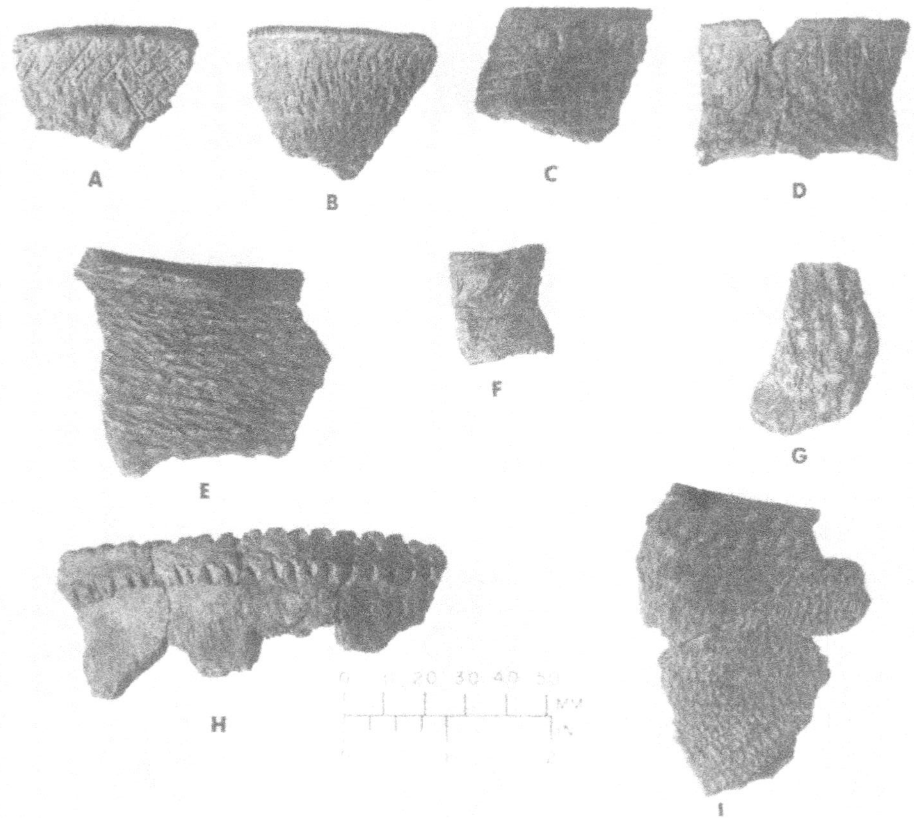

Unusual vessels: *a–d*—vessels decorated with incisions over cord-marking; *e,i*—vessels decorated with horizontal cord-marking or horizontal cord-wrapped stick impressions; *f,g*—temperless miniature vessels; *h*—vessel with notches along the edge and cord-wrapped stick impressions along upper edge of rim.

TABLE 5

VESSELS FROM SPRING CREEK

Distributions of the Three Main Vessel Types From Areas of Known Provenience at the Spring Creek Site with the Percentages From Each Area and From the Rest of the Site

	Area I		Area II		East Unit		Rest of Site	
	N	Per Cent	N	Per Cent	N	Per Cent	N	Per Cent
Spring Creek Collared	58	34	39	24	9	43	124	23
Cord-marked No. 1 . .	88	52	96	60	10	48	315	58
Cord-marked No. 2 . .	24	14	25	16	2	9	102	19
Total	170	...	160	...	21		541	

The frequencies of the three main vessel types from the site are given in Table 5 and the areal distributions are plotted on a cumulative graph in Figure 7. It can readily be seen that there is not a great deal of variation in type frequencies between various areas on the site. Again, the eastern unit, N50 E100, is the most divergent and, again, we can point to a relatively small sample from this unit. To get such a small amount of variation with multiple occupations you would almost have to assume later occupants were breaking pots whenever they found a broken pot from a previous occupation.

There is a much simpler explanation. The Spring Creek Collared vessels are the largest vessels on the site and the Cord-marked No. 2 vessels are the smallest. There is a progressive increase in the percentage of Spring Creek Collared and a consistent decrease in the frequency of Cord-marked No. 2 vessels with increased distance from Spring Creek, the local water source. This appears to be a simple functional difference rather than multiple occupations. One could carry more water in fewer trips with the larger collared vessels.

The density of vessels per square foot of excavated area on the site was also greater in the eastern unit. Where the rest of the site averaged about .4 vessels per square foot, the east unit yielded .6 vessels per square foot. Not only were the vessels larger but there were more of them in areas more distant from the creek.

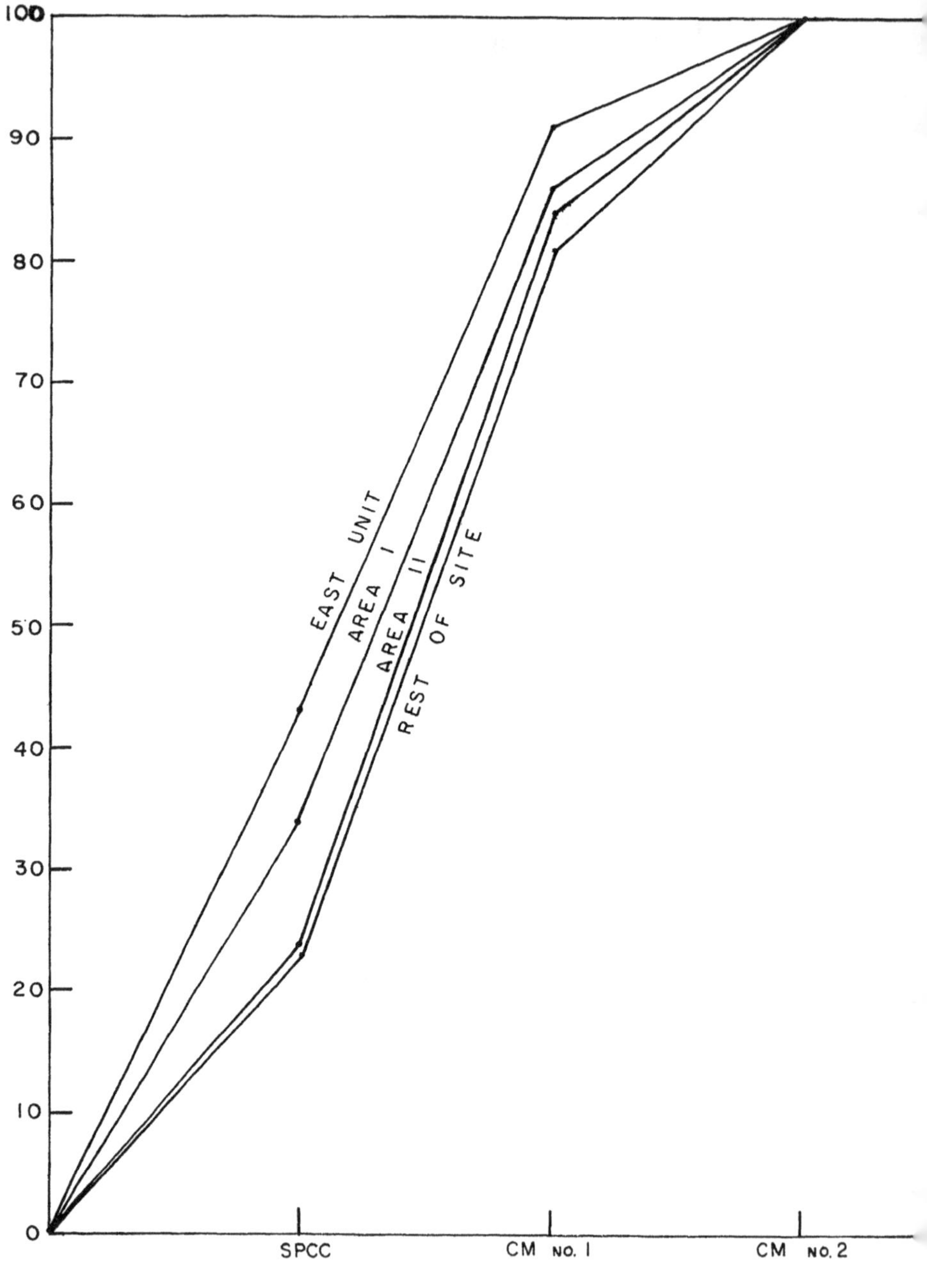

FIG. 7. Frequencies of Spring Creek Collared and Wayne Cord-marked variants at Spring Creek.

Social Implications

The social implications of the Spring Creek ceramics are difficult to interpret. Deetz (1965:2) has suggested that, "under matrilocal residence, reinforced by matrilineal descent, one might well expect a large degree of consistent patterning of design attributes since these would be passed from mothers to daughters, and preserved by continuous manufacture in the same household." McPherron (1965) has suggested that weak clustering of stylistic attributes in the Mackinac phase at the Juntunen site may be related to virilocal residence. Since his Mackinac phase is contemporary with the Spring Creek occupation this model needs to be viewed more closely. Actually, neither model is directly applicable to the Spring Creek situation where there is neither obvious localized attribute clustering nor stylistic overlap of distinctive attributes. There are simply no decorative attributes to cluster or overlap.

There is only the homogeneity of the collection and a small degree of functional variation within a single tradition. This is in an area where we could expect only central Algonquian groups which have a strong tradition for virilocality, with apparently, a considerable time depth (McPherron, 1965). Spring Creek stands in strong contrast to the sites reported by Wright (1965) along the north shore of Lake Superior which have a great deal of ceramic diversity. These groups, however, would probably have had a similar virilocal postmarital residence pattern.

Perhaps the significant variable here is the population density. Less than one-third the number of rim sherds were recovered from Wright's 6 components than from a single component, representing a short occupation, at Spring Creek. Given the same postmarital residence patterns, we would expect a great deal more homogeneity from groups in a densely settled agricultural area than in the more sparsely settled boreal forests.

The widespread southern ceramic tradition to which the Spring Creek site ceramics belong argues for a generally greater homogeneity for the more densely settled groups in the Carolinian deciduous forest area. At the same time period there are many local traditions within the less densely populated northern areas where we could postulate a hunting, fishing, and gathering economy with low population density.

IV

LITHIC MATERIAL

There were 1,841 fragments of chipped stone in the loan collection from the Spring Creek site including 1,497 flakes of various types, 91 small cores and core fragments, and 253 whole or fragmentary artifacts. No large cores nor massive quarry debris were recovered suggesting that this was not a workshop site. Indeed, the lithic industry seems insignificant when compared to the ceramic industry. There are 2 pieces of chipped stone for every vessel recovered from the site and more than 10 body sherds for every scrap of flint debris.

There was a tremendous variation in chert type. All 91 small cores were from different nodules with distinctive appearances, and the flakes showed even greater variation. Therefore, for the study of chippage, no specific data on chert variants will be included.

The kind of flakes in the debris is indicative of the kind of knapping activity that took place at the site. Flakes were classified as decoration flakes, block flakes, flat flakes without striking platforms, and several types of flakes with striking platforms and bulbs of percussion. The category of flakes with striking platforms was subdivided into those showing evidence of having been struck with a hard hammer and those which were struck off with a soft hammer. Among the soft hammer flakes was one group with a right angle striking platform and a second group with an acute angle between the striking platform and the outer surface of the flake. This last group will be referred to as flakes of bifacial retouch.

Decortication flakes have been defined by White (1963:5) and Binford and Quimby (1963:287). They are flakes removed from the exterior surface. The small size of these flakes at Spring Creek, a little over 4 grams, suggests that small pebble sources were worked on the site.

Block flakes have been defined by Fitting (Fitting, DeVisscher and Wahla, 1966) in a study of the Holcombe site chippage. The category includes White's (1963:13-4) tabular flakes and tabular flakes from broken nodules. It probably includes flakes which

Binford and Quimby (1963:286-87) called "primary shatter" and what Wittoft (1952:474) referred to as "blocky spalls of chert, triangular or prismatic in cross-section, tapered and of no regular form. . . ." Evidence at the Holcombe site seemed to indicate that some of these block flakes were formed as a result of heat fracture. Many of the block flakes from the Holcombe site, were darker than the rest of the chert, and many showed obvious high temperature heat alteration, fire pops, and irregular surfaces. Some of the Spring Creek block flakes may have been heat-altered but the majority were not. These were probably formed by the coarse trimming suggested by White (1963:13) and Witthoft (1952: 474), perhaps along old frost cracks as suggested by Binford and Quimby (1963:286). Such frost-cracking was very evident in a sample from a small core-chipping station near Hamlin Lake (Fitting, n.d.), which appears to date to the same time period, and where several nodules could be reconstructed from the debris. This flake type was illustrated by Fitting (Fitting, DeVisscher, and Wahla, 1966:Plate II) in the Holcombe site report.

The largest flake category at the site is that of flat flakes without readily identifiable striking platforms, or at least without striking platforms which could be associated with a particular technique of manufacture. While many of these may have been flakes of bifacial retouch, others were the by-products of small core preparation. This is, admittedly, a residual category and could probably be broken down into a number of subcategories.

Flakes with hard hammer platforms are distinctive with a bulb of percussion starting near the point of impact, no lip or overhang, a prominent bulb of percussion, shatter lines along the cone of percussion, and an impact scar on the striking platform at the point of impact.

When a soft hammer is used a less prominent bulb of percussion is found, although the weight of the hammer has an effect on this. Impact scars and shatter lines along the cone of percussion are usually absent. One of the diagnostic features of this flake type is the occurrence of a lip or overhang of the striking platform on the interior surface of the flake.

Two variants of soft hammer flakes are recognized in this study: those with right-angled and those with acute-angled striking platforms. Those with right-angled striking platforms reflect rough flint-working activity such as core and preform preparation. Those with acute angles and ground edges, the flakes of bifacial retouch, reflect the finishing of preforms into bifacial tools. Flakes of bifacial retouch have been illustrated by Fitting (Fitting, DeVisscher, and Wahla, 1966:Fig. 4).

Both complete small cores and fragments were counted and weighed. Small cores have been recognized in Great Lakes lithic assemblages within the last decade. They have been reported on Paleo-Indian (Fitting, DeVisscher, and Wahla, 1966), Archaic (Harrison, 1966:61), Middle Woodland (Flanders, 1965:333-36, Fitting, n.d.), and Late Woodland sites (Binford and Quimby, 1963; Wright, 1965:201) so the mere presence of such tools has no chronological significance.

The over-all flake type counts and weights are given in the last columns of Table 6 and Table 7. Rough flint-working activities account for only a minor part of the flint-working on the site as shown by relatively low frequencies of decortication and block flakes. The small size of the block flakes would seem to relate many of them to the preparation of small cores and small core tools. The high numbers of flat flakes, particularly flakes of bifacial retouch, suggests that the flint for bifacial artifacts was brought to the site in the form of preforms.

TABLE 6

COUNTS AND PERCENTAGES OF FLAKES

Counts and Percentages of Flakes and Small Cores from Various Areas of the Spring Creek Site

	Area I	Area II	Rest of site	Total
Decortication flakes . . .	20	28	98	146
Percentage	9 per cent	10 per cent	9 per cent	9 per cent
Block flakes	46	41	160	247
Percentage	20 per cent	15 per cent	15 per cent	16 per cent
Flat Flakes	106	131	485	722
Percentage	46 per cent	49 per cent	45 per cent	45 per cent
Hard hammer flakes . . .	4	3	12	19
Percentage	2 per cent	1 per cent	1 per cent	1 per cent
Soft hammer flakes. . . .	17	13	103	133
Percentage	7 per cent	5 per cent	9 per cent	8 per cent
Bifacial retouch flakes .	27	44	159	230
Percentage	12 per cent	16 per cent	15 per cent	14 per cent
Small cores and fragments	10	9	72	91
Percentage	4 per cent	3 per cent	7 per cent	6 per cent
Total count	230	269	1089	1588

TABLE 7

WEIGHTS AND PERCENTAGES OF FLAKES

Weight, in Grams, and Percentage of Weights of Flakes and Small Cores from Various Areas of the Spring Creek Site and the Average Weight of Complete Small Cores from Those Areas

	Area I	Area II	Rest of site	Total
Decortication flakes . . .	53	62	533	648
Percentages	13 per cent	17 per cent	21 per cent	19 per cent
Block flakes	155	86	682	923
Percentages	37 per cent	24 per cent	26 per cent	27 per cent
Flat flakes	104	113	635	852
Percentages	25 per cent	31 per cent	24 per cent	25 per cent
Hard hammer flakes . . .	9	8	31	48
Percentages	2 per cent	2 per cent	1 per cent	1 per cent
Soft hammer flakes . . .	34	18	194	246
Percentages	8 per cent	5 per cent	7 per cent	7 per cent
Bifacial retouch flakes .	29	57	237	323
Percentages	7 per cent	16 per cent	9 per cent	10 per cent
Small cores and fragments	35	18	283	336
Percentages	8 per cent	5 per cent	11 per cent	10 per cent
Average Weight of Complete small cores	4.0	2.2	4.4	4.2
Total weight	419	362	2595	3376

Most of the bifacial tools at the site were ultimately derived from large cores. Although they were absent from the Spring Creek collection, block cores occurred with burials of this time period at the Riviere au Vase site (Fitting, 1965:52-54) in association with bifacial preforms. Block cores have been reported from the Eastport site (Binford and Papworth, 1963:83) and Summer Island (Binford and Quimby, 1963:300). In 1965 University of Michigan field parties collected similar cores from Sand Bay (called Point Detour Bay by Binford and Quimby), Sack Bay and a site near the store in Fairport, all on the Garden Peninsula along the north shore of Lake Michigan. Small cores were also recovered from all of these sites with the exception of Riviere au Vase. There is either direct or indirect evidence for the association of both large and small core techniques at both the Holcombe (Fitting, DeVisscher, and Wahla, 1966) and Schmidt (Harrison, 1966: 67-68) sites, so the use of both techniques by Spring Creek peoples would not be unusual.

Some of the flaking debris could be clearly assigned to either Area I or Area II. Only 5 flakes were in the collection from N50E100, the east unit, so they were grouped with the residual category representing the main body of the site. The flake counts and percentages are presented in Table 6, and the weights and percentages are given in Table 7. When we look at percentages of flake types we find a great deal of homogeneity. In only one instance do we have as much as 5 per cent variation between areas. All other variation is 4 per cent or less.

There is a slight difference between Area I and Area II with more block flakes of bifacial retouch in Area II. This might indicate more small core preparation in Area I and more bifacial tool preparation in Area II.

The trends noted for flake counts are magnified by a comparison of flake weights (Table 7). This is a result of differential weights for the flake groups. We would also conclude from the weights of flake groups that more small core preparation took place in Area I and more bifacial tool preparation in Area II. Even the few small cores in the sample from Area II weighed only slightly over half as much as those from Area I.

A special study was made of the 68 complete small cores in the sample (Table 8). They were separated according to the small core classification developed by Binford and Quimby (1963:289-96). All six categories were found at Spring Creek but there was only

TABLE 8

SMALL CORE TYPES

Types of Small Cores Present at the Spring Creek Site Classed After the Types Defined by Binford and Quimby (1963)

	Total Number	Number Diminutive	Number Utilized	Total Weight	Total Weight Excluding Diminutive	x̄ Weight	x̄ Weight Excluding Diminutive
				Grams	Grams	Grams	Grams
Ridge core . . .	18	1	11	99	98	5.5	5.8
Point core. . . .	5	...	...	28	28	5.6	5.6
Ridge point . . .	9	2	9	25	23	2.8	3.3
Ridge ridge . . .	30	11	30	97	82	3.2	4.3
Point point . . .	6	3	3	20	16	3.3	5.3
Totals . .	68	17	53	...	...	...	...

one with right-angled striking surfaces. This was probably originally double-ridged, but had been worked to a ridge point right-angled form so it was grouped with the ridge point small cores.

A number of the small cores were far below the average size for the site. The number of these diminutive small cores, those with weights of 1.5 grams or less, is given for each core group in Table 8. Binford and Quimby, McPherron, and others have suggested that many of these small cores might have been used as tools. Wright (1965:201) and Harrison (1966:61) have actually referred to them as "wedges." The small cores from Spring Creek were examined for extensive nibbling such as might result from use as wedges or bone-splitting tools. Fifty-three, or 78 per cent, of the complete small cores were found to have this attribute and must also be classed as tools.

All of the ridge ridge and ridge point cores from the site appear to have been used as tools. Much smaller frequencies of single ridge and bipointed cores and none of the single-pointed cores showed any evidence of such use.

The 253 chipped-stone artifacts were separated into 20 artifact categories used in the Schultz site analysis (Fitting, n.d.) and several references will be made to this report. Spring Creek has a lithic industry which seems to be a logical development out of the Late Woodland levels at the Schultz site. There are, of course, reflections of the local situation and economy, but the stylistic trends noted at Schultz continue at this site.

The metric attributes of the measurable artifact categories are presented in Table 10. Table 9 contains the distribution of artifacts at the site, but I would suspect that collecting and cataloging bias might have destroyed part of the value of this distribution.

The bifacial artifact groups consisted of whole and fragmentary preforms; large triangular pointed bifaces; groups of large, medium and small expanding stemmed points; side-notched points; small triangular points; crude triangular pointed bifaces and drills. We also had a group of point tips, a group of finished biface fragments and 3 other bifacial tools, 2 argillite knives, and an ovate quartzite knife.

Seven of the preforms were complete and 41 were fragmentary (Plate VIII, *e-h*, Fig. 8, *a-b*). Several showed signs of possible use as scraping tools, but this was rare. A group of 19 fragmentary preforms (46 per cent) showed signs of heat alteration; heat spalls, blocky fractures, oxidation of trace elements, and actual alteration of the chert structure were present on some. This was the only artifact class that showed such a high percentage of

TABLE 9

ARTIFACTS FROM SPRING CREEK

Distribution, Counts and Percentages of Chipped Stone Artifacts from the Spring Creek Site

	Area I		Area II		Rest of site		Total	
	N	Per cent	N	Per cent	N	Per cent	N	Per cent
Bipolar cores	10	22.2	9	17.3	72	29.1	91	26.5
Complete preforms	...	...	1	2.0	6	2.4	7	2.0
Fragmentary preforms	9	20.0	7	13.5	25	10.1	41	11.9
Large triangular	...	...	...	...	7	2.8	7	2.0
Large expanding stem	2	4.4	2	3.8	8	3.2	12	3.5
Medium expanding stem	...	...	1	1.9	16	6.5	17	4.9
Narrow expanding stem	...	...	2	.3	6	2.4	8	2.3
Small expanding stem	...	...	1	1.9	3	1.2	4	1.2
Side notched	1	2.2	2	3.8	5	2.0	8	2.3
Small triangular	8	19.8	1	1.9	19	7.7	28	8.1
Crude triangular	...	...	1	1.9	4	1.6	5	1.5
Drills	...	...	1	1.9	4	1.6	5	1.5
Point tips	1	2.2	2	3.8	18	7.3	21	6.1
Finished fragment	1	2.2	2	3.8	10	4.0	13	3.8
Other bifaces	1	...	...	...	3	1.2	3	.9
Total biface	22	48.9	23	44.2	134	54.3	179	52.0
Steep endscraper	3	6.7	7	13.5	13	5.7	23	6.7
Sloping endscraper	2	4.4	3	5.8	4	1.6	9	2.6
Side scraper on flakes	5	11.1	5	9.6	12	5.3	22	6.4
Pointed unifaces	3	6.7	2	3.8	7	2.8	12	3.5
Concave scraper	...	...	1	1.9	2	.8	3	.9
Retouched flakes	...	...	2	3.8	3	1.2	5	1.5
Total unifaces	13	28.9	20	38.5	41	16.6	74	21.5
Total	45	...	52	...	247	...	344	...
Percent of grand total for site		13		15		72		

heat alteration. It was not possible to carry out a controlled study of chert discoloration such as was done at the Holcombe site (Fitting, DeVisscher, and Wahla, 1966) because of the greater variation of basic chert sources and the lack of control of feature materials.

Similar preforms have been reported in Late Woodland context at Riviere au Vase (Fitting, 1965:53) and the Juntunen site (McPherron, 1967*a*:232).

TABLE 10

METRIC ATTRIBUTES

Metric Attributes, in Centimeters, of Some Chipped-stone Artifact Groups from the Spring Creek Site

	Length	Width	Hafting Width	Thickness
Complete preforms				
N	5	7	...	7
X̄	58.4	34.7	...	13.2
Range.	45-76	24-42	...	12-20
Large triangular				
N	5	7	...	7
X̄	46.8	26.9	...	7.3
Range	40-54	22-30	...	6-8
Large expanding stem				
N	6	9	11	11
X̄	48.7	27.0	11.3	8.4
Range.	44-54	23-35	14-20	7-10
Medium expanding stem				
N	10	13	13	16
X̄	33.3	22.8	14.0	7.4
Range.	28-39	20-26	12-17	5-10
Narrow expanding stem				
N	8	8	8	8
X̄	33.9	16.1	9.5	6.3
Range.	29-44	14-18	8-12	4-9
Small expanding stem				
N	3	4	4	4
X̄	24.0	13.8	8.5	5.5
Range.	23-26	12-15	7-10	5-6
Side-notched				
N	4	8	8	8
X̄	40.8	22.3	15.4	6.5
Range.	35-55	19-27	13-19	4-8
Small triangular				
N	21	27	...	28
X̄	26.0	18.8	...	5.1
Range.	17-42	16-25	...	3-10

A number of triangular pointed bifaces (several used as knives) were recovered (Plate VIII, *a*, Fig. 8, *c*-*e*). As a group, they were smaller than the triangular bifaces from the Schultz site. Each of the 5 from Spring Creek, however, has a counterpart among those from the Schultz site. At first glance they appear similar to Late Archaic "Pomranky points." They are,

PLATE VIII

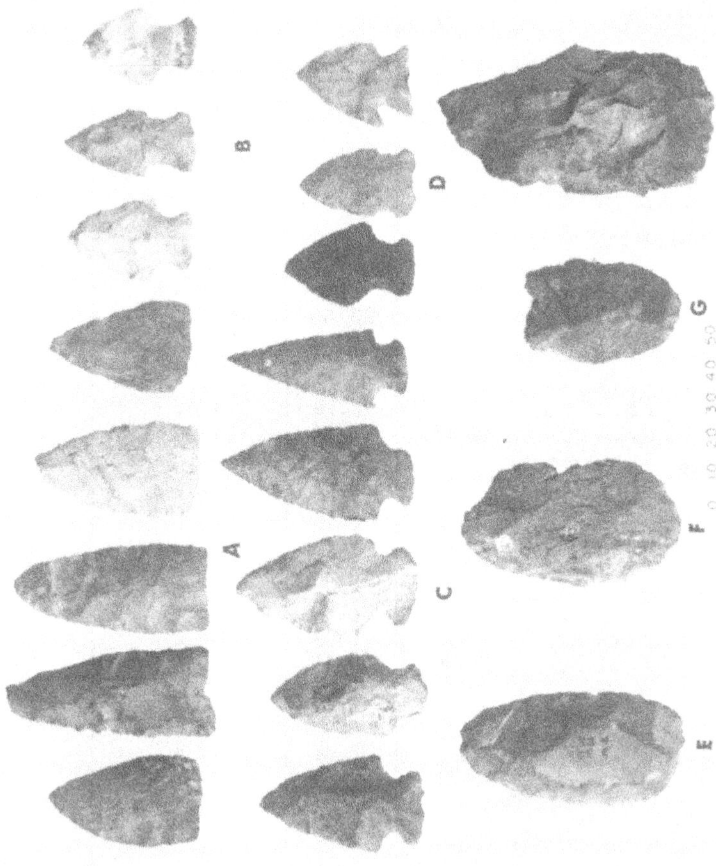

Chipped-stone artifacts: *a*—triangular pointed bifaces; *c*—large expanding-stemmed points; *b,d*—medium expanding-stemmed points; *e-h*—preforms.

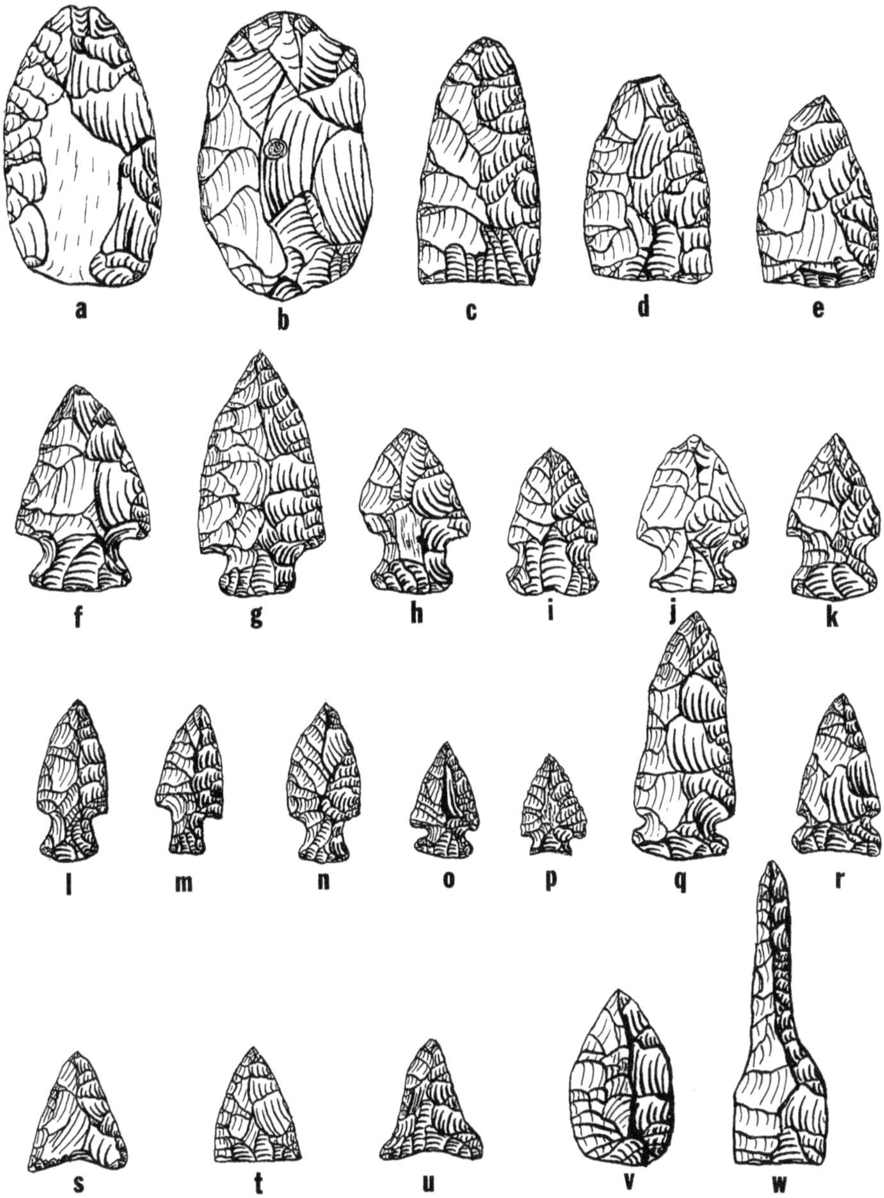

FIG. 8. Chipped-stone artifacts.

a,b—preforms; *c-e*—triangular pointed bifaces; *f,g*—large expanding-stemmed points; *h-k*—medium expanding-stemmed points; *l-n*—narrow expanding-stemmed points; *o,p*—small expanding-stemmed points; *q,r*—side-notched points; *s-u*—small triangular points; *v*—thick triangular pointed biface; *w*—expanding base drill.

however, larger. Among the 27 measurements on Pomranky points of various chert types from the Pomranky site (Binford, 1963:165) only one exceeds the Spring Creek series. The greater thickness of the Spring Creek artifacts is particularly significant. McPherron noted similar "Cache Points" at the Juntunen site and observed that "for some reason artifacts not representative of their period seem to cluster in the later occupations,. . . ." (1967*a*:232). Recent excavations at the Bussinger site in Saginaw have produced caches of nearly identical pointed bifaces in an unquestionable Late Woodland burial context. In my mind there can be no question that these are legitimate Late Woodland artifacts. It is unfortunate that the detailed analysis of lithic materials so characteristic of reports on Archaic sites is not carried over to ceramic sites. As a result, the majority of named projectile point types are Archaic types (Ritchie, 1961: 74 per cent Archaic types; Bell 1958, 1960: 63 per cent Archaic types, and so on) and since they are so named they remain "Archaic" when found on ceramic sites. The wary archaeologist is forced to conjure primitive relic collectors or myriad occupations to account for anything other than small triangular points (which are not limited to Late Woodland sites anyway). This is well demonstrated by the projectile points from Spring Creek.

The projectile points from the site were divided into 6 groups. Four of these groups were variations on the basic expanding-stem point pattern common at the Schultz site. The categories of large expanding-stemmed (Plate VIII, *c*, Fig. 8, *f-g*) and medium expanding-stemmed (Plate VIII, *d*, Fig. 8, *h-k*) were slightly shorter and wider than the comparable groups at the Schultz site. The narrow expanding-stemmed group (Plate IX, *b*, Fig. 8, *l-n*) was also smaller. Four expanding-stemmed points were smaller than any found at the Schultz site (Plate IX, *a,c*, Fig. 8, *o-p*) which would fit in well with the trend toward diminished size in the later horizons at the Schultz site.

The narrow expanding-stemmed points bear a resemblance to the Late Archaic "Lamoka Point" (Ritchie, 1961:29) or the Michigan "Dustin Point" (Binford and Papworth, 1963:105). The occurrence of these narrow expanding-stemmed forms was limited to late Middle Woodland and Late Woodland levels at the Schultz site. McPherron has reported a "Dustin Point" from the Late Woodland Juntunen site (1967:526). They also occur on Late Woodland sites in Ohio (Prufer and Sofsky, 1965:20-21).

Eight side-notched points were recovered from the site (Plate X, *a*, Fig. 8, *q-r*). Turning again to the published point type definitions, it is Ritchie's "Meadowood Point" that first draws ones eye

PLATE IX

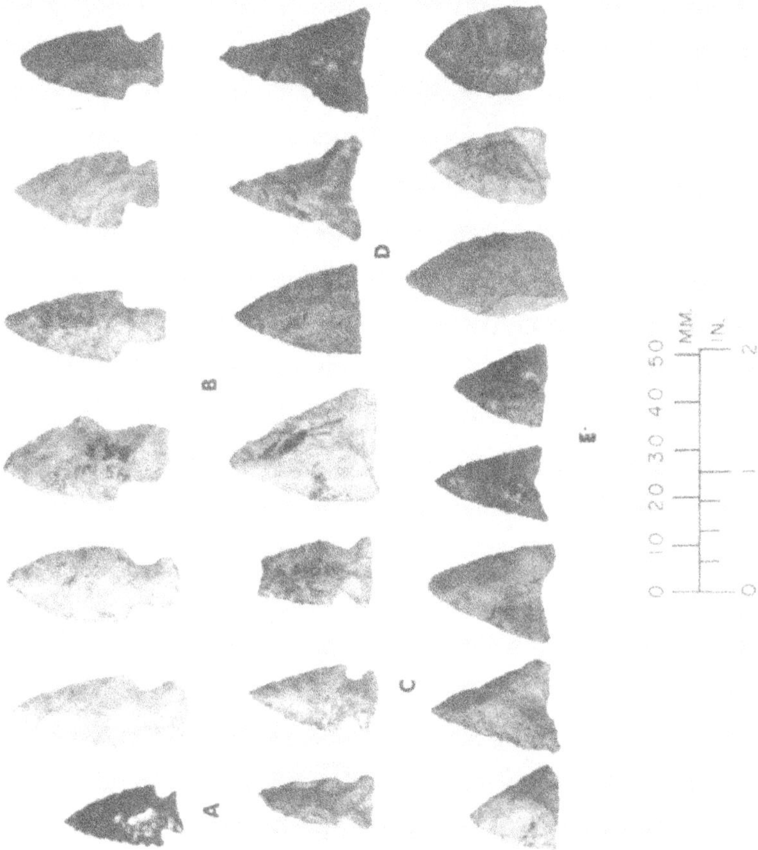

Chipped-stone artifacts: *a,c*—small expanding-stemmed points; *b*—narrow expanding-stemmed points; *d-e*—small triangular points.

PLATE X

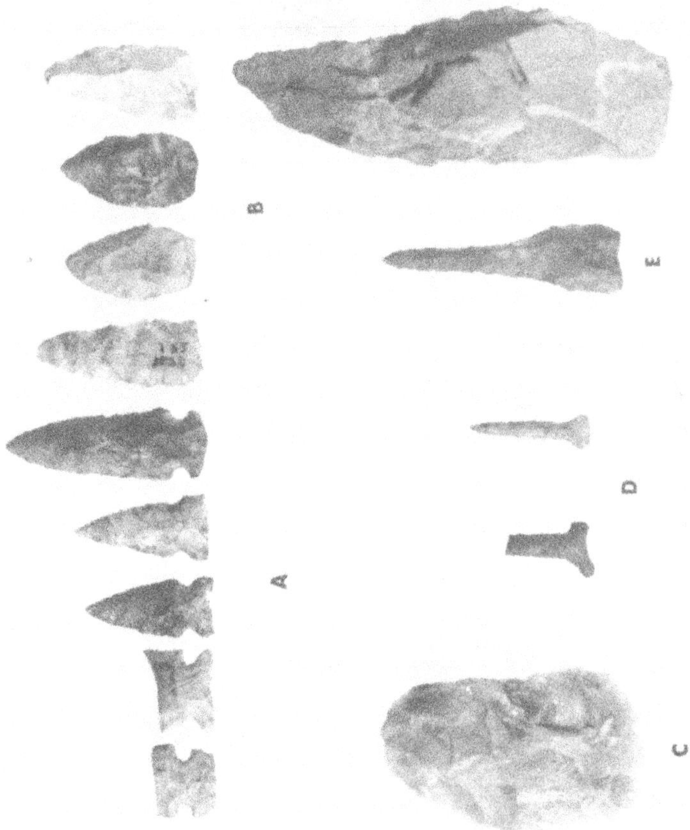

Chipped-stone artifacts: *a*—side-notched points; *b*—thick triangular pointed bifaces; *c*—quartzite knife; *d,e*—expanding base drill; *f*—argillite knife.

Ritchie (1961:35), however, noted that, "The thickness, even of the largest points, rarely exceeds 3/16 of an inch" (.46 centimeters), while the mean thickness of the side-notched points from Spring Creek is .65 centimeters. In actuality we need not look to New York sites for similarities. In Michigan similar side-notched points have been found in Late Woodland context at Riviere au Vase (Fitting, 1965:51), Juntunen (McPherron, 1967:526), and with the West Twin Lake burial (Hinsdale, 1930:Plate XXXII, Fig. 2) which has been radiocarbon dated at A.D. 950 (M-1084).

The most common points on the site are small triangular points (Plate IX, *d,e*, Fig. 8, *s-u*) represented by 28 specimens. Such points are usually considered typical Late Woodland forms although they have been found in earlier context at a number of sites (Fitting, n.d., Harrison, 1966:60, Pi-Sunyer, 1965:84).

There were 5 crudely made, thick triangular pointed bifaces (Plate X, *b*, Fig. 8, *v*), similar to many artifacts in the miscellaneous biface category at the Schultz site; 5 expanding-base drills (Plate X, *d,e*, Fig. 8, *w*), 21 projectile point tips; and 13 fragments of thin, finished bifacial implements. The other bifacial tools consisted of 2 argillite knives (Plate X, *f*, Fig. 9, *a*), 1 complete and 1 fragmentary, and a quartzite knife (Plate X, *c*, Fig. 9, *b*) with a great deal of wear on the edge.

The unifacial tools consisted of steep retouch endscrapers (Plate XI, Fig. 9, *c-f*), sloping retouch endscrapers, and four categories of retouch flakes: side scrapers on flakes, pointed unifacial objects, concave scrapers, and other retouch flakes. Two steep retouch endscrapers were manufactured on blades (Fig. 9,*f*), but such small blades were probably manufactured in the process of small core manufacture rather than from blade cores. We have grouped them with the endscrapers from the site.

In terms of simple chronological placement, the site fits well as an extension of the Schultz site (Table 11, Fig. 10). Spring Creek can be viewed as representing a stylistic successor to the Late Woodland occupation at the Schultz site.

Functional interpretations of the chipped stone artifacts follow those noted for the chippage. Bifacial tools outnumber unifacial tools by a ratio of more than 2-to-1. The largest biface category is that of fragmentary preforms. The large flakes necessary for the manufacture of unifacial tools were rare. The ratio of bifacial to unifacial tools, following the trends at the Schultz site, would suggest a lithic industry with an emphasis on hunting. Not all the "hunting artifacts" suggested at the Schultz site are present in the same frequencies. There are more finished bifaces and a much higher percentage of small cores

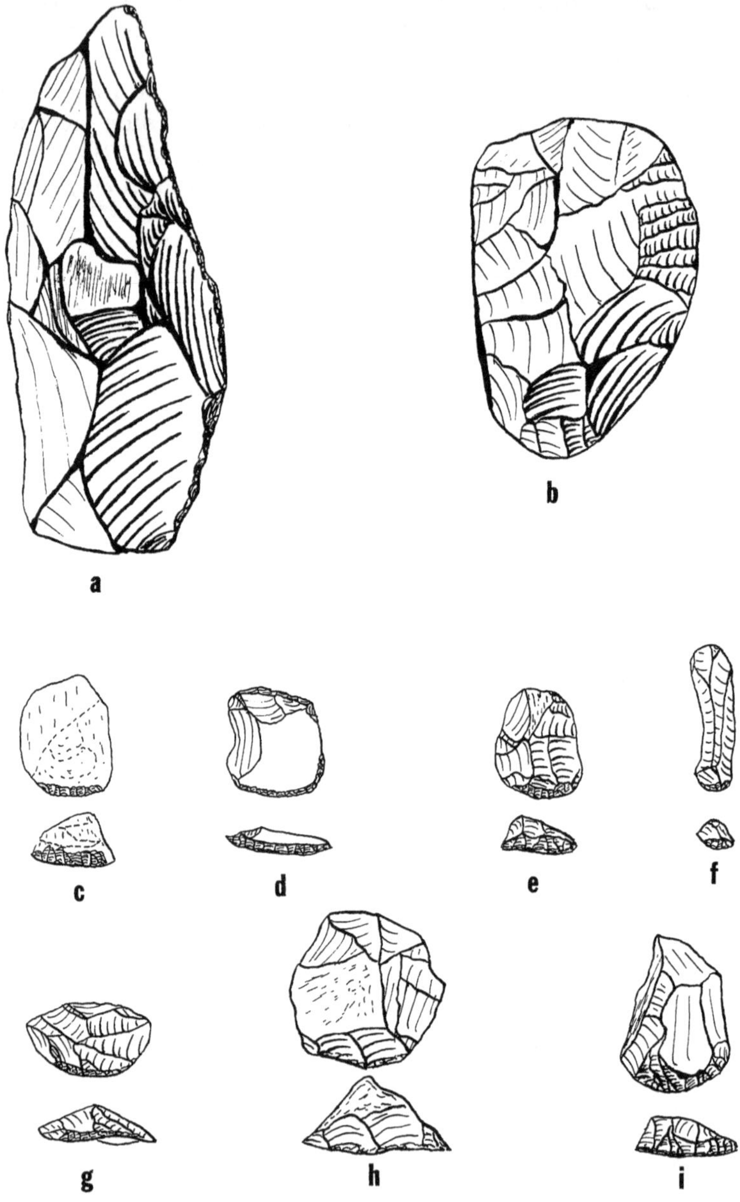

FIG. 9. Chipped-stone artifacts.

a—argillite knife; *b*—quartzite knife; *c-f*—steep retouch endscrapers; *g-i*—sloping retouch endscrapers.

PLATE XI

Scrapers from the Spring Creek site.

(wedges?). There are fewer point tips suggesting that game was not sought in the site area. The scraper frequencies are very close, which is remarkable in light of the sparse number of all unifacial tools at Spring Creek. The lithic industry is numerically insignificant next to the ceramic industry. Little industrial activity was carried out on the site; the ratio of 6 flakes to each artifact is amazing when we consider the Schultz site counts

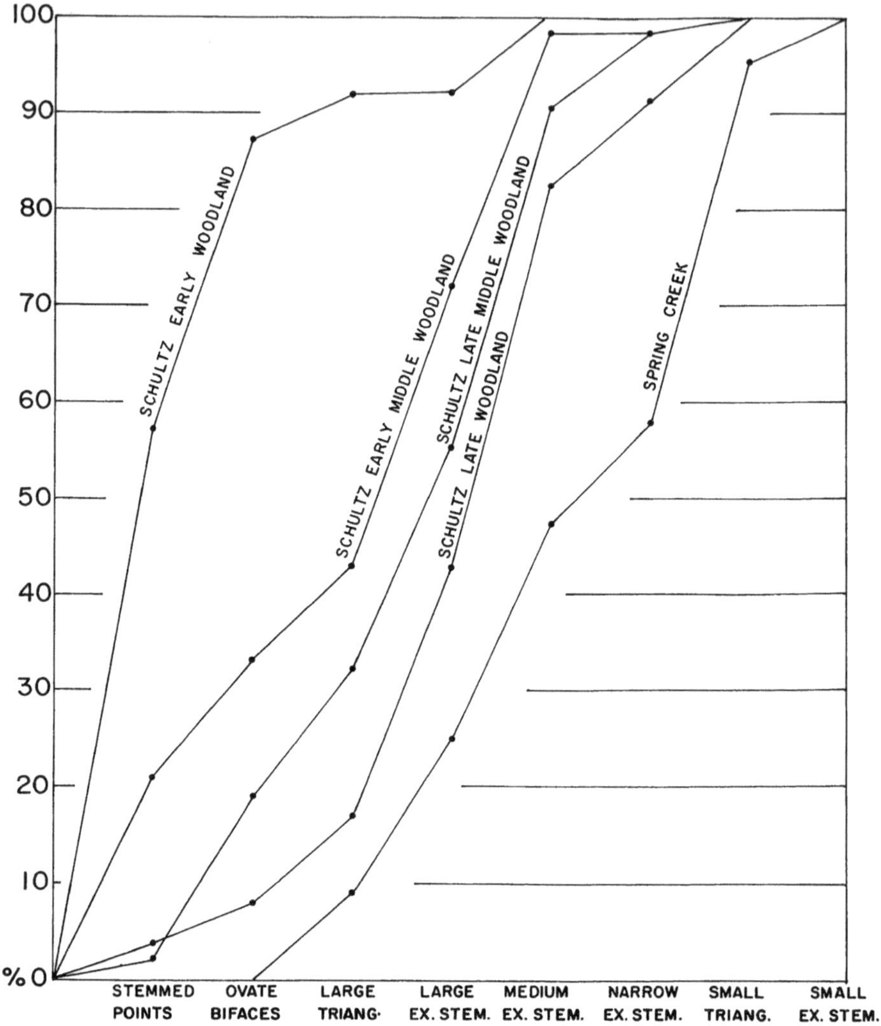

FIG. 10. Succession of projectile point forms at the Schultz and Spring Creek sites.

range between 93 and 212 flakes to each artifact. Most of the artifacts must have been brought to the site in finished form.

There are some differences in artifact frequencies between the different areas on the site. The high concentration of small triangular points in Area I and the variety of points in Area II are the most obvious differences. The ratio of bifaces to unifaces is also quite variable. Almost all of the large, complete

TABLE 11

PROJECTILE POINT SERIATION

Comparison of Key Projectile Point Frequencies from the Four Main Occupations at the Schultz Site and the Spring Creek Site

	SCHULTZ								SPRING CREEK	
	Early Woodland		Early Middle Woodland		Late Middle Woodland		Late Woodland			
	N	Per cent	N	Per cent	N	Per cent	N	Per cent	N	Per cent
Stemmed points .	27	57	9	21	1	2	1	4		
Ovate bifaces. . .	14	30	5	12	9	17	1	4		
Large triangular	3	6	4	10	7	13	2	9	7	9
Large expanding stem	...	...	12	29	12	23	6	26	12	16
Medium expanding stem.	3	6	11	26	18	35	9	39	17	22
Narrow expanding stem.	...	...	...	...	4	8	2	9	8	11
Small triangular	...	...	1	2	1	2	2	9	28	37
									4	5
Total	47		42		52		23		76	
Date	550 B.C.		A.D. 300		A.D. 450		*A.D.700		A.D.950	

*A Radiocarbon date of A.D. 1180 ± 100 (M-1648) has been obtained for the latest material on the site. The majority of early Late Woodland material predates this time and, presumably, predates Spring Creek.

projectile points were in a single box with no marked provenience. This, coupled with the small sample size (less than 100 artifacts) to fill 42 category cells for areas of known provenience, has led me to discount any functional differences suggested by chipped-stone artifacts and base my functional interpretation on the larger samples of chippage and ceramics.

V

OTHER ARTIFACTS

Artifacts other than chipped-stone and ceramics were rare at the Spring Creek site. The loan collection contained only 10 other stone tools, 12 fragments of worked bone representing only 2 objects, and 13 clay elbow pipes and pipe fragments.

There were 2 ground sandstone fragments (Plate XII, *i-j*) which were ground as if used as abraders. Two small slate disks (Plate XII, *g-h*) were chipped all around the edges. Similar objects have been found in burial caches at the Fort Wayne Mound and at the Bussinger site. They were probably part of a flint knappers kit. These other sites are approximately the same age as the Spring Creek site, but this tool type was probably used over a long time period in the Great Lakes.

Five gorget fragments were recovered including one of slate that was roughly chipped before it broke (Plate XII, *e*), a second of slate which broke longitudinally after polishing (Plate XII, *a*), and 3 fragments with evidences of perforation. One of these, (Plate XII, *c*), was of schist, 1 of an igneous rock (Plate XII, *b*), the last of slate (Plate XII, *f*). This type of object has been dated to approximately the same time period as the Riviere au Vase site (Fitting 1965:56-57).

A single adze bit (Plate XII, *d*) rounds out the ground stone tool assemblage from the Spring Creek site.

The bone industry from the site consists of 11 fragments of a highly polished section of long bone (Plate XIII, *b-c*) which has been cut at both ends and a cut and polished bone sliver 3.5 centimeters long with a slight notch at one end (Plate XIII, *a*). This last object may have been a fish gorge.

Three restorable elbow pipes (Plate XIII, *d-f*), 3 bowl fragments and 7 stem fragments were found at Spring Creek. The paste appears to be similar to that of the ceramics but all of the pipes are temperless. Several of the fragmentary stems suggest that the pipes were made by rolling a flattened piece of clay until it was round, smoothing the outer surface, flattening the base and piercing the stem with a twig or stick.

PLATE XII

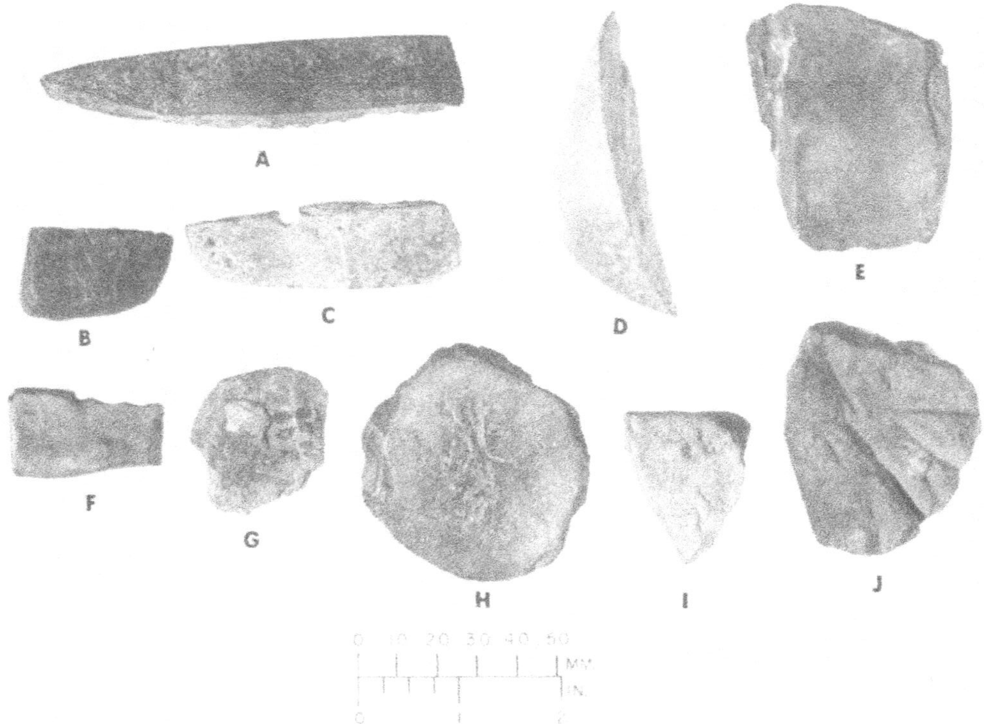

Ground-stone implements: *a–c, e,f*—gorget fragments; *d*—adze bit; *g,h*—slate disks; *i,j*—ground sandstone fragments.

PLATE XIII

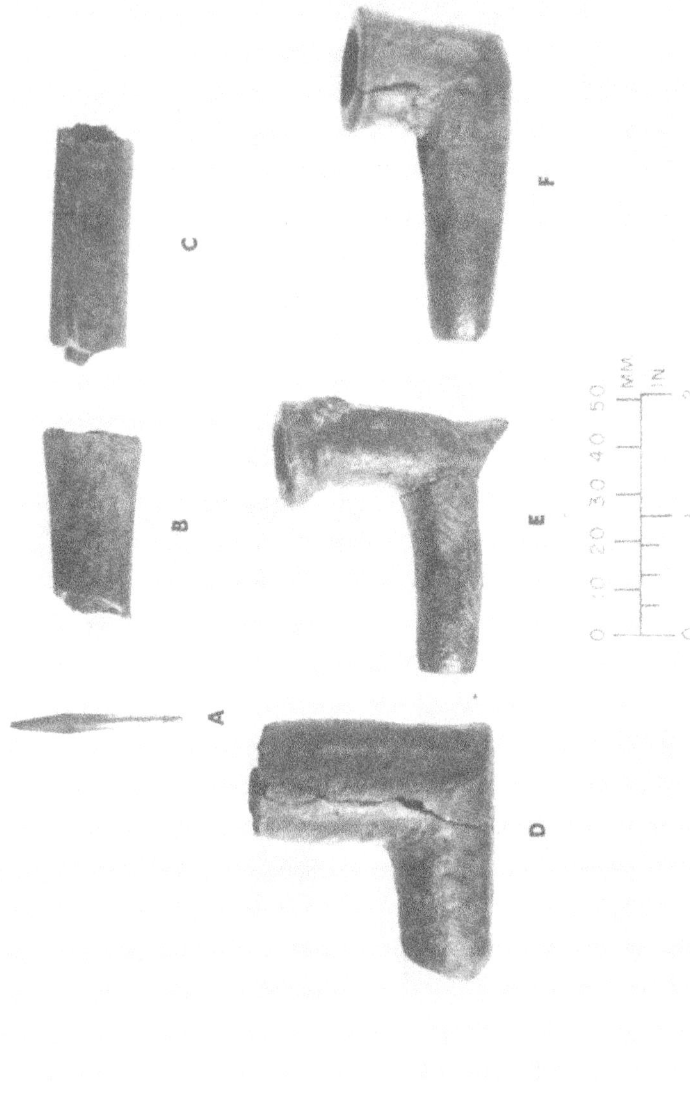

Pipes and bone from Spring Creek: *a*—polished bone sliver; *b–c*—highly polished sections of long bone; *d–f*—elbow pipes.

The bowls appear to have been scraped with a stick or twig.

In contrast to the elbow pipes from the Younge site (Greenman, 1937:74-81) and the Riviere au Vase site (Fitting, 1965:58-62) the bowls of the pipes from Spring Creek all had smooth surfaces. On only one did there appear to be any attempt at decoration. This pipe (Plate XIII, *e*) had a spur projecting beyond the base and 2 clay projections below the bowl rim which suggest eyes. Several other pipes with suggestions of human faces have been found in Michigan and date to the same time period as the Spring Creek occupation (McPherron, 1967:270, Griffin, 1963). The metric attributes of the 3 complete pipes are given in Table 12.

TABLE 12

PIPES

Metric Attributes, in Centimeters, of Complete Elbow Pipes from the Spring Creek Site

	Plate	Length	Height	Width	Bowl Diameter	Stem Diameter
Pipe No. 1	XIII, *e*	5.5	4.7	2.3	.9	.3
Pipe No. 2	XIII, *f*	6.5	3.1	2.7	1.5	.3
Pipe No. 3	XIII, *d*	5.4	4.7	2.6	1.7	.4

VI

FAUNAL REMAINS

Megan Biesele

In a few rare cases, anthropologists possess historical records which supply unequivocal information about past historical extensions of fauna. Makers of anthropological voyages of discovery who do not have recourse to such records for their particular sites, however, must rely upon an analysis of faunal remains as the basis for an educated guess concerning the food economy of an ancient people.

Faunal remains in the form of kitchen midden bones and shells reflect, first the availability of various animal foods and second the food preferences of the people. An analysis of the *available* fauna gives us a detailed indication of the ecological situation prevalent in the region at the time of habitation, as well as of ancient geography and of past extensions of faunal ranges. If we study the *preferred* fauna we gain information about taste preference (which reflects to some extent, at least, the quantity of nutritive value provided by a given animal per man-hour of hunting, trapping, preparing, etc.), traditions and superstitions bearing upon food choice, and conditions of trade and/or barter. The faunal remains further reflect the economic organization of an ancient people, such as the presence of specialized economic activity within the group or of the group as a whole, or division of labor and its importance in the economy. Then, too, they often answer the question of the permanence of a specific site as opposed to merely seasonal use.

The food economy of a past people is elucidated not only by noting the presence of certain animal remains but also by their relative abundance or scarcity. It is important, too, to note conspicuous absences of animals which might have been expected in a given region and to explain why they are absent. A plotting of the spatial distribution of faunal remains at a site is often helpful--in conjunction with plottings of the cultural remains--in mapping features such as dumping grounds in order to see their relationships to living areas. Finally, the total number of faunal fragments at any one site is an indication of the intensity of the habitation, for the presence of many fragments at a site is generally taken to mean the use of many animals rather than the extensive dismemberment of a few animals. Unless we are dealing with a cave or rockshelter site, we may to a great extent disregard the possibility that some animals may have merely wandered to the site and died, for "in an open village site it is reasonably certain that most, if not all, of the bone debris was concentrated by the people occupying the site and that it represents the remains of animals actually utilized by them" (Guilday and Tanner, 1962:136).

The site presently under consideration is located along Spring Creek, which flows into the Muskegon River in Muskegon County, Michigan. A radiocarbon date which has been obtained on charcoal from the Spring Creek site is A.D. 960 ± 75 (M-512, Crane and Griffin, 1958), and in the light of the geological evidence it would seem reasonable to assume that the geography and the ecology of the region have changed little since then except by the encroachments of modern America. The pre-Columbian carbon date is corroborated by the total absence of the remains of domesticated animals except for what is perhaps the remains of an Indian dog or two.

This area presents mostly a low-relief geography with rolling hills; underlying rocks rarely appear at the surface. Glacial features such as lakes, moraines, drumlins, eskers, etc., are common. The winters are, in general, long and severe with snow for the most, if not all, of the season. The region is north of the cyclone belt for the winter but not for the summer. Burt (1957) tells us that the mammals we can expect to find in this region are primarily boreal in their relationships, but also show a strong southeastern element. While there has been little recent natural change in extensions of most faunal ranges in Michigan, animals such as black bear, beaver, and white-tailed deer, among others, have moved northward in the state, retreating before the advance of Caucasian agriculture and hunting and trapping.

The faunal remains collected from the Spring Creek site comprise some 7000 bone and shell fragments, roughly half of which are identifiable and are mostly small bits of mammal bone in the deer/bear size range. A drawback of the collection is that the provenience materials were not taken from all areas of the site but apparently only from those which it was felt afforded the richest middens. Finally, the large percentage of identifiable fragments at this site (most sites have a figure of 15 per cent or so) leads one to suspect some sort of preferential selection.

The great majority of the bone remains fall into 7 mammalian species. These are white-tailed deer (*Odocoileus virginianus borealis*), beaver (*Castor canadensis michiganensis*), black bear (*Ursus americanus americanus*), raccoon (*Procyon lotor lotor*), gray fox (*Urocyon cinereoargenteus cinereoargenteus*), muskrat (*Ondatra zibethica zibethica*), and what may be Indian dog (*Canis familiaris*). In addition, there is a considerable number of bivalve shell fragments which comprise 7 species: Wabash pig-tow (*Fusconaia flava*), three-ridge (*Amblema costata*), pink nigger-head (*Pleurobema cordatum coccineum*), spike or lady-finger (*Elliptio dilatatus*), mucket (*Actinonaias carinata*), fat mucket (*Mampsillis siliquoidea*), and black sand shell (*Ligumia recta latissima*). The third type of remains important in the food economy is a large quantity of shell fragments from the turtle *Pseudemys graptemys*. The availability of these animals gives certain fairly direct clues as to the natural ecology of the immediate vicinity of the site.

Odocoileus virginianus

Formerly the white-tailed deer ranged all over Michigan. At present this species is found in Newaygo County but is absent from the southern two tiers of Michigan counties, driven northward by White agriculture and hunting. Its preferred habitat consists of the border area between forests and openings. The diet of *Odocoileus*, says Burt, is highly varied and changes with the seasons: in early spring it nibbles on tender young grass and in later spring the summer herbs, shrubs, tree leaves, and fungi furnish its food. In the autumn, it subsists almost entirely upon acorns, while they last, and in winter it browses upon small shrub-twigs, mosses, and green cedar tips.

From the site as a whole, a minimum of 21 *Odocoileus* individuals have been collected,--50 per cent of the total minimum number of individual mammals collected. This number represents 2100 pounds of edible meat, which is 73 per cent of the total number of pounds of edible meat for the site (Table 13). Obviously, the white-tailed deer formed a large part of the diet of these people as well as providing hides and sinews. All ages of deer were well represented in the teeth except the very young, of which, however, there was some evidence in the other bones. None of the deer long bones collected were anywhere near complete; such bones, apparently, were always fractured for their marrow. There was a marked scarcity of the larger deer skeletal elements in the collection, but sometimes such large animals were killed away from the camp and only the lighter parts were brought back. White (1953) states that metapodials, pelves, vertebrae, and skulls were usually left at the kill site.

The antler fragments collected were invariably of the mature antler growth expected in fall and winter. Antlers are generally shed from January to June, with new growth beginning in early summer. This piece of evidence, especially when coupled with the usual abundance of deer in the fall, after the fat summer season and before winter privation, might lead us to conclude that hunting was a seasonal activity. This conclusion seems to gain support from the relative scarcity of fawn-sized remains, for fawns would naturally be more abundant in the spring.

Ursus americanus

The minimum possible number of black bear individuals represented at the site is 2. However, since the unidentifiable elements of the collection may in part represent bear, the number may be somewhat larger. Assuming 2 bear kills, or 4.8 per cent of the total number of individual animals killed, we can conclude that 420 pounds of edible meat (or 14 per cent of the total number of pounds of edible meat for the site) were furnished by black bear. Two kills hardly seems a reasonable total for more than one season, so if the collection is anywhere near complete, we cannot with much certainty postulate a longer period of occupation for any sizeable human group. Bear meat, high in energy content, doubtless was a highly-prized food, and was probably easy to obtain during the months of hibernation. The presence of bear argues for the nearby existence of densely wooded areas, for bear prefer heavy cover. It is interesting that many of the identifiable bear remains were skull parts, indicating the labor of carrying such a heavy part from the kill site to the camp. We might conclude that some ceremonial significance may have been attached to the bear skulls. Formerly bear were all over the state of Michigan but they have in general retreated north in recent times, until at present they occupy only the Upper Peninsula and the northern-most parts of the Lower.

Procyon lotor

A minimum of 6 raccoon individuals is represented in the bones recovered; at an average of 17.5 pounds of edible meat per animal the site should have been furnished with 105 pounds of raccoon meat. The raccoon remains represented 14.4 per cent of the total number of individual mammals from the site and 3.4 per cent of the total weight of edible meat. Raccoons were prized as items of diet and fairly easy to take, especially with the help of dogs. Their state of semihibernation in winter made them especially vulnerable during that season.

Raccoons are semiarboreal and omnivorous, and streams or lakes are almost indispensable to their existence, due to their habit of washing food and their preference for aquatic diet. They inhabit wooded areas near water, especially where provided with large hollow trees as homes. At present, as formerly, they are found throughout Michigan, but are more common in the Lower than in the Upper Peninsula.

Castor canadensis

The bones of 6 beavers, as a minimum, were collected from the site, which represent 14.4 per cent of the total number of individuals killed. Beavers provided 231 pounds of edible meat, or 7 per cent of the total for the site. Certainly utilized as food, the beaver must also have been of help to Indians in the creation of ponds, which have the dual economic function of retaining water against dry seasons and of acting as a natural regional condenser of fish populations. The habitat of the beaver is wooded streams and lake shores. Nearby stands of small timber are an absolute requirement, and the preferred types are aspen, birch, maple or willow. If the supply of trees is depleted, the beaver will travel up to 200 yards from water to obtain them. Beaver colonies consume the trees along streams or around the lakes they clear, and water with their dams rich meadow-land which is perfect for deer-grazing. Formerly beaver ranged all over the state of Michigan, but are now absent from the southern 2 tiers of counties.

Ondatra zibethica

Four muskrat individuals were represented in the jaw fragments found. This number is 9.6 per cent of the total number of individual mammals killed, and provided 8 pounds of edible meat or 0.2 per cent of the total. One maxilla found has a complete complement of milk teeth, which probably shows that the underwater muskrat houses were raided by the Indians, because the young were much less likely to travel abroad. Muskrats inhabit marshes, ponds, lakes, and streams, especially where there are havey growths of rushes or cattails. They are chiefly aquatic; and open water, at least during part of the year, is essential for them. Muskrats generally eat the stems and roots of aquatic vegetation, but may turn carnivorous for a time and eat mussels, frogs, or turtles. They build houses of available aquatic vegetation under water. During the late summer and early fall muskrats crossed country searching for home sites and were presumably easily taken at that time. The animal may have been very important to the Indians for its fur, if not so much for its meat. It is distributed throughout the state of Michigan.

Urocyon cinereoargenteus

Two gray foxes are represented, or 4.8 per cent of the total number of mammals killed. If this animal was indeed utilized for food, it provided 9 pounds of meat (or 0.3 per cent of the total) to the site. It seems more probable, that it was killed primarily for its pelt, which was highly valued. The fox is sly and cunning

TABLE 13

SPRING CREEK MAMMALS

From Entire Site, Including Provenience and Nonprovenience Materials

	Minimum Number of Individuals		Pounds of Meat per Individual		Total Pounds of Meat	Per cent of Total No. of Individuals	Per cent of Total Pounds of Meat
Odocoileus (from rt. tibial tarsal).	21	x	100	=	2100	50	73
Ursus (from l. maxilla fragment). . .	2	x	210	=	420	4.8	14
Castor (from jaw teeth)	6	x	38.5	=	231	14.4	7
Procyon (from l. mandible fragment)	6	x	17.5	=	105	14.4	3.4
Urocyon (from l. mandible fragment)	2	x	4.5	=	9	4.8	0.3
Ondatra (from jaw fragments)	4	x	2	=	8	9.6	0.2
Canis (from phalanges)	1					2.4	.....
Total	42				2873		

and the small amount of food value is hardly compensation for the labor involved in its capture. This theory is further supported by its rarity, although it was sparsely distributed throughout the lower peninsula. The pelt may thus have been prized as an object for ceremony or barter. The habitat of the gray fox is the forest and fairly open brushland.

Canis

The few elements in the collection may represent the remains of an Indian dog or two, but since it is nearly impossible to identify the postcranial elements of *Canis* as to species, they may well be the remains of wolves.

Pelecypods

The habits of the fresh-water bivalves found in conjunction with the site seem to indicate the fairly close presence of nearby bodies of water ranging in size from smaller streams to larger rivers, with variable bottom material. The preferred depths of the 7 species range from 0.3 to 8 meters and preferred current speeds range from quiet water to 8 mph. In spite of variations in preferred habitat, however, it is conceivable that all 7 species could have inhabited one nearby shallow stream of variable bottom and current speed. In fact, it hardly seems likely that the Indians would have bothered to gather bivalves from more than the closest stream if that one remained sufficient.

The presence of certain of these bivalves in the midden material indicates, in turn, the concomitant presence of certain fish hosts in the nearby streams and, presumably, in the Indians' diets, although no fish bones are included in the collection. These hosts are white crappie (*Pomoxis annularis*), black crappie (*Pomoxis sparoides*), bluegill (*Lepomis pallidus*), yellow perch (*Perca flavescens*), and wall-eyed pike (*Stizostedion vitreum*).

The bivalve shells, of which more than 1500 grams were collected at the site, seem to constitute an important article of the Indian diet. Bivalves are easily obtainable and are available throughout the year. They represent women's work almost entirely, because the males killed the vertebrate food.

Gastropods

In addition to the bivalves, a few terrestrial snails (*Anguispira alternata*) were found on the site. It is generally agreed that where such terrestrial snails are found in less than inordinat numbers, they probably became part of the kitchen middens while seeking food, and do not have any bearing upon the Indian economy.

Reptiles

The only reptile represented at Spring Creek is the turtle *Pseudemys graptemys*, present in a number of shell fragments which are probably the remains of only 1 or 2 individuals. Scrape-marks on the concave inner surfaces of these fragments indicate its use as food. This turtle is rather large and may have provided several pounds of edible meat per individual. Careful scrutiny by John Halsey failed to reveal the etching or design sometimes found on the outsides of turtle shell implements from archaeological sites in Michigan.

Two major recovery areas are represented in the provenience material. A chi-square run on the different amounts of deer and bivalve material from the two areas revealed no significant differences from the nonprovenience collection, except that only half the amount of bivalve material expected was found in the provenience areas. This discrepancy reflects, in my opinion, the small size of the sample rather than any significant cultural difference between the site as a whole and the two recovery areas. Further, cumulative graphs of the relative amounts of mammal material in the diet (Fig. 11) show little in the way of important differences, except that Area II is devoid of raccoon and muskrat remains, which may again reflect only the small size of the sample.

The quantity of bone remains recovered from this site—a minimum of 42 mammals—demonstrates that this is not primarily a hunting camp. A hunting camp might conceivably have consisted only of males, but the bivalve remains as evidence of womens work, and the cultural remains, seem to suggest other use for this camp.

What we are able to conclude from the faunal remains of the Spring Creek site is that they represent an open village encampment of fairly low economic intensity, as far as hunting is concerned. We can presume that the geography of the region at the time of occupation was much as it is today. The remains of food animals indicate that the site must have been in the immediate vicinity of a wooded stream of variable character with fairly easy access to the small timber stands required by beaver and to the dense cover preferred by bear. A forest habitat is suggested but it may also have had open glade areas and some brushland.

TABLE 14

DETAILED RECOVERY NOTES

A. Nonprovenience

Odocoileus

17 antler fragments
2826 grams long bone fragments
14 left tibial tarsals
14 right tibial tarsals
3 right scapula fragments
1 left scapula fragment
5 left fibular tarsal fragments
4 right fibular tarsal fragments
41 phalanges
3 distal ends of femur
2 distal ends of metatarsal
4 proximal ends of ulna
20 humerus fragments
31 metacarpal fragments
17 assorted carpals and tarsals
15 vertebral fragments
11 distal ends of tibia
1 distal end of radio-ulna
1 vestigial metacarpal
1 phalanx (fawn-size)
7 mandible fragments
2 basioccipitals
37 cranial fragments (mainly from occipital region)

Castor

4 right mandible fragments with teeth
2 left mandible fragments with teeth
palatine process of 1 maxilla
proximal ends of 4 left ulnae
proximal ends of 1 right ulna
1 tibial tarsal
1 unguis
15 phalanges
73 jaw teeth
19 incisors

Procyon

2 right mandible fragments with teeth
3 left mandible fragments with teeth
1 right maxilla fragment with teeth
3 canine teeth
3 molars
5 premolars

Urocyon

1 left mandible nearly complete, with 4 teeth

Ondatra

1 left pelvis fragment (ilium, acetabulum, parts of ischium, pubis)
8 jaw fragments; one a left maxilla with milk dentition
8 incisors

Ursus

1 left mandible fragment
2 left maxilla fragments
1 right maxilla fragment
6 molars
2 premolars
2 canines
1 incisor
proximal end of 1 right ulna
1 distal end of metacarpal
2 first phalanges (one mangled or diseased)
2 second phalanges
1 right tibial tarsal

TABLE 14 (Cont'd.)

B. Provenience Area I

Castor

7 jaw teeth	2 incisors
1 unguis	1 phalanx
1 tarsal	

Procyon

2 left mandible fragments, each with 1 molar	1 left tibia (proximal end)
1 right mandible with 3 premolars and 2 molars	1 phalanx
	1 left mandible fragment
	1 right mandible fragment with molar

Urocyon

1 proximal end of tibia	1 tibial tarsal

Ondatra

1 maxilla with teeth	1 left mandible with teeth
1 incisor	

Ursus

4 phalanges	1 unguis

Canis

1 sagittal crest fragment	5 phalanges
1 right molar	

C. Provenience Area II

Castor

3 phalanges	6 jaw teeth
1 vertebra	1 maxilla with 3 jaw teeth

Procyon

none

Ondatra

none

Urocyon

1 left mandible with 2 molars, 1 premolar

Ursus

3 phalanges	1 tarsal
1 carpal	4 ungues

Canis

1 carnassial

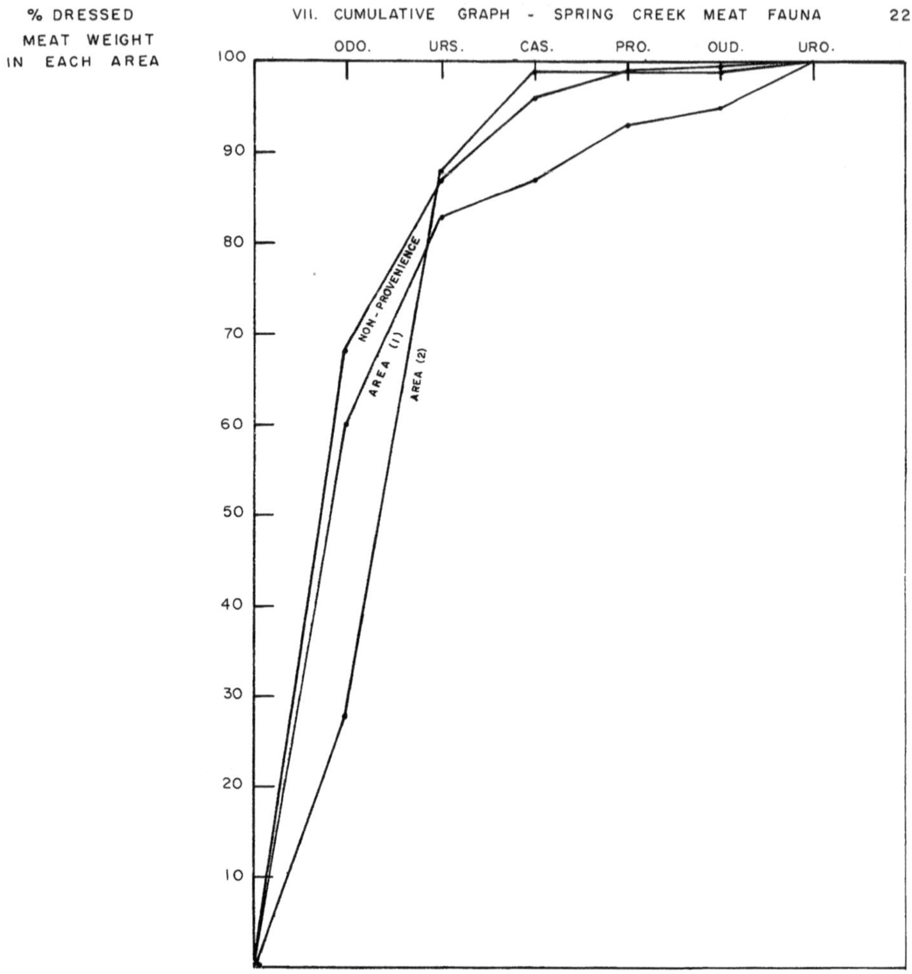

FIG. 11. Faunal remains from Spring Creek.

VII

CONCLUSIONS

Cultural and Chronological Significance

During the past few years the prime focus of many Michigan prehistorians has been on the cultural and ecological significance of the Carolinian-Canadian transition area in lower Michigan (Fitting, 1966). It now appears that no single variable can be used to define this zone. It also appears that cultural as well as environmental factors can be used for defining the transitional area as a whole.

Although Dice (1943) would have included the Spring Creek site in the Canadian Biotic Province, our examination of soils, forest cover, and fauna (Hinsdale, 1932:Map 1) indicate more of a Carolinian situation near the mouth of the Muskegon. Actually the Muskegon River penetrates the edge area, and the entire valley must be viewed as a unit and a transition between these two areas.

The cultural material from the sites indicates a series of close cultural relations to the south. The ceramics in particular point to the Carolinian and Illinoian biotic provinces. In Michigan there is a strong division between cultural forms in these areas starting at least as early as the Middle Woodland period. In the southern part of the state are Havana Tradition materials; in the northern part are manifestations of what I have referred to as the Lake Forest Middle Woodland.

The division of cultural material in these two areas of the state carries over into Late Woodland times. Again, because of the prevalence of ceramics at these sites, the ceramic style zones are most evident. The northern early Late Woodland ceramics are Mackinac wares or similar to Mackinac wares (McPherron, 1967) there southern equivalents are, again, Wayne wares, early Riviere wares, and such types as Spring Creek Collared. The emphasis on elaboration of ceramic decoration found on the northern Middle Woodland materials carries over into the Late Woodland period. The extent of decoration, the elaboration of rim form and decoration, and the variety of motifs are particularly significant. In contrast, the majority of Wayne Ware vessels are undecorated. What decoration is present consists of incising, punctations, or cord impressions. There are more rounded rims and the thickened and slightly everted rims are impressed with a paddle edge or cord-wrapped stick. Even these decorations are subdued in comparison with their northern contemporaries.

Actual Mackinac wares have been found at the Ekdahl-Goudreau site on Seul Choix Point on Lake Michigan, from the beach at Naomikong Point in Lake Superior, and the Juntunen site itself. Related forms have been found at Skegemog Point in the Traverse Bay area and the Butterfield site in Bay County. Many of the sherds from Mason's (1966) Heins Creek site also resemble Mackinac wares.

In eastern Michigan there is an overlap of these types with Wayne wares along the Lake Huron shore. I would consider the vessel from the West Twin Lake burial mound to be a Wayne ware variant (Hinsdale, 1930: not illustrated). The vessel in Plate XXXIII, Figure 1 is from the Brooks Group (Plate XXXVI, same article). This site is north of the Butterfield site. In eastern Michigan, however, the entire Lake Huron shore must be considered as a part of the Canadian-Carolinian transition area. The relative north-south position is not as important as the existence of both forms in the transition area.

Wayne wares are common in southeastern Michigan at the Gibraltar site, the Fort Wayne Mound, and in the Riviere au Vase site (Fitting, 1965:131-37). In this area Wayne ware variants are found in an early Late Woodland context. A burial area with grave lots and ceramics virtually identical to those from Gibraltar has been recently excavated in Saginaw. This site, the Bussinger site, was excavated by a University of Michigan field party in 1965 and by members of the Saginaw Valley Chapter of the Michigan Archaeological Society working with Arthur Graves. At this site the Late Woodland burials intrude into a Middle Woodland village site.

Spring Creek contains the largest sample of the southern ceramic types found along the Muskegon River, but Prahl has also found them with burials in the Brunett and Mallon Mounds near Newaygo.

Many of the sherds illustrated by Flanders from the Spoonville site along the Grand River (Flanders, 1965:346) resemble Wayne wares. There are two radiocarbon dates from Spoonville which would indicate that this is a Middle Woodland Village site. Perhaps we have a situation similar to that in southeastern Michigan with early Late Woodland ceramics having their origin in Middle Woodland cord-marked types.

With the exception of the Spoonville dates, the corroborative radiocarbon dates from comparative sites are very uniform. The Fort Wayne Mound has been dated to A.D. 750 ± 120 (M-1843). The West Twin Lake Mound in Montmorency County has been radiocarbon dated to A.D. 950 ± 100 (M-1084). The Riviere au Vase Phase in southeastern Michigan has been radiocarbon dated to A.D. 700 ± 120 (M-1519). Low-collared rims with a slightly greater degree of elaboration were found in the Whorely earthwork (Speth, 1966) and have been radiocarbon dated to A.D. 1070 ± 100 (M-1758). A feature at the Bussinger site in Saginaw containing a small vessel with a crosshatched rim and rocker-stamped body has been dated to A.D. 590 ± 120 (M-1756). The Late Woodland occupation at Bussinger is intrusive into this level and must be later than this.

Going beyond the range of dated Michigan materials we can note that Maxwell (1959:27) suggested that Late Woodland materials in Illinois postdate A.D. 700. Winters (1963:81) has suggested that the Albee complex falls between A.D. 800 and A.D. 1000.

Looking to the northern Mackinac wares we find radiocarbon dates of A.D. 835 ± 75 (M-1142, Crane and Griffin, 1961), and A.D. 910 ± 75 years (M-1141, Crane and Griffin, 1961) for McPherron's Mackinac Phase at the Juntunen site. Mason has a radiocarbon date of A.D. 720 ± 150 years (I-678, Mason, 1966) from the Heins Creek site.

The Spring Creek site with its radiocarbon date of A.D. 960 ± 75 (M-512, Crane and Griffin, 1958) falls nicely into place, in terms of cultural and chronological divisions, with what we know of similar sites in the upper Great Lakes. It is representative of one of the northernmost occurrences of a generally more southern cultural form which may be correlated with the favorable Neo-Atlantic climatic episode (Baerreis and Bryson, 1965:215-16). It serves as an important site in the correlation of cultural types and environmental zones in prehistoric Michigan.

Economy

Cleland (1966:42-45) has recently contrasted focal and diffuse economies of prehistoric peoples of the Great Lakes area. Focal economies are directed toward the exploitation of one or a few kinds of resources, while diffuse economies are directed toward a number of resources. As Cleland pointed out, the polar extremes are seldom encountered. Most groups fall somewhere along the continuum between these points.

During the Late Woodland period Cleland has noted the existence of both the focal and diffuse patterns in the Upper Great Lakes. The hunters and fishers of the Canadian Biotic Province are an excellent example of a diffuse adaptation; the farmers of the Carolinian Biotic Province are focal agriculturalists. The edge area between these zones was occupied by peoples with economies varying between those of their northern and southern neighbors.

Cleland has found that focal agricultural sites are marked by a selective hunting pattern with emphasis on a few food species. This increasing emphasis on fewer food species is seen throughout the stratified Schultz site sequence, and is seen at its fullest at the Moccasin Bluff site in Barrien County (Cleland, 1966:211-23) and the Silver Lake site in Oceana County (Cleland, 1966:79-80). The faunal assemblage from Spring Creek follows the pattern of these sites.

In light of the vast amounts of cultural material, it seems clear that hunting was not the main subsistence activity. Biesele has estimated that a total of 2873 pounds of dressed meat was obtained from the animals represented by the bone refuse from Spring Creek. Using Hinsdale's (1932:9) estimate that a full grown man requires 2.6 pounds of lean meat per day we arrive at a population estimate of three males if we assume a one-year occupation. Mollusks were, no doubt, an important food item but Hinsdale (1932:9) has also noted that it would take 13.4 pounds of clams to support a man for one day.

In addition to the limited amount of animal bone refuse there are a limited number of food species. Biesele believes that all ages of deer were represented at the Spring Creek site. A single reptile was found and no fishbone was recovered from the site. The conclusion that this was a focal agricultural site seems clear in spite of the fact that we have no direct evidence of agriculture to support this contention. An alternative might be maize agriculture with an important dependence on wild rice--see Hinsdale (1932:21) for a discussion of the importance of wild rice in Michigan, particularly in the Muskegon River Valley.

The hunting activities of the Spring Creek site occupants, as represented by the refuse, sounds familiar when we read accounts of historic groups in the area. Biesele noted the absence of deer long bones and suggested that much meat was brought back to camp already dressed. Alexander Henry (cited from Quimby, 1962:225) noted the practice of moving to the site of an elk kill, butchering it and carrying the dried and smoked meat back to the site. If this were being done at Spring Creek (as I believe it was) our previous estimate of meat in their diets, based on animal bone refuse, would be far short of the actual amount consumed at the site.

Just as Quimby has noted for historic Chippewa (1962:223) bear, raccoon, and beaver follow deer and elk in order of importance. Biesele's comments on the bear skull fragments from the site recall Henry's description of a bear hunt among a Chippewa group in 1763 and the following ceremonies (Quimby, 1962: 227). The skin, the meat, the fat and the *head* were taken back to camp. The skull was treated with ceremonial respect for three days and then "put in the kettle." While the hunting activities described by Henry deal with the diffuse economy of the Chippewa, it would seem that the secondary hunting activities of an agricultural group in the same area would be similar.

Some further comment is also required on the specific functions of various areas on the site. Biesele found that the only statistically significant difference in the distribution of food remains was that "only half the amount of bivalve material expected was found in the provenience areas." If we go back to the distribution of ceramics on the site, the "rest of the site," the nonprovenience areas, was the part of the site closest to the creek with the preponderance of small vessels. Mollusks were, apparently, eaten near the creek and not carried to the east end of the site in large numbers.

No raccoon or muskrat remains were found in Area II. This was the area with the larger projectile point forms. The abundance of small triangular projectile points correlates with the provenience area with greater frequency of small game remains. Again, a simple functional explanation for artifact distribution seems preferable to postulating multiple occupations.

Social Organization

While the nature of the Spring Creek collection does not allow us to draw conclusions about the social organization with the degree of refinement found in McPherron (1967) and Pilling (1965) it does allow some generalizations on community patterning.

The nature of the Spring Creek settlement is striking. It is generally assumed that among aboriginal groups in the Upper Great Lakes ceramics were made by the women and chipped-stone implements were made and used by men. The relative frequencies of these artifact classes might reflect the ratio of men to women at any particular site. We noted at Spring Creek a ratio of almost 4 vessels for each finished flint artifact and 10 sherds for every scrap of flint debris of any type. This would suggest an emphasis on female activity, that more females than males were actually present in the site area. This would further be supported by the nature of the lithic industry. Almost no actual flint knapping took place on the site. I noted a similar but even more obvious skew at Riviere au Vase (Fitting, 1965:47) but did not realize its possible significance.

Going back to Cleland's assessment of economic types in the Upper Great Lakes, it follows that there is a similar division of community patterning. The Chippewa are an example of a diffuse economy. Their seasonal activities involved a breaking up into family hunting parties during the winter months with a gathering of family groups for specific economic activities, such as fishing, in the summer. Quimby (1962) has dealt with the nature of this economic cycle and the type of sites which the archaeologist could expect to find from such a cycle. We have sites corresponding to two of the types suggested by Quimby. Wright (1965) has compared a series of sites along the north shore of Lake Superior and Lake Huron which seem to fit Quimby's small camp description. McPherron (1967) has reported on a summer fishing village in the straits of Mackinac which would be analogous to the site which Quimby suggested should be found on St. Martin's Island.

At the northern Chippewa hunting sites Wright (1965:207) noted ". . .that stone tools were more abundant relative to rimsherds than is characteristic of most ceramic producing sites." The actual ratios might reflect a higher ratio of males to females than that suggested by the Spring Creek assemblage. McPherron found an abundance of ceramics over finished stone tools but there was other evidence that males were present on the site but engaged in an economic activity, fishing, which did not require extensive preparation of a variety of stone tools. There is no evidence at Spring Creek that any fishing took place.

Cleland has used the Miami as an example of a group with a focal agricultural economy with seasonal hunting. The Miami were semisedentary with large permanent villages occupied during the summer months while they tended the fields (Kinietz, 1940:171). During the late autumn months the entire population, with the exception of those too old to take part, left for several months of communal hunting. In Michigan the Moccasin Bluff site may represent this type of village site.

The later occupations at the Schultz site in Saginaw might serve, with some qualifications. This site, as we have noted before, was probably occupied somewhat before the Spring Creek site. In the same way that the lithic material from Schultz suggested a base from which something like the Spring Creek assemblage could develop, so the Spring Creek economy is a logical development of the trend represented at the Schultz site. There are indications of seasonal occupations of large groups containing complete family units throughout the Schultz sequence. While not an exact analogy, the spring-summer occupation of the late Middle Woodland levels at Schultz might be similar to the summer village occupation of a group like the Miami. The Schultz Late Woodland occupation might reflect a situation similar to that of the Miami winter hunting camp with short occupations by numerous complete family units.

In the summer camp, even with increased artifact density, the ratios of ceramics to finished stone tools are closer to those of Wright's Lake Superior sites than to Spring Creek. In the Late Woodland levels at Schultz this trend is even more evident. The degree of industrial activity at Schultz is reflected in the ratio of chippage to artifacts: 212 chips to each flint artifact in the late Middle Woodland level, 93 chips to each flint artifact in the late Middle Woodland level, as opposed to only 7 chips to each artifact at Spring Creek.

From this discussion it would appear that Spring Creek is not typical of either a group with a diffuse economy and settlement pattern like that of the Chippewa or of a group with a focal economy and a settlement pattern like that of the Miami. I can, however, see similarities of the settlement pattern recorded for the Ottawa.

Kinietz (1940:236) has noted that the Ottawa were semisedentary with permanent villages which were frequently moved because of fear of hostile tribes. The women practiced agriculture assisted only by older men no longer capable of going out with the hunting parties. In contrast to both the Miami and Chippewa the hunting parties were almost exclusively male affairs:

> Hunting parties went out from the village during the summer and also in the winter. In the summer the men usually left the greater part of their families at the village and did not travel as far as on the winter hunts—ordinarily only seventy-five to a hundred miles from the village. The summer hunts were of less importance than were those in the winter. . . ."
>
> The principle animals sought were deer, bear, and beaver. . . . Lahontan reported that the Ottawa did not hunt in the same region every year. The country around Glen Lake, for instance, was only hunted every third year, whereas the valley of the Saginaw was visited every other year.
>
> Hunting grounds were assigned to families or to members by the

head of the family every autumn (for winter hunting). Usually, eight or ten men, probably related, lived together in a cabin erected near the center of their territory (Kinietz, 1940:236-37).

If Spring Creek were the central village of a group with a settlement pattern like that described for the Ottawa, where are the hunting camps? Hinsdale (1932:33-34) has suggested that the dune areas along the shore of Lake Michigan played an important part in the economic lives of the people of Lower Michigan. He has further suggested that these were summer fishing and hunting camps. I recently studied one such camp between Hamlin Lake and Lake Michigan (Fitting, 1967) and found that it was a locality for preparation of preforms which were taken elsewhere to be finished into artifacts, a perfect balance for the limited industry at Spring Creek. While ceramics have been found in the dunes around Hamlin Lake they are sparse compared to the lithic material in the area (the Ottawa took part of their families with them on summer hunts), and the chipping station which I studied produced no such material. From the close similarities of cores, preforms, and general chipping techniques I would suggest that this was a nonceramic Late Woodland male camp rather than a preceramic site.

The winter camps, like those of the Chippewa, were probably inland, very likely further up the Muskegon River. To quote Hinsdale, ". . .in the late fall and until early spring the shore villages were generally abandoned for winter quarters upstream away from the piercing winds and cutting sands as they were driven in whatever direction the breeze might be blowing" (1932:34). Prahl has found several little chipping sites with few or no ceramics in the upper reaches of the Muskegon River during a survey carried out in this area in 1965 and 1966. None of these have been excavated but if they were, we might expect the camps of "eight or ten men probably related." Prufer, in his report of Chesser Cave in Ohio (1967), has found just this type of men's winter hunting camp. From a detailed analysis of the archaeological material and animal bone he concluded that it was repeatedly occupied as a winter hunting camp by a group of 6 to 8 males.

One could go further and speculate on the type of family structure that would develop with the males absent from the camp for much of the year. It is possible that the women developed a strong dominant hierarchy among themselves which could enforce a great deal of conformity to social norms including, perhaps, the production of pottery vessels. The accounts of the treatment of prisoners by Ottawa women does not suggest that they were a group of retiring, passive homebodies (Kinietz, 1940:255-57).

I do not wish to imply that the inhabitants of the Spring Creek site were Ottawa. The site is much too ancient to assign an ethnic identification anymore specific than central Algonquian. It does, however, represent a type of cultural adaptation later found among the Ottawa. It is an adaptation to the Carolinian-Canadian edge area in central Michigan. The Spring Creek site was occupied during the Neo-Atlantic climatic, one of the most favorable periods possible for such an occupation in the Muskegon River Valley. Cleland has stated (1966:73-74), in relation to the Ottawa but just as applicable to the people of Spring Creek, that, "their adaptation to this ecological zone was neither a simple one, nor marginal to the more highly agricultural societies to the south." Spring Creek has added a temporal dimension to this type of adaptation.

Summary

The Spring Creek village site was excavated in the 1950's by members of the Wright L. Coffinberry Chapter of the Michigan Archaeological Society. The site was radiocarbon dated to the tenth century of our era.

The site is a typical densely settled Late Woodland village of this period with an abundance of characteristic ceramics and a more limited amount of lithic material.

An analysis of animal bone indicated that this was a village with a focal type of economy, probably based on agriculture or agriculture and ricing. The settlement pattern seems to indicate a type of social organization similar to that of the historic Ottawa who also occupied the transition area between the Carolinian and Canadian biotic provinces. Spring Creek indicates some time depth for this way of life.

REFERENCES

Baby, Raymond S., and Martha A. Potter
1965 The Cole Complex: A Preliminary Analysis of the Late Woodland Ceramics in Ohio and their Relationship to the Ohio Hopewell Phase. Papers in Archaeology of the Ohio Historical Society, Number 2. Columbus.

Baerris, David A., and Ried A. Bryson
1965 Climatic Episodes and the Dating of Mississippian Cultures. The Wisconsin Archaeologist, Vol. 46, No. 4, pp. 203-20. Lake Mills.

Baerreis, David A., and Joan E. Freeman
1958 Late Woodland Pottery in Wisconsin as Seen from Aztalan. *Ibid.*, Vol. 39, No. 1, pp. 35-61. Lake Mills.

Bell, Robert E.
1958 Guide to the Identification of Certain American Indian Projectile Points. Special Bulletin No. 1. Oklahoma Anthropological Society. Norman.
1960 Guide to the Identification of Certain American Indian Projectile Points. *Ibid.*, No. 2. Oklahoma Anthropological Society. Norman.

Binford, Lewis R.
1963 The Pomranky Site. A Late Archaic Burial Station. Anthropological Papers, Museum of Anthropology, The University of Michigan, No. 19, pp. 149-92. Ann Arbor.

Binford, Lewis R., and Mark L. Papworth
1963 The Eastport Site, Antrim County, Michigan. *Ibid.*, pp. 71-123. Ann Arbor.

Binford, Lewis R., and George I. Quimby
1963 Indian Sites and Chipped Stone Materials in the Northern Lake Michigan Area. Fieldiana: Anthropology, Vol. 36, No. 12, pp. 277-307. Chicago.

Brose, David
1966 The Valley Sweets Site, 20 SA 24, Saginaw County, Michigan. The Michigan Archaeologist, Vol. 12, No. 1, pp. 1-21. Ann Arbor.

Burt, William H.
1957 Mammals of the Great Lakes Region. The University of Michigan Press. Ann Arbor.

Cleland, Charles E.
1966 The Prehistoric Animal Ecology and Ethnozoology of the Upper Great Lakes Region. Anthropological Papers, Museum of Anthropology, University of Michigan, No. 29. Ann Arbor.

Crane, H. R., and James B. Griffin
1958 University of Michigan Radiocarbon Dates III. Science, Vol. 128, No. 332, pp. 1117-23. Lancaster.

Crane, H. R., and James B. Griffin
1961 University of Michigan Radiocarbon Dates VI. *In:* Radiocarbon, Vol. 3, pp. 105-25. New Haven.

Deetz, James
1965 The Dynamics of Stylistic Change in Arikara Ceramics. Illinois Studies in Anthropology No. 4. Urbana.

Dice, Lee R.
1943 The Biotic Provinces of North America. The University of Michigan Press. Ann Arbor.

Fenner, Gloria J.
1961 The Bowmanville Site. *In:* Chicago Area Archaeology, edited by Elaine A. Bluhm. Illinois Archaeological Survey Bulletin No. 3. Urbana.

Fitting, James E.
1965 Late Woodland Cultures in Southeastern Michigan. Anthropological Papers, Museum of Anthropology, University of Michigan, No. 24. Ann Arbor
1966 Archaeological Investigation of the Carolinian-Canadian Edge Area in Central Michigan. The Michigan Archaeologist, Vol. 12, No. 4, pp. 143-49. Ann Arbor.
1967 The Camp of the Careful Indian: An Upper Great Lakes Chipping Station. Papers of the Michigan Academy of Science, Arts, and Letters, Vol. 52, pp. 237-242. Ann Arbor.
n.d. Lithic Industries of the Schultz site. To be published in "Culture and Ecology of the Schultz site." Anthropological Papers, Museum of Anthropology, University of Michigan. Ann Arbor.

Fitting, James E., and John R. Halsey
1966 Rim Diameter and Vessel Size in Wayne Ware Vessels. The Wisconsin Archaeologist, Vol. 47, No. 4, pp. 208-11. Lake Mills.

Fitting, James E., Jerry DeVisscher, and Edward J. Wahla.
1966 The Paleo-Indian Occupation of the Holcombe Beach. Anthropological Papers, Museum of Anthropology, University of Michigan, No. 27. Ann Arbor.

Flanders, Richard E.
1965 A Comparison of Some Middle Woodland Materials from Illinois and Michigan. Doctoral Dissertation, The University of Michigan. University Microfilms.

Fowler, Melvin L.
1952 The Clear Lake Site: Hopewellian Occupation. *In:* Hopewellian Communities in Illinois, edited by Thorn Deuel. Illinois State Museum Scientific Papers, Vol. 5, pp. 131-74. Springfield.

Gillis, Edward V.
1959 Bone Awls and Pottery Types. The Coffinberry News Bulletin, Vol. 6, No. 11, p. 130. Grand Rapids.

Greenman, Emerson F.
1937 The Younge Site: An Archaeological Record from Michigan. Occasional Contributions from the Museum of Anthropology of the University of Michigan, No. 6. Ann Arbor.

Griffin, Leonard
1963 The Eisen Site: A New Concept in Amateur Archaeological Endeavor. Michigan Archaeologist, Vol. 9, No. 4, pp. 73-78. Ann Arbor.

Guilday, John E., and Donald P. Tanner
1962 Animal Remains from the Quaker State Rock Shelter. Pennsylvania Archaeologist, Vol. 32, No. 3-4, pp. 131-37. Lancaster.

Harrison, Sidney
1966 The Schmidt Site (20 SA 192), Saginaw County, Michigan. The Michigan Archaeologist, Vol. 12, No. 2, pp. 49-70. Ann Arbor.

Hinsdale, Wilbert B.
1930 Reports of Archaeological Field Work in the Summer of 1928 in Montmorency, Newaygo and Lake Counties, Michigan. Papers of the Michigan Academy of Science, Arts, and Letters, Vol. 12, pp. 127-35. Ann Arbor.
1932 Distribution of the Aboriginal Population of Michigan. Occasional Contributions from the Museum of Anthropology of the University of Michigan, No. 2. Ann Arbor.

Keslin, Richard O.
1964 Archaeological Implications on the Role of Salt as an Element of Cultural Diffusion. The Missouri Archaeologist, Vol. 26 (whole volume). Columbia.

Kinietz, W. Vernon
1940 The Indians of the Western Great Lakes, 1615-1760. Occasional Contributions from the Museum of Anthropology of the University of Michigan, No. 10. Ann Arbor.

Leestma, Roger Arnold
1951 The Muskegon River Basin, Michigan: A Region of Contrasts. Doctoral Dissertation, The University of Michigan. University Microfilms. Ann Arbor.

McPherron, Alan L.
1965 Pottery Style Clustering, Marital Residence, and Cultural Adaptations at an Algonkian/Iroquoian Interface. Unpublished Manuscript in possession of author.
1967 The Juntunen Site and the Late Woodland Prehistory of the Upper Great Lakes Area. Anthropological Papers, Museum of Anthropology, University of Michigan, No. 30.

Mason, Ronald J.
1966 Two Stratified Sites on the Door Peninsula. *Ibid.*, No. 26, Ann Arbor.

Maxwell, Moreau S.
1951 Woodland Cultures of Southern Illinois. Logan Museum Publications in Anthropology, Bulletin No. 7. Beloit.
1959 The Late Woodland Period. Illinois Archaeological Survey, Bulletin No. 1, pp. 27-32. Carbondale.

Mayer-Oakes, William J.
1955 Prehistory of the Upper Ohio Valley; An Introductory Archaeological Study. Annals of Carnegie Museum, Vol. 34. Pittsburgh.

Munsell Soil Color Charts
1954 Munsell Color Company, Inc. Baltimore.

Pilling, Arnold R.
1965 Life at Porter Site 8, Midland County, Michigan. The Totem Pole, Vol. 48, No. 4, pp. 31-45. Detroit.

Pi-Sunyer, Oriol
1965 The Flint Industry. *In:* The McGraw Site: A Study of Hopewellian Dynamics, by Olaf H. Prufer and others. Scientific Publications of the Cleveland Museum of Natural History, Vol. 4 (N.S.), No. 1, pp. 60-89. Cleveland.

Prahl, Earl J.
1966 The Muskegon River Survey. The Michigan Archaeologist, Vol. 12, No. 4, pp. 183-209. Ann Arbor.

Prufer, Olaf H.
1967 Chesser Cave: A Late Woodland Phase in Southern Ohio. *In:* Studies in Ohio Archaeology, pp. 1-62. The Western Reserve University Press. Cleveland.

Prufer, Olaf H., and Charles Sofsky
1965 The McKibben Site (33 TR-57), Trumbull County, Ohio: A Conbribution to the Late Paleo-Indian and Archaic Phases of Ohio. The Michigan Archaeologist, Vol. 11, No. 1, pp. 9-40. Ann Arbor.

Quimby, George I.
1961 Cord Marking Versus Fabric Impressing of Woodland Pottery. American Antiquity, Vol. 26, No. 3, 426-28. Salt Lake City.
1962 A Year with a Chippewa Family, 1763-1764. Ethnohistory, Vol. 9, No. 3, pp. 217-39. Bloomington.
1965 An Indian Earthwork in Muskegon County, Michigan. The Michigan Archaeologist, Vol. 11, Nos. 3-4, pp. 165-69. Ann Arbor.

Ritchie, William A.
1961 A Typology and Nomenclature for New York Projectile Points. New York State Museum and Science Service Bulletin, No. 384. Albany.

Speth, John D.
1966 The Whorley Earthwork. The Michigan Archaeologist, Vol. 12, No. 4, pp. 211-28. Ann Arbor.

White, Anta M.
1963 Analytic Description of Chipped-Stone Industry from Snyders Site, Calhoun County, Illinois. Museum of Anthropology, The University of Michigan, Anthropological Paper, No. 19, pp. 1-70. Ann Arbor.

White, T.
1953 A Method of Calculating Dietary Percentages of Various Food Animals Utilized by Aboriginal Peoples. American Antiquity, Vol. 18, No. 4, pp. 396-98. Salt Lake City.

Winters, Howard D.
1963 An Archaeological Survey of the Wabash Valley in Illinois. Illinois State Museum, Reports of Investigation, No. 10. Springfield.

Witthoft, John
1952 A Paleo-Indian Site in Eastern Pennsylvania: An Early Hunting Culture. Proceedings of the American Philosophical Society, Vol. 96, No. 4, pp. 464-95. Philadelphia.

Wright, James E.
1965 A Regional Examination of Ojibway Culture History. Anthropologica, Vol. 7, No. 2, pp. 189-228. Ottawa.

Part II

THE SPRINGWELLS MOUND GROUP OF WAYNE COUNTY, MICHIGAN

John R. Halsey

I

PREFACE

THE body of knowledge on which this study is based was accumulated over a period of 150 years. Careful gleaning and examination of the remaining material reveals an archaeological succession in the mounds covering at least 1500 years. The growth of the Detroit area has eliminated all but one of these mounds. No recorded excavation was done in this area between 1876 and 1944, and there was no published synthesis until the late 1950s. Many writers have attempted to describe the Fort Wayne Mound, only to turn to other sites and areas. It is hoped that this report will draw together some of this information, collected over so long a time.

I owe much to the staff of the University of Michigan Museum of Anthropology, particularly to Dr. James B. Griffin and Dr. James E. Fitting, who critically read the manuscript. Mr. Richard G. Wilkinson analyzed the human skeletal remains while sharing an office with me and enduring my numerous groping questions. He too indulged in the eye-opening research of old records and was able to utilize some of Gillman's data in his analysis.

Mr. Donald E. Janzen aided in the identification of a portion of the faunal material and Mr. David S. Brose contributed to the identification of the historic material. I also benefited greatly from conversations of a more general nature with Miss Carole L. Crumley, Mr. Earl J. Prahl, Mr. Martin A. Wobst, and Mr. John D. Speth. The plates are the work of Mr. George Stuber.

Many thanks are extended to Mr. Carl E. Holmquist and other members of the Aboriginal Research Club of Detroit who generously loaned the copious notes and collections from the Fort Wayne Mound to the Museum of Anthropology for the present analysis.

Dr. Arnold R. Pilling's articles in the *Michigan Archaeologist* provided an invaluable research base. His thorough researching sets a standard that is difficult to achieve.

Dr. W. E. Taylor's excellent maps made work and analysis much easier and quicker.

My wife, Linda B. Halsey, did the final editing.

The National Science Foundation provided the funds that supported the 1965 excavations at the Central Mound and my support while writing this report.

Had it not been for others now long dead, this report would have a mere fraction of its significance and excitement. It is to the memory of Mr. John Blois, Mr. Bela Hubbard and Mr. Henry Gillman that this report is dedicated.

II

EARLY REPORTS AND EXCAVATIONS AT SPRINGWELLS, THE CARSTEN MOUND, AND THE GREAT MOUND AT THE RIVER ROUGE

The Detroit area was the scene of the earliest known archaeological research in Michigan and all but one mound of those herein reported have been destroyed—most well before the turn of the century. It is an unfortunate fact, but there is not one traceable artifact from the excavations reported herein. Hence, although these early reports have a significance well out of proportion to their reporting excellence, it is only through the publications of Gillman, Hubbard, and Blois that we get the slightest glimmer of what was found in these mounds. I have included the reports of McKenney and Witherell, although they only describe the physical condition of the mounds and legends concerning them, because they indicate that even at these early times, concern was expressed about the total destruction of the mounds.

A further reason for the length of the quotations is that even though some have been reprinted in such sources as the *Michigan Archaeologist* and the *Report of the Pioneer Society of the State of Michigan*, these publications are going out of print and leave the basic source material almost unobtainable.

Although Blois' account is the first personal account of mound excavation, Samuel R. Brown in *The Western Gazetteer; or Emigrants Directory* published in 1817 reports that, "At *Belle-Fontaine*, or Spring-Wells, three miles below Detroit, are three small mounds, or tumuli, standing in a direct line, about ten rods apart. One of these having been opened, bones, stone axes, arrow-heads, etc., were found in abundance. About one-fourth of a mile below these, are still to be seen the remains of an ancient fortification. A breast-work, in some places three or four feet high, encloses several acres of firm ground, in the centre of an extensive marsh." (Brown, 1817:170.)

In this case Brown is greatly in error concerning his measurements, as an examination of Army maps of the period when the mounds were still extant shows that a distance of 10 rods between each of the three mounds is quite clearly impossible. Unfortunately Brown does not give us a date for the opening of this mound.

Nine years later the mounds at Springwells received a visit by Thomas L. McKenney while he was preparing his *Sketches of a Tour of the Lakes* (McKenney, 1827).

> Soon after Breakfast, Major F. called, and invited me to join him in a ride to the Governor's farm, about six mile down the river. I accepted the invitation—the ride was agreeable, as such, but the road passing through what is called Spring Wells, and over mounds, once the burial places of the Indians of this quarter, made it one of peculiar interest. . . .
>
> On our return from the Governor's very valuable farm, we rode upon one of the mounds to which I have referred. There appears to have been three of them, but only one retained much of its original conical figure, and this, like the other two, is fast finding its level. A principal cause of the mounds wasting away, is, the cattle go upon them from the river, near the shore of which they are—and to get rid of the flies. The soil being light and sand, is kept stirred by them, and the rains wash it off. Hence the exposure of human bones from time to time, as the several layers or strata, are reached; for they appear to have been buried at different depths, and upon one another. I picked up some ribs, a bit of *os frontis,* and pieces of vertebrae, but all in a state of decay, so much so, that they crumbled at the touch. Major F. told me he had taken from the same mound a skull of enormous dimensions, and so much above the common size, as to be a matter of curiosity. This is promised to me—"if it can be found." Should I get it, you shall see it; and it will be the first skull of man or woman, whose death could not have happened short of a hundred years ago, that you will have seen. It will not answer, however, for a test of the doctrine of phrenology, because no mortal lives, now, who can tell what the character of the man was, who once wore this crown (McKenney, 1827:120,122).

The first personal report of an excavation at Springwells was given by John Blois in 1838. His first paragraph is quite obviously a paraphrase of Brown's article (Pilling, 1961*a*:28). After that however is Blois' own account of what he found:

> In Spring Wells township, (Belle Fountaine) three miles below Detroit exist a group of mounds on the right bank of the river. Several years ago, one of these mounds was opened and found to contain bones, arrowheads, stone axes, etc. in abundance.
>
> In the spring of 1837, the author in company with a scientific friend, resolved to excavate another of them, in order to obtain a more minute information concerning their contents.
>
> On repairing to the spot, they were found to be located upon a sandy elevation, or bluff, which gradually projected into the river, and rose above the surrounding country, a prospect of which it commanded for some distance to the interior, and of the river both above and below, a distance of at least seven miles. A selection of one was made for excavation. The shape of it was conical, and the height about eight feet. In surveying the surface upon the top, small fragments of pottery, pieces of human bone, and several of the molar teeth were discovered, the latter of which, in apparent perfection; but on examination, only the enamel remained, which is a phosphate of lime, a substance said to oppose a stronger resistance to decay than any other part of the human system. The excavation was commenced on the top and continued

to a depth of four feet below the base. The soil like the country around the mound was sandy, but exhibited a mixture of decomposed animal matter, and occasionally fragments of bone, some of which had evidently undergone the process of calcination. At a depth of about two and one half feet, in distinct positions, were found the remains of six different human skeletons, that appeared to have been buried in a promiscuous manner. Deposited near each were arrowheads, stone axes, spearheads, and some other utensils of stone of such uncouth shape as to be difficult to imagine their use, much more to name. There was likewise found a kind of rouge, that had the appearance of the earth called Spanish brown, and supposed to have been used as a pigment. It was in a friable state, and colored a deep red by applying it to any substance. In each deposit there were several pounds. About one foot from the base of the mound, a stratum of charcoal, three inches thick, was penetrated. Immediately below this were found six other human skeletons, not collectively, but lying in as many separate places, in different parts of the mound. Each one had the appearance of having been inhumed in a kneeling or rather sitting posture, with the knees so far bent as to leave a space of only four inches between the tibial and femoral bones of the lower limbs, with the body a little reclined backward, with the head pointing invariably towards the north and supporting with the hands an earthen vessel in the manner of a person in the act of preparing to drink from a ponderous vessel. The bones were generally decayed, except the larger ones of the lower limbs, arms, some of the ribs, and of the cranium, yet these were more or less imperfectly preserved. In all cases, that portion of the cranium which lay under was decomposed, while the superior part was sound. . . . From some calculations made on the femoral bones, it was judged that the stature of none would exceed five feet three inches. Arrowheads, small pieces of hornstone and some of a silicious kind, (the same that manufactured into gun flints) and quartz, wrought and unwrought, of the rudest kind, used undoubtedly as a substitute for knives, were found buried beside them. Some of these were so sharp as to cut flannel and several other substances, with the same facility as a knife. No metal was discovered; but the oxyd, or rust of iron, was traced in the shape of a vessel, holding some two or three gallons, which proved it to have been of iron.[1]

By the side of one was found the remains of an uncommonly large white marine shell. Around the bodies of two were found 30 or 40 rosaries, or beads made of the same kind of shell just mentioned. Their shape was cylindrical, three fourths of an inch and an inch in length [*sic*] and half an inch

---

[1]Bela Hubbard in *Memorials of a Half-Century* has some interesting observations on this particular item. "The most remarkable feature of this find [Blois' excavation] is the presence of an oxide of iron supposed to represent a vessel of that metal. It suggests a very difficult subject of inquiry, for if these bodies really belonged to the prehistoric race, as every other circumstance would imply, then are we in conflict with the apparently well founded opinion that the art of smelting metals, either iron or copper, was unknown to that early race. Iron is very perishable and would probably be wholly consumed by rust, long before human bones deposited at that remote era would have crumbled away.

"In a letter from Mr. Blois written to me in 1877, he confirms his statement made in 1839, regarding the supposed iron vessel, by the recollection of Mr. H. Ransom, who was present [Blois' scientific friend?]. He says he had 'broken one side of the top before he noticed anything peculiar. He then scraped the sand from the hollow interior, but there was not sufficient strength in it to hold together.' The appearance, he adds, was certainly that of indurated oxide of iron and yet the circumstance seems to him incredible" (Hubbard 1887:223-24).

More recent excavations at Ft. Wayne indicate that this "indurated oxide of iron" is probably a ground-water percolation feature.

thick, with a perforation through them in a longitudinal direction. It is probable there were many more. They lay on different parts of the skeleton, and six were found enclosed in the mouth. From the latter circumstance, it is inferred that they were amulets, supposed to possess the talismanic property of preserving and defending the soul of the deceased from evil. The vessels were generally too much broken to preserve their natural shape. They appeared to be in the shape of half an egg, abruptly contracted toward the mouth, with a flaring brim, and without a handle, smooth on the inside, carved and marked with various fantastic figures on the exterior, and with the capacity of holding two or three gallons. Their composition was argile, or clay, and pounded quartz and other stone. In place of broken quartz, sometimes coarse sand was substituted. Their appearance showed that they had been subjected to the action of fire, and perhapd used for culinary purposes. They appeared to be of the same kind which the author has found in Tennessee, Ohio, and New England, and which are common to western tumuli (Blois, 1838:168-72).

In 1882 Benjamin Witherell published a report that he had prepared in 1857. Pilling (1961*a*:23) believes it concerns the condition of the mounds around 1810.

Mounds of the Dead, on Springwells Sand Hill.—It is called "Springwells," from the fact that from the river side of the hill there formerly gushed many springs of pure water, and for the same reason the French called it "Belle Fontaine." The place was so called long before the territory was divided into townships. In the days before ice houses were known, the good people of the hamlet of Detroit were accustomed to have parties of pleasure, picnics, etc., on the hill on hot summer days, where they quaffed the bubbling waters, sparkling and bright, as they well up at the fountainhead.

On this sand hill stood three mounds of the dead—one near the present copper works, another in the center of the ground now occupied by the Fort, and the third midway between them. In my boyhood, that standing in the fort was covered with oak trees, and apparently had been undisturbed for many, many generations. The middle mound was a great age, and was covered with oak trees of smaller size; the third, near the copper works, was of more recent date, and on it was neither tree nor shrub. In my childhood I have seen the children of the wilderness deposit the remains of their departed friends on its bosom. They scooped out a shallow grave in the center of the top of the mound, and covered the body with some sand, brought from the neighboring sand bank. After covering the body, the friends of the dead man went into the river and waded about in a zigzag or circular course, for sometime, until they thought the spirit had departed on its long, long journey to the setting sun. Their object in wading in the river was that the spirit might not be able to follow their tracks in the sand. They were a superstitious people.

The three mounds were all nearly of the same size; they were some thirty feet in diameter at the base, and about ten feet high, and perfectly circular in form, and were filled with "dead men's bones" (Witherell, 1884:4-5).

Bela Hubbard, who came to Detroit in 1835, and who was a very active participant in the retrieval of Detroit's prehistory, left the following account of the condition of the mounds as he first saw them.

Allusion has already been made to tumuli at Springwell. A group of these existed on the river in front of the Reeder farm. Just below the copper works the bank was very bold and elevated about thirty feet above the water. On this bank were two mounds of conical form, of which one still existed at the time of my first visit, though injured by pilferers of Indian relics. It was then about ten feet in height with a base diameter of forty feet. Large excavations were in progress for gravel, and for clay used in the manufacture of brick. These encroachments had destroyed one of the tumuli, and the whole have since disappeared.

On and around this spot, for the extent of an acre, were thickly strewn bones and broken pottery, mingled with shell beads, stone knives and arrow-points. Several rods below was a smaller tumulus in a field, then covered with forest. It did not exceed six feet in height, and is still in good preservation, within the grounds of the United States reservation (Hubbard, 1887:220-22).

Finally in 1876 Henry Gillman came on the Springwells scene and Michigan in general, where he worked and published for many years. Although obsessed with the discovery of platycnemia and tracing its distribution, Gillman's reports are the first with a suggestion of modern archaeological technique. Gillman's burials are plotted along with those of Holmquist in Figure 1.

The mound of which with its contents a description is here given, is situated on the North or Michigan bank of the Detroit River, a few hundred feet from the shore-line, and within the limits of Fort Wayne, occupying the southeast corner of the Parade Ground, and being immediately westward of the fort proper.

Though the permission of the War Department to examine the mound had been obtained by the Detroit Scientific Association in the latter part of the autumn of 1875, various circumstances occurred to delay the investigation, which was not commenced until May 22, 1876. The work was conducted by the Association, several members specially interested participating, under the immediate direction of the writer, and, agreeably to the orders of the War Department, with the general supervision of the Post Commandant.

The courteous and efficient manner with which the objects of the work were facilitated on the part of General Stanley deserves more than merely passing notice. The valuable aid rendered, and the kind personal interest and attentions constantly bestowed, throughout, by this distinguished soldier and accomplished gentleman, as well as by the several members of his command, place the Association under the most grateful obligations, and call for unqualified praise and thanks. Nor of the representatives of the Association whose assistance was of the most useful character, must I omit to mention the Messrs. Bela and C. B. Hubbard, and especially Mr. H. G. Hubbard, who was unremitting in his efforts.

The Structure at the date of this examination could hardly be supposed to present its original features. Though its location afforded it a certain kind of protection, it also exposed it to some dangers from which a more secluded site would have exempted it. There can be little question that at least in height the mound is much reduced. Its rounded summit is at present but five feet above the general level of the parade ground. Almost circular, its east and west diameter, nearly seventy feet in length, is slightly in excess of its north and south diameter. This includes an outlying rim or border ten to

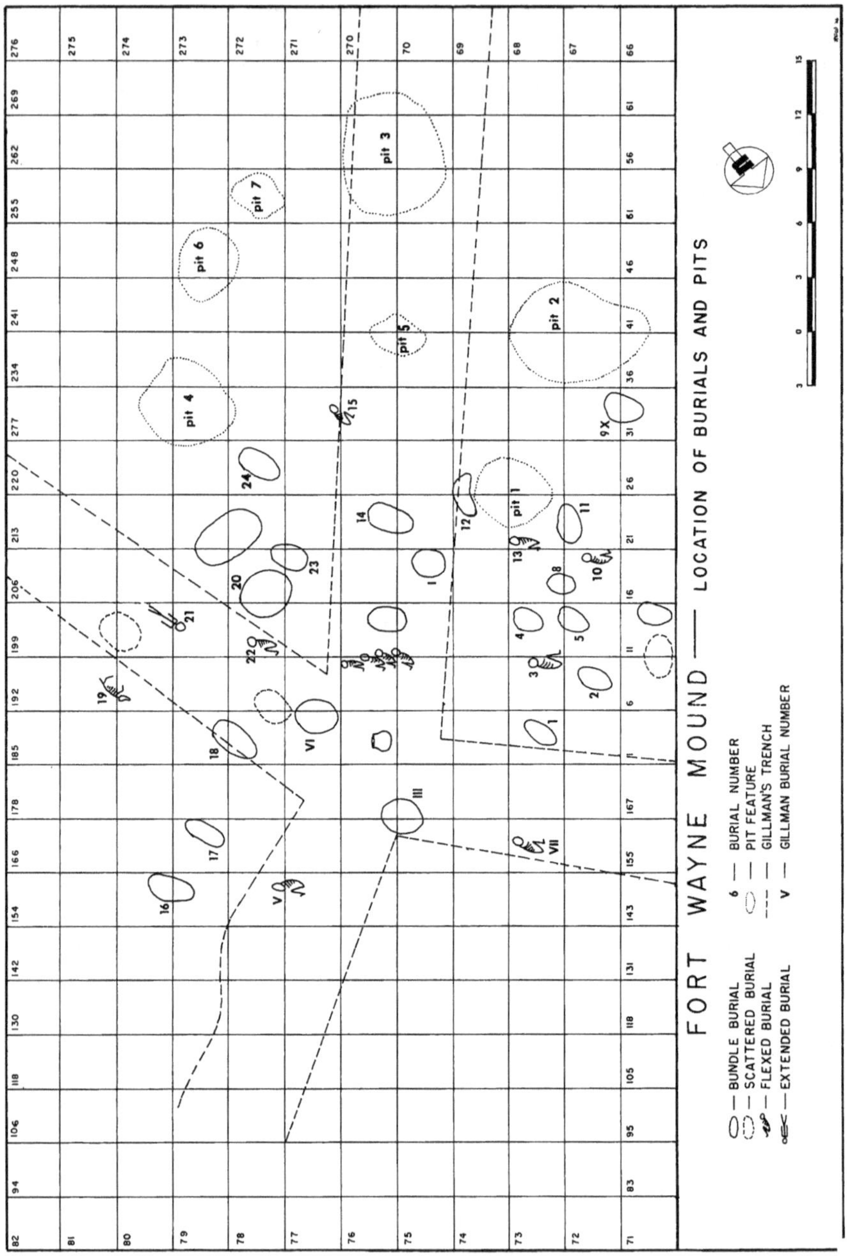
FORT WAYNE MOUND — LOCATION OF BURIALS AND PITS
— BUNDLE BURIAL
— SCATTERED BURIAL
— FLEXED BURIAL
— EXTENDED BURIAL
6 — BURIAL NUMBER
— PIT FEATURE
— GILLMAN'S TRENCH
V — GILLMAN BURIAL NUMBER
pit 1
pit 2
pit 3
pit 4
pit 5
pit 6
pit 7

FIG. 1

twelve feet in width and one foot above the general level, and which, surrounding the mound, has apparently been formed by the many years' washing down of the sand of which it is composed. Previous to the year 1870 the process of erosion must have proceeded with considerable rapidity. In that year attention was called to the process, and with the object of causing its arrest, the entire mound was sodded over, a small oak tree being planted near the centre. A few oaks of no great age (probably not over fifty years) are scattered in proximity to the limits of the mound; but no tree grew on the structure with the exception of the single oak the planting of which we have mentioned.

The investigation was commenced by running a drift or trench seven feet wide, east and west through the centre of the tumulus.

Within a foot or so of the surface small fragments of skulls and long bones with broken pottery were found, promiscuously mingled, being suggestive of a previous disturbance at this point of this place of sepulture. With these were exhumed the greater portions of a skull and pot, both in quite a fragmentary condition. The skull is very thin, and does not seem to be that of an adult. It is significant that this is the only one of the crania which comes within the brachycephalic range.

Extending from within a foot of the surface to a depth of 2 and 1/2 feet, we found a belt of charcoal of over a foot in width, running northward and southward across the mound, a little to the westward of centre. This appeared to be the remnants of the trunk of a burnt oak; and with the exception of an isolated instance of fireplace a short distance to the west of this, no other marked indication of fire having been used on the spot occured, although there were occasional stains in the sand which may have been produced by the action of fire. A few pieces of charcoal were, however, not seldom found with each burial. Toward the centre of this belt of charcoal, at the depth of two feet, was exhumed Skull No. 2. This fragmentary, roof-shaped cranium falls within the dolicocephalic range, presenting the cephalic index of .725, and has prominent superciliary ridges and traces of an epactal bone. Beside it was found what may be called a chisel made from apparently a species of grindstone. The implement is, I think, the only one of the kind which has been taken from the mounds of this vicinity, and is neatly made. It is nearly 5 inches in length, and 3/4 of an inch wide at the centre, the thickness at the same point being nearly 1/2 an inch. It is formed by being ground square on the sides, and it gradually tapers to the extremities, one of which remains blunt and unfinished, while the other, though injured from use, had been brought to an effective wedge-like blade.

Further toward the centre of the mound, at the depth of 2-1/2 feet, four crania with other bones were exhumed, each individual being provided with a burial vase or pot, probably for food, and the remains being massed within a very small space. As far as could be seen, the bodies had been interred in a crouching posture. In one instance this was quite apparent, the body lying on its side with head to the east. A small stone axe or hatchet, slightly polished, the cutting edge broken from use, lay beside; and the accompanying burial vase is of a finer quality than usual, resembling the pottery from the mounds farther south (Ohio and Missouri). It is marked with an evenly indented cord pattern, the intersecting lines being laid on at wide and regular intervals, so as to form large diamond-shaped figures. With the other interments of this group the only stone implements discovered were a carved knife, very rudely chipped from flint, and so-called sinker made from a flat piece of shale, ground smooth on the sides, edges, and ends, and perforated at one extremity—the perforation having plainly been made from opposite sides.

At 2 feet below the surface, and at 3-1/2 feet northward and 4 feet eastward of the centre were encountered the fragments of skull (No. 3), much distorted from the pressure of the sand, with which burial had been deposited four well-wrought flint arrowheads and a lance head of the same material. The lance and arrowheads have the peculiar spiral twist, designed to give a rotary motion to the missile. In the latter is this peculiarity so finely developed, that on the front or pointed end being presented to view, the continuous curved line of the chipped edge, (resembling a greatly elongated letter S, the arrowpoint at the centre) exhibits a perfect representation of Hogarth's line of grace and beauty.

At 11 feet east of the centre and 33 inches in depth, the cranium No. 5 and other bones were exhumed. This rather coarse roof-shaped skull slopes decidedly in the parietal region from the central longitudinal ridge, while the sides are vertical. It is the most perfect, and appears to be one of the largest, if not the largest of the skulls exhumed here. The cephalic index is .773, the altitudinal index being inferior, or .719, thus placing it within the orthocephalic range. The position of the foramen magnum is well advanced forward, in this respect sustaining the important distinction to which on former occasions I have called attention. The index of the foramen in this instance .502, and as the skull is well preserved, and free from any flattening or distortion, there can be no question as to the value of the evidence thus reiterated. . . . The body appeared to have been buried in a crouching but upright posture, subsequently falling slightly to one side, the head to the east. The pot placed with it also slanted in the same direction. It is of the ruder description of mound pottery, the ornamentation mostly constituting of indented lines inartistically produced by the indiscriminate application of a cord. As usual in our mounds, the base is rounded or semi-conical, so that the vessel is incapable of standing upright without support. It is the only specimen of the ceramic art which we were able to secure in a tolerably perfect condition, but a small portion of the rim at the mouth being wanting. A thin crust of a blackish substance adhered to the sides and bottom, within.

There now occurred an intermediate space, without a burial. Nothing but the pure fine sand of the structure was met with till we reached the depth of 3 feet 2 inches, when, at the exact centre of the mound, we uncovered a burial vase containing the remains of a human body mostly reduced to ashes. This proved to be one of the most decided isolated instances of cremation which has been met with in our mounds. Though it had crumbled to pieces this cinerary urn remained in position, upright, and holding in place its contents. It is of the common pottery of the mounds, and is ornamented with ordinary cord pattern; and as the base of the urn was not reached short of the depth of 4 feet, this vessel which was about 8 inches in diameter, must have been 10 inches in height. Incompletely consumed fragments of the leg bones indicated the incinerated subject to have been marked with platycnemism. Within the vase had been deposited a copper knife, of which only two small portions almost destroyed by oxidation, one of them being the point remained. Like all other articles made of copper which have been recovered from our mounds, this knife had unquestionably been formed of the virgin metal from Lake Superior. If we may pronounce from the evidence afforded by this relic, the tool had simply been rudely hammered into shape. Two pieces of *Pyrula* shell were also taken from the urn. The shell, the fragments of which were too far decayed to testify as to whether it had been worked or not, must originally have been brought from the sea-coast.

Further excavation revealed no other interments beneath the depth here attained. The clear fine sand, of a pale yellowish hue, bleaching to a grayish white on exposure to the air and sunshine, continued to the depth of six feet, when a hard compact stratum of ferruginous-like sand, half a foot in thickness, was reached. It was evident that this level had never been disturbed. We had, therefore, penetrated below the level of the interments, and, in fact, below the level of the surrounding land. The cut was, however, deepened to 7-1/2 feet in order to satisfy all doubt on the subject. For the remaining depth, only coarse sand and gravel of the drift (pebbles intermixed) were met with.

From what we have described, together with what the remainder of the excavation revealed, it would appear that the single case of cremation—the ashes, etc., deposited in burial-urn at the exact centre of the mound, at a depth greater than that of any of the other inhumations—constitutes the first interment in this place of sepulture; and that therefore, in all probability the remains are those of the individual in whose honor the mound was originally erected.

The work was continued by opening, about 2-1/2 feet to the eastward of the centre of the mound, a trench running south from the first cut, thus giving the entire excavation a T-shape.

At a foot below the surface, and but a short distance south of the first excavation, the remains of a pot and skull with other bones, all in a fragmentary condition were dug out. The skull, No. 6 of series, is evidently of less antiquity than the other crania from this place. The superciliary arches are not prominent. It is too imperfect to afford the usual dimensions. At six feet south of the centre, and two feet below the surface, two mingled burials one on top of the other, also much decayed, occurred. There was no pottery or stone implement found with these last relics. South of the centre 14-1/2 feet, and 1-3/4 foot from the surface, pieces of a skull, much decayed, with other bones beneath, were taken out. To the depth of 3 feet a few scattered fragments of human bones were encountered; beneath which no further interments were met with, though the excavation was carried below the level of the base of the mound.

A trench similar to the other cuts we have described was now opened northward from the north line of the east and west excavation at its intersection with the centre of the mound,—thus giving the entire of the work the form of an irregular cross. Within from one foot to two feet of the surface broken pottery and pieces of charcoal with a quantity of reddish-colored sand, the color supposed to be the stain produced by the remains of some pigment, were uncovered. About seven feet northward of the centre of the mound, and at the depth of 20 inches we reached an interment in which the body had been placed in a much crouched semi-sitting posture. The leg bones were drawn over the arm bone, and the skull (No. 7), which had fallen forward partly on its face, lay, base upward resting on its feet. Most of the bones were badly decayed. These last were all on, or slightly to eastward of, the east line of this cut.

As no other relics were discovered on this side of the mound, work was resumed on the south side, by widening the cut to the westward, it having, in the first instance, been made somewhat to the eastward of centre. This necessitated the removal of the oak tree already referred to as having been planted on the mound, and which stood about 4 feet south of centre. Beneath this tree, at 2-1/2 feet from the surface, were found two arrowheads chipped from stone, of the rudest workmanship, and a little to the east of these, a few bones of a bird. Immediately beneath, at the depth of 3 feet, we reached a pot finely and very regularly marked with the cord pattern, giving to it quite a distinctive appearance. Like all the others, with the single exception we have noted, it was in a fractured condition. About one foot to the northward of this pot and 2 feet from the surface portions of a coarser pot, somewhat similarly marked occurred. A few small pieces of human bones, much decayed, were found nearby. The three skulls, Nos. 8, 9, and 10, with fragments of other bones, and a broken pot of a different pattern, were next disinterred, at that part of the mound 6 feet to west and 7 feet to south of the centre, being about 2 feet below the surface. The only other relic found associated with them was the greater part of a thick Unio shell. All were within an area of 2 feet square.

Further investigations of the mound afforded no results worthy of mention, and operations were brought to a close. . . .

In conclusion, I would dwell on the special interest pertaining to those relics, associated as they were in a single mound, and exhumed so that their relations are preserved.

No indications are found here, such as are seen so abundantly present in the Rouge River tumulus, of this structure having been used as a dwelling place or point of observation. It is clearly a sepulchral mound, and as such I have named it and classed it.

A further study and comparison of the relics may possibly disclose points of interest which I have overlooked; but I have endeavored to make this discussion of the remains as exhaustive as their important nature demanded, and the very limited time at my command would permit.

The age of the mound is undoubtedly not so great as that of the River Rouge mound. The most ancient interments in the latter have no representation in the Fort Wayne mound. I feel safe, from the evidences afforded, in placing the age of this mound, or the date of its earliest interment—the single instance of cremation—at or toward the close of the period indicated by those isolated cases of cremation which I have described as occurring in the Rouge River mound.

The corroborative testimony is valuable. It affords us a standard not to be despised, for the establishing of a comparative chronology for, at least, our own region, about which other facts may group themselves, thus building up a system which at length may obtain an importance entitling it to a more general recognition and application.

The Rouge River mound presents unquestionable evidence that 1., There was a time when cremation was not practised here, as indicated by the chalky or lime-like concretions of the earliest interments.

2., That the custom slowly grew up, or was gradually introduced, till, at length, it apparently largely prevailed; to be succeeded by,

3., Burial in the crouching posture, as practised by those platycnemic men, who were generally marked by small orthocephalic crania; and which, in turn gave place to,

4., Those later interments which with their accompanying relics, stone implements and rude pottery, and the entire absence of the tools or metals used by the White man, indicate a period, be it of greater or less remoteness at least antecedent to the advent of the European to these shores.

To these might be subjoined,

5., That denoted by the remains of the various nomadic Indian tribes—the red man as known to the early colonists, and when the sites of now populous cities were an unbroken wilderness.

It scarcely remains necessary for me to add that I consider the Fort Wayne mound to represent the 2nd, 3rd, and 4th of the periods here mentioned. And, I would suggest, may not the scale indicated prove to be already applicable in the case of a large number of the sepulchral monuments throughout our country, and thus become the entering wedge in reducing to order and system many of the apparently heterogeneous elements which so constantly thwart the American archaeologist? (Gillman, 1877:311-24).

Bela Hubbard writing in July of 1876 evidently had participated in the excavations with Gillman and left his summation of the mound contents.

There are (or have been, for little remains,) several tumuli upon and near the bank of the Detroit River, from two to four miles below the city. All are burial mounds. They occupy sandy elevations, fifteen to twenty feet above the water, are conical in shape, five to twenty-five feet in height, and thirty to fifty feet broad. All contain numerous skeletons, both original and intrusive. The former are found on or near the original surface, and are mostly in a sitting posture, and the faces toward the East, and sometimes a dozen or more are found arranged around the centre in a circle.

In one case, each held in his arms a pot, of unusual size, having a capacity of about two gallons. In other cases, pots are found near the heads. These are all composed of the materials common to the mounds—clay, mixed with ground shells and micaceous stones; black within, reddish without. They have regularly rounded bases, with wide mouths, somewhat flaring, and in part or whole ornamented with rude patchwork. With these are the usual stone implements, hammers, celts, chisels, fleshers, slings, pendants, spear and arrowheads, with, rarely, sea shells and copper knives. The hammers and celts are mostly of greenstone, the arrow heads of quartzose rocks, of various colors, and often very large and beautifully constructed.

The human remains were mostly much decayed and only a few skulls have been preserved. These are mostly dolicocephalic, of good size and well formed. The skeletons show an average size of about 57 feet 10 inches [*sic*]. In most cases the tibia is very much flattened. No idols or images, nor any sculptures, have been found in this neighborhood, to my knowledge (Hubbard, 1887:233-34).

Silas Farmer added the following observations in 1884:

In the township of Springwells, just below Detroit, were four of these mounds; one of them still remains inside the grounds of Fort Wayne; the second was on property now occupied by the Copper Smelting Works, and the third lay between the other two. They were circular in form, from thirty to seventy feet in diameter, and varying from three to ten feet in height. Two parallel embankments, about four feet high, led to them from the east. One of these mounds was opened in 1837, and the one inside the fort, by permission of the War Department, on May 22, 1876 (p. 321).

Perhaps the most enigmatic of the mounds in the Fort Wayne or Springwells area is that known as the Great Circular Mound or the

Carsten Mound. The description of artifacts given by Hubbard and Gillman are so similar as to indicate that even though there are two different names they are talking about the same mound. Gillman's articles are remarkable for their redundancy but are included because so little is known about this mound.

> About three-quarters of a mile to the north and eastward of the Great Rouge Mound, and only a few hundred feet to the westward of Fort Wayne, being over a third of a mile from the shore of the Detroit River, occurs the monument which I have named for distinction and from its originally symmetrical shape "The Great Circular Mound." This also appears to have been one of a numerous series, many of which have been removed for various purposes, but the present occupation of the land prevents a satisfactory examination of its character.
>
> A few years ago a greater part of the mound was removed, and some important results were obtained, the relics being of unusual interest. Eleven skeletons were exhumed, with a large number of burial vases, stone implements in great variety and of superior workmanship, consisting chiefly of axes, spears, arrowheads, chisels, drillers, and sinkers; pipes; ornaments of shell and stone; also, a peculiar implement of unknown use formed from an antler; and two articles manufactured from copper, one the remains of a necklace, consisting of a number of beads; the other a needle several inches in length (Gillman, 1874:367-68).

> A few years ago the great part of this large circular mound in the vicinity of Fort Wayne was removed and most important results were obtained. Eleven human skeletons were exhumed; a large number of buried vases, stone implements in great variety and of superior workmanship, consisting chiefly of axes, fleshers, spearpoints, arrow heads, chisels, drillers and sinkers; pipes, a peculiar implement of unknown use, formed of an antler, with duplicate perforations at its thickest end; and two articles manufactured from copper, one the remains of a necklace, formed of a number of beads strung on a two-stranded cord, a few fragments of which remained sufficiently preserved to satisfy me that it was made from a vegetable fiber, probably from the basswood (Tilia Americana, L. [*sic*]). The other article of copper consisted of a needle, or borer, several inches in length, quadrangular at the base and well wrought. One of the skulls is remarkable for its diminutive size, though adult, its capacity being only 56 cubic inches, or less than 76 per cent of that of the average Indian cranium, which is given as 84 cubic inches by Morton and Meigs, the minimum observed by them being 69 cubic inches (Gillman, 1880:42-43).

Hubbard contributed his observations in 1887 on this mound. It is interesting to note the relatively greater detail of Hubbard:

> By the side of each of the numerous skeletons found in what is known as the Carsten Mound, Springwells, lay a pot or urn, of which three only were obtained entire. Two of these were uncommonly fine specimens, in good preservation, and about a foot in height. The neck was about five inches wide, with a collar below the rim, of two inches breadth. Below this the body swelled into a graceful curve, rounded at the base into a gourd form. The composition was clay, largely mixed with pounded stone, which contained

much mica, and on the inside was black throughout. On the exterior was a thin coating of reddish clay, quite distinct from the remainder. These vases were purchased by Mr. Gillman, and presented to the Archaeological Museum at Cambridge, Mass.[2]

In the year 1870, in digging away a section from one of these ridges, on land of Mr. J. H. Carstens, opposite Fort Wayne, one of the ancient tombs was disturbed, and the skeletons of fourteen bodies disinterred. They were in the usual contracted posture, and beside the head of each was an earthen crock. Two of these which were quite perfect, were the vases described in a former page, and now in the Archaeological Museum at Cambridge.

Among a large number of arrow-points and other articles common to the mounds were several lance heads of unusual size and beauty. They were of milk white quartz, about 7 inches long by 3 wide, and very finely and evenly serrated.

Among the relics was a long needle of copper, and a necklace of copper beads, but no vestige of iron.

There was the usual report of big bones. In this case the large individual measured seven and a half feet in height.

The original surface of the ground was about fifteen feet above the general level, and consisted of drift gravel, overlaid by yellow sand. The bodies were found at a depth of six or seven feet from this original surface, and were, of course, interred in these deep graves before the tumulus, which was only three or four feet high, was heaped above (Hubbard, 1887:213-15, 225-26).

One of the potentially most important sites in the interpretation of southeastern Michigan prehistory was the Great Mound at the mouth of the River Rouge. There are indications that this mound participated in every cultural tradition from Hopewell to the British occupation of Detroit. Today no trace of this huge mound exists. The first report dates from 1874 in Henry Gillman's article on *The Mound-Builder and Platycnemism in Michigan.*

---

[2]From the Sixth Annual Report of the Peabody Museum of American Archaeology and Ethnology we have the following description of material presented by Gillman.

"A collection made by Mr. Henry Gillman from a mound on the Detroit River, Michigan, explored by him, has been purchased. This consists of human remains and various objects buried with the dead. The latter are of the common kinds, such as stone chisels, one of much beauty made of diorite and highly polished, a spear point, arrowpoints, stone pendants, a stone boring tool, beads and ornaments made of shell and copper, an implement made of antler, a miniature vase of the size of a common thimble, and two large and perfect vases of the oval pattern and ornamented over the whole surface with cord marks. One of the skulls, that of a fully adult person, is worthy of notice for its diminutive size, and for a remarkable extension of the lines for the attachment of the temporal muscle towards the top of the head. The average capacity of the Indian cranium as given by the tables of Morton and Meigs is eighty-four cubic inches, and the minimum observed by them only sixty-nine cubic inches. That from the Detroit River Mound measures only fifty-six cubic inches, or less than sixty-seven per cent of that of the average Indian. In ordinary skulls the ridges of the temporal muscles on the two sides of the head are separated by a space of from three to four inches, seldom less than two, while in the Detroit mound skull this space measures only three quarters of an inch; and in this respect presents about the same conditions as the skull of chimpanzee. As the other two crania from the same mound offered no such peculiarities, the skull which just has been described must be considered simply as an extreme case of individual variation from the ordinary form. There are no signs of artificial deformity.

"The single tibia accompanying this collection is somewhat flattened" (1873:12-13).

One of the most interesting works of this region, and which, till a few years ago, formed a member of a numerous series of mounds in the immediate vicinity, is the tumulus which I have named "The Great Mound of the River Rouge." This, in many respects, remarkable work is situated on the eastern bank of the Rouge River, a tributary of the Detroit, and near the point of junction of the former with the latter river, or about four and one-half miles from the city hall in Detroit.

The size, shape, and well-defined outline of the monument could hardly fail to attract the attention of even the superficial observer, and impress him as to its being the work of man. With a height of 20 feet, it must originally have measured about 300 feet in length by 200 feet in width; but large quantities of sand have been removed from it from time to time, greatly reducing its proportions, and scattering or destroying a large number of interesting relics.

The series of smaller mounds, extending from the great mound to the eastward, has long since been entirely removed; so has the greater number of other similar mounds which once stood immediately below the southern city limits. Those which remain are fast disappearing before the march of civilization, the sand, of which they are principally composed, being in demand for building and other purposes. . . .

The relics exhumed from the great mound (which has not even yet been thoroughly explored) consist of stone implements, such as axes, scrapers, chisels, arrow-heads and knives; fragments of pottery of a great variety of pattern, including the favorite cord-pattern; and the bones of man, generally much decayed, and exhibiting other indications of antiquity. From the fragments of burned bone and charcoal found it would appear that in the earlier interments cremation was practiced. . . . (Gillman, 1874:365-67).

Gillman's scattered reference to the Great Mound in 1876 in *Certain Characteristics Pertaining to Ancient Man in Michigan* produced a most interesting description of a piece of bone that superficially appears to exhibit Hopewellian influences:

During last summer (1874) in some further excavations made in the Great Mound at the Rouge River, Michigan, among other relics exhumed were eight crania, two of which had this aperture. Of the remaining bones pertaining to the two skulls in question, I specially noticed that many were wanting, and that those present were heaped *en masse* and not in the usual manner of burial, seeming to imply that they were interred subsequently to being denuded of the flesh and the other soft parts of the body (Gillman, 1876*a* :237).

In this connection, and in concluding, I have considered worthy of being mentioned the fragment of carved bone represented in Fig. 11, a side view of which is seen in Fig. 12. This was lately taken by me from the Great Mound at the Rouge River, and it is the only relic of the kind which I have seen from the mounds in Michigan. Though but a small fragment remains, it is sufficient to prove the workmanship to have been of no mean order and of remarkably neat finish surprisingly so when we consider the rude implements which in all probability, alone were available for its manufacture. The illustration scarcely does it justice. The front or carved surface is convex, as shown in Fig. 13, while the back is flat and perfectly plain and smooth. In its perfect state, it was probably intended to be worn as an ornament, the remains of a finely-drilled hole at one side appearing to have been one of the means for its attachment to the person (1876*a*:244-45).

This description and the illustrations are remarkably similar to carved bone fork handles in vogue in the nineteenth century.

From Gillman's *The Ancient Men of the Great Lakes* we learn something of the physical characteristics and anomalies and various modes of burial observed in the Great Mound:

The Great Mound on the River Rouge near its junction with the Detroit River, has proved a fruitful source of relics of the most valuable description. Some flattened tibiae here exhumed by the writer first called attention to the fact of platycnemism being a characteristic of our northern aborigines. . . . [long discussion on platycnemism]

It is worthy of note that from the same mound on the Detroit River, from which were exhumed the flattest tibiae, were also taken several crania, of which one (though evidently adult) presented the hitherto, I think I may say, unprecedented feature of its capacity being only fifty-six cubic inches. . . . (Gillman, 1876*b*:316); (*see also* p. 91).

The first instance of its perforated crania being brought to my knowledge was in the year 1869, when I took from the Great Mound on the River Rouge two fragments of crania, each of which exhibited this perforation. . . . During the summer of 1874, in some further excavations made in the Great Mound at the River Rouge, Michigan, among other relics exhumed were eight crania, two of which had this aperture. Of the remaining bones belonging with the two skulls in question, I specially noticed that many were wanting, and that those present were heaped *en masse* and not in the usual manner of burial, seeming to imply that they were interred subsequently to being denuded of the flesh and other soft parts of the body.

In resuming the excavation of the Great Mound at the River Rouge, the opening was made at what was presumed to be its original centre. At the depth of three feet, human bones, much decayed (though including the eight nearly perfect crania, already mentioned) with fragments of pottery and a few stone implements were exhumed. At a depth of four feet occurred abundant evidence of cremation in the presence of masses of burnt human remains and ashes with charcoal-compact, discolored agglomerations, separated from each other by the surrounding pure sand of the mound. The average bulk of those spheroidal bodies, in which fragments of burnt bone abounded, gave a length of two feet, a breadth of one and one half feet, and a height of one and one-quarter feet. Beneath those peculiar interments which had remained undisturbed, nothing but sand was encountered for four feet additional depth, or a total of eight feet from the surface. At this depth white limelike masses, each of a few inches in circumference were reached. They had little resemblance to bone, though subsequent examination proved them to be such, and of man. In a few cases the remains of the exfoliated cellular tissue were quite apparent, while the outlines of portions of some of the principal bones could be sufficiently recognized to determine whether they belonged to femur, tibia, fibula, humerus, or ulna. But in the majority of instances, those remains of our brother man (of which there were considerable quantities) had returned to "dying Nature's earth and lime"—had obeyed the infinite decree. "Dust thou art, and unto dust shall thou return." These, in general, ball-like masses continued to the depth of ten and one-half feet, where operations were suspended.

Over the greater part of what is left of this mound, at about eighteen inches from the present surface, occurs an almost continuous bed or stratum of burnt bones and ashes with intermingled fragments of pottery. I have already (in 1869 and subsequently) called attention to the evidences of the practice of cremation in the burials here, and it is unnecessary that I should at present dwell on the subject. It must be borne in mind that this mound has been much disturbed, and large quantities of sand, its chief component, removed (Gillman 1876*b*:325-29).

The following article written by Hubbard in 1876, but not published until 1880 is of historical interest only:

One and by far the largest of the mounds in the vicinity of Detroit, seems somewhat exceptional in character. It is situated at the junction of the River Rouge with the Detroit, and was originally probably not less than four hundred feet long by two hundred broad and thirty or forty high. It is built of the light sand of the neighborhood, and contained many hundreds, if not thousands of skeletons, in every stage of decay and burial. It had two or more *pits*, filled with great numbers of bones, promiscuously disposed, and apparently corresponding with those used by the Hurons, and some other tribes at their "Festivals of the Dead," for which purpose bodies were preserved and brought from long distance. It is hardly possible to dig into the mound at any point, and to any depth, from two to ten feet, or even more, without disinterring human bones.

Evidence of *cremation* abound in some parts of the mound, and at various depths, consisting of beds and strata of coal, burned bone and ashes. Nothing certainly indicative of "altars" have been discovered, but the modes of interment are without uniform system (Hubbard, 1880:234).

In 1887 Hubbard published his *Memorials of a Half-Century* with the following lyrical and fairly detailed report of the excavations in the Great Mound:

I shall close these remarks with some account of the Great Mound near the junction of the River Rouge with the Detroit, at Del Rey, three miles below the city.

Ever since the settlement of the country this mound has been a well-known and conspicuous feature. To the old French inhabitants it was also known that it had been used by the Indians as a burial-place. Yet its true character seems never to have been fully appreciated, and the interest which attaches to it may warrant me in occupying some further pages in its description.

For nearly half a century, portion after portion has been dug away and removed, by wagon load and boat load, and little notice taken of its contents, until it is but a miniature of its former self. Mr. Bourdeno who has lived in the vicinity for more than sixty years, says the mound originally extended from its present limits westerly fully 500 feet, to where a bend in the Rouge brings that river close to the highway. The mound or hill was then 700 or 800 feet long, 400 feet wide, and not less than forty feet high. The south side bordered close on the river for its whole length. It was symmetrical in form, and the slopes were about as steep as the sand, of which most of it was composed, could be retained. Not only has it been reduced more than half the entire length, but more than half also of its width on the river side. Little of the original shape now remains, and the present extreme height nowhere exceeds thirty feet above the stream.

But little examination is needed to show that some part at least of the elevation is natural, for the stratum of gravel appears below ten or more feet of sand, which evidently belongs to the drift that has left many similar deposits over this region. A portion of the overlying sand may be ascribed to the same source, but I think the fact will be made evident that a considerable part of the original, and even of the present elevation, is artificial.

The situation is such as would be chosen by the Mound-Builders, over all others, for a resting place and monument to their dead. It is most picturesque. At the base, circling nearly two sides of the mound, lay the deep waters of the river Rouge. Beyond stretched a field of natural meadow, to the river Detroit, half a mile distant, and visible for many miles of its course. To the south and west were seen Grosse Isle and the channel leading past Malden to Lake Erie. Above stretched the straits, as far as the site of the city, while northward the view commands many miles of rolling country. The tumulus must have been visible from a great distance, in every direction.

Much as has been lost by the wanton destruction of this instructive monument, enough is disclosed to show that this huge mound has been the memorial of many interesting and marvellous events. From the immense number of skeletons found within it, and the mode of their occurrance, there can be little doubt that it was one of these national sepulchres of the Hurons and other Algonquin tribes, where were deposited the remains of their dead, that had been carefully kept for the purpose, until the flesh had disappeared, and the proper season had arrived for the great "Festival of the Dead."

This was attended, amid the general gathering of the tribes, with many ceremonies, to which I shall only briefly allude. The festival has been so well described in the 15th Canto of *Teuch-sa-Grandie*, by our lamented townsman, Levi Bishop, that I refer the curious to that poem for its full illustration.

Until this ceremony had taken place the spirits of the dead were supposed to wander restlessly about, as did the unburied Romans on the borders of the Styx.

"Departed spirits linger still,—
Their vacant place in cabin fill;
Awaiting for the festal day,
To speed them on their destined way,—
To final home—to land afar—
To land beyond the evening star."

When the appointed time has arrived

—"the recent dead
Are lifted from their temporary bed,
The relics—shapeless forms, in swift decay,
The mouldy bones, without the lifeless clay,
Of both the sexes, and of young and old;
The child, the lover, sachem, chieftan bold,—
A frightful throng, a melancholy train,
Come forth their final resting-place to gain."

The dismal process of cleansing the bones—the exposure of the remains to the view of mourning friends—the decoration in the richest furs—the display of gifts destined for sacrifice,—the procession—the harangue—the dance—the games—the feast—the solemn song, broken at intervals by the long-measured, dreary funeral wail, simulating voices of disembodied souls, winging their way to the land of spirits,—the promiscuous casting of remains into one general pit, amid "a weeping, shrieking, howling concourse" of guests and mourners, gathered from the whole nation, all illuminated by the midnight glare of blazing torches and camp-fires, constituted a scene unique as it was solemn and awful; one of those mysteries of the past that is never to return.

"Two fathoms deep the burial pit,
And twice two ample fathoms wide;
A circle that might well admit
A thousand bodies, side by side!"

The *Jesuit Relations* of 1636 tell us of a place of this kind set apart among the Hurons in Canada, before their fatal dispersion by the Iroquous, where they were accustomed to inter their dead in one common sepulchre, heaping above them the funeral mound. This ceremony took place once in ten or twelve years.

That the river Rouge mound was of this character there is much cumulative evidence to prove. Mr. Bourdeno has seen hundreds of skeletons removed in the digging down of the hill. He says that in some parts there seems to have been a "cellar" which was filled with bones, mingled indiscriminately.

Squire Ludlow, an old resident, also gives similar accounts of the number of skeletons disinterred. His statement goes further, as to their immense quantities, much of which he collected and buried elsewhere. Thousands of fragments of human bones still lie bleaching on the sand, mingled with sherds of pottery and other relics.

Powerful as is the interest which attaches to this hill of the dead from this proof of its character, it presents other points of interest. It affords certain evidence that *cremation* was practiced by the Mound-Builders of this region. It was also, in all probability, a sacred or "altar" Mound. In the account given me by Bourdeno he states, that in other parts of the mound than those containing the "cellars," much charcoal and ashes were found, mingled with burned bones. With these were many pieces of large pots, but all were broken. The latter fact is consonant with the theory of cremation, for on these occasions the relics, instead of being buried whole with the dead, as in ordinary casės, were thrown upon the burning pile, and of course suffered partial destruction.

Another phase in the history of this mound is related by Bourdeno, viz., that in Pontiac's time, and before the fatal ambuscade at Bloody run, there occurred at this place a massacre of British soldiers by the Indians, and that the dead were buried in this mound. I am not aware that history alludes to this event, but the fact that many bodies of white soldiers have been interred in the hill is evident, from the character of the skulls found in a certain part of it, and from the attendant relics, such as pieces of scabbards, buttons and other portions of military equipment, which have escaped decay.

During old territorial times the mound was made to subserve the living. A house was erected on the summit, near the east end, which was at first a trading-post for the Indians. It has been gone many years,—all except a large quantity of bricks and mortar, and other rubbish. The relic hunter finds over the whole surface a curious intermingling of the old and the new;—glass, pieces of crockery, iron and other articles of modern housekeeping are in close communion with flint implements, antique pot sherds, and Indian trinkets, and with bits of brass and iron that once belonged to the accoutrements of the British soldier.

Desirous of more fully determining the true character of the mound, a few years ago I proceeded in company with Messrs. Henry Gillman and H. G. Hubbard, to a practical investigation.

Having determined, as nearly as possible, the central axis of the original mound, we proceeded to open a trench near to it, and through the highest part now remaining, a portion of which seemed to have been undisturbed and was still covered with sod.

This trench was commenced on the river side, near the top, six feet wide and five deep, and was continued northerly for a distance of ten feet before anything appeared to reward the labor, except an English half-penny of George III, and a United States cent of 1829. These were found about four feet below the surface of the digging. We then struck a skull. This was dug carefully around, and the skeleton exposed. It lay with the head to the east, and was so doubled together and crushed, that the whole occupied a space not more than two feet long by four inches thick.

It had evidently originally been placed in a sitting posture. The skull was so much flattened and decayed as to render it impossible to determine the shape or size. The ribs and most of the vertebrae and smaller bones had perished, but the larger bones of the arms and legs were sufficiently perfect to be removed. The flattening of the tibia, first pointed out by Mr. Gillman as characteristic of the most ancient human remains in this region, was very observable.

On the south side of the head was a small pot, composed of baked clay, which was also so flattened and decayed that it could be removed only in fragments. This skeleton was only three feet below the surface, but how many feet had been originally heaped over it was impossible to say.

To the west, and about two feet from the above and one foot deeper, was a mass apparently composed of burned human remains. It formed a dark, reddish soil, several inches thick, and quite hard and compact. It occupied a space two feet by one and a half and four inches thick. Close to this were a few unburned portions of a skeleton, and a perfectly formed greenstone celt.

At about the same distance from the skeleton first mentioned, and a foot lower down, was another mass of cinders. Still deeper, and at a foot removed to the west, was another mass of considerably larger extent, and a foot thick.

Among these masses of compacted cinder were several large nodules of irregular form, and of a yellowish red color, which seemed held together by a cement of iron rust. Nothing, however, beyond this indicated that these might once have composed vessels of iron. The lowest of the compacted masses was five feet beneath the present surface. That they consisted in part of burned human bones there could be no doubt, and they establish the fact of cremation beyond question.

In excavating another trench at a lower part of the mound, we came, at a depth of two feet, upon what appeared, from its color and character, to have at one period constituted the original surface. A few inches below this was disclosed a stratum of black earth, composed of cinders and burned bones, the extent of which was traced at several points, and found to constitute a bed not less than twenty feet square. On the disturbed surface was found a spot covered with broken fragments of clay. This, as the matrix is entirely sand, may be presumed to be an artificial deposit. It may have formed part of an "altar," or clay hearth, such as are pointed out by Squier in his so-called "Altar Mounds" of Ohio.

Continuing the excavations beneath the sodded portion of the mound, at three feet from the surface we uncovered numerous skeletons. They were disposed irregularly, as though hastily buried. The skulls and some of the bones were in tolerably perfect preservation. Quite a number were those of babes. Some of the crania were shattered, as if from heavy blows. Two of them exhibited a round hold at the apex, made by some sharp instrument after death. The rimming is plainly visible, and the holes are about half an inch in diameter.

We now sunk a shaft or well into the sand at the place where the hard, cemented masses were discovered. This was continued to the depth of eight feet, and here were found numerous nodules or lumps of a white substance which proved to be disintegrated bone. These continued in considerable numbers through the succeeding three feet, when the digging was discontinued. How much lower still these singular masses continue was left undetermined.

There was no appearance of the sand having ever been disturbed, yet the presence of these bones made evident either that interments had taken place at this great depth of more than ten feet, or that the earth had accumulated since the deposition. It is entirely improbable that any of the Indian races buried their dead in graves of that extreme depth, for no such custom is known. And as these occur immediately below the undoubted Indian remains first mentioned, it is apparent that interments took place during long intervals of time, the earth heaped above the first being sometimes buried entire and sometimes burned, the remains being covered, like the others, with a fresh deposit of sand. Thus year by year, and cycle by cycle, the mound grew in height and proportions.

Since the discovery of the two perforated skulls others have come to light, similarly treated, elsewhere in the State. The condition of these crania indicates that they are fairly modern. For what purpose were these perforations. A suggestion has been made, and it accords with the known anxieties of the Indian, that the holes were for giving more speedy release to the spirit from its earthy tenement. Another supposition is of a very practical kind, that they were intended as a means of suspending the skull in view of the friends of the deceased, until the time of the great festival of inhumation.

We must regard this great mound now being so ruthlessly destroyed—as a fast necropolis, containing the dead of many centuries, belonging both to the prehistoric past and to our modern era (Hubbard, 1887:228-36).

It is perhaps most apt at this point to apply a modern viewpoint or terminology to the findings of Gillman, Hubbard and Blois. It is evident from the statements of each that the mounds they investigated saw use well up into historic times. But they also mention that the mounds were much mutilated by the time they got to them and as Pilling points out ". . .relic hunters were digging into this site for souvenirs within a few years, if not months or days after deceased Indians had been buried. . . ." (Pilling, 1961*a*:28). Thus most of the historic burials had probably been removed or destroyed and account for much of the bone on the surfaces of the mounds.

The first burials described by Blois had no real diagnostic traits except those of a generalized Late Woodland context containing projectile points, ground stone tools and red ochre. He mentions no distinct burial posture and conjecture here is pointless. However the burials that occurred under the charcoal layer at the base of the mound present a different problem. Blois describes them as being in a flexed position, each having a pot in the hands. This has never been reported by any competent observer. He mentions no ground stone with these burials, but states that there were projectile points, knives, shall beads and a large shell container. Blois' interpretation was that some of the shell beads were amulets because they were found in the mouth. However it is not at all unusual for beads that obviously form part of a necklace to become lodged in such a position after burial. The pottery interpretation of the burials is the key to the piece. I have examined all of the pottery known to exist from the Springwells mounds and have not seen one piece that could be construed as being "carved and marked with various fantastic figures." This fits no known Late Woodland pottery assemblage, but is strongly reminiscent of a Middle Woodland or Hopewell description.

A description such as Blois' represents an almost absolute minimum of knowledge, but as stated above, it is all that remains of the Central Mound at Springwells. All of Blois' description with the exception of the rusty bucket (which he views as an anomalie) is quite probable and leaves no room for the consideration of scientific fraud.

Henry Gillman's excavations represent a considerable advance over those of John Blois. There is more attention paid to the description of excavation technique and the relation of one thing to another, but Gillman did not number his burials consecutively, apparently considering them significant only when the skull was relatively complete.

The burial complex described by Gillman appears to be fairly uniform even though the bulk of the burials appear to be intrusive. Each burial is associated with one or more pottery vessels. One pot described by Gillman as being "marked with an evenly indented cord pattern, the intersecting lines being laid on at wide and regular intervals so as to form large diamond-shaped figures..." (Gillman, 1877:314) is particularly interesting since it seems to correspond to what Fitting (1965:158) has called Wayne Cross-hatched ware. Gillman's "so-called sinker" would appear to be a gorget.

As Gillman pointed out cremation was confined to a single instance in which the cremated remains had been placed in a funerary urn. Gillman interpreted this burial as the one precipitating the building of the mound, however the Holmquist excavations, discussed below, tend to shed some doubt on this interpretation.

Not a great deal can be said about the Circular or Carstens Mound except that the descriptions by Hubbard and Gillman coincide fairly well. Unfortunately the excavation of this mound was accidental and description of the artifacts is even scantier than Blois'.

The Great Mound at the River Rouge is an enigma no matter how viewed. Cremations and mass burials arrest one's attention. Unfortunately no reliable estimate for the age of these two types of burial can be made because of the mutilation and attrition this mound suffered and also because Gillman gave no depths on the ones he discovered. If the mass burials are the remains of various "Feasts of the Dead" as Hubbard labors so eloquently to prove, the evidence is strong if somewhat obscured.

The perforated crania while strongly suggestive of some burial or preburial ritual are not very culturally diagnostic, although they do appear to be more prevalent in Late Woodland. Perforation by drilling appears to be restricted to Late Woodland and later. Puncturing or plaque removal of the skull however has a long history extending back into Middle Woodland times and is fairly common at the Norton Mounds near Grand Rapids, Michigan, where 13 of 29 burials have plaque removal. This is usually along the top of the occiput or near bregma.

The mound appears to be stratified to some degree, but we are unable to make any cultural associations with it except for the fact that one level covers a cremation area; but it is impossible to say if this level pertains to all the cremations in the mound. The description of artifacts also is not detailed enough to make any cultural distinctions. It is also evident that not all of the mound's height was artificial since there is mention of an undisturbed gravel level and supports the theory that the mound augmented the height of a pre-existing knoll or ridge.

The following list will enable the reader to see at a glance the traits occurring in each of the Springwells mounds:

TABLE 1

TRAIT LIST FOR DETROIT MOUNDS

	Fort Wayne Mound	Central Mound	Great Mound	Carsten Mound
Burial Mode				
Flexed	X	X	X	X
Bundle	X		X	
Mass			X	
Cremation				
one	X		X	
more than one .			X	
Ground Stone				
Celts	X	X	X	X
Gorgets	X			X
Pottery				
Cord-marked . .	X	X	X	X
Other.	X	X		
Shell				
Beads.	X	X	?	X
Column.	X(?)			
Container	X	X		
Skeletal Anomalies				
Drilled crania . .	X		X	
Platycnemia . . .	X		X	
Flint				
Projectile points	X	X	X	X
Other.	X	X	X	?
Ochre	X	X	X	
Copper.	X			X
Bone-antler Artifacts	X		X	X
Mound				
Sand	X	X	X	X

III

THE FORT WAYNE MOUND

The Fort Wayne Mound is located at the Fort Wayne Ordinance Depot, Detroit, Michigan. It is west of the old fort between Gibbs Street and the Officer's Row, immediately in front of the former site of Barracks Number 13. As previously described, it was excavated by Henry Gillman and members of the Detroit Scientific Association in 1876.

In the years that followed, Gillman's report faded from memory and the true nature of the mound was forgotten. One commandant had made up his mind to have it removed "deeming it an eyesore on the Parade Grounds," but he was dissuaded (Holmquist, 1946:1).

In 1944 the commandant of Fort Wayne, Colonel Harry Adamson instructed his adjutant, Major Donald Wanless, to discover just what the mound was. Major Wanless checked all the available records and found nothing. Assured that there was nothing in the title to the land that barred excavation, he applied to Washington for permission to excavate. This permission was received and it was decided to open the mound on July 1, 1944, with the excavation to be done by the Aboriginal Research Club of Detroit.

The mound exhibited several depressions that the officers believed were caused by children playing on the mound and which had been resodded only a few years earlier. It had also been truncated on its northern side by a northeast-southwest sidewalk. Mr. Carl Holmquist took charge of the excavators and decided to start a test trench 28 feet from the intersecting eastern sidewalk heading toward the highest point of the mound as the approximate center. This trench was 3.5 feet wide and was begun at sidewalk level where bone and pottery were found. The trench was troweled down to where the soil showed only clear beach sand. This point, 11 inches below the sidewalk grade, was taken as the base of the mound. When surveyed, this base was found to be 596.3 feet above sea level. Beneath this, 14 inches of beach sand overlay a 6- to 8-inch "hardpan" of red clay and gravel, and below this, several feet of fine sharp grey gravel (Fig. 2). The excavation of 32 square feet confirmed the base level of the mound.

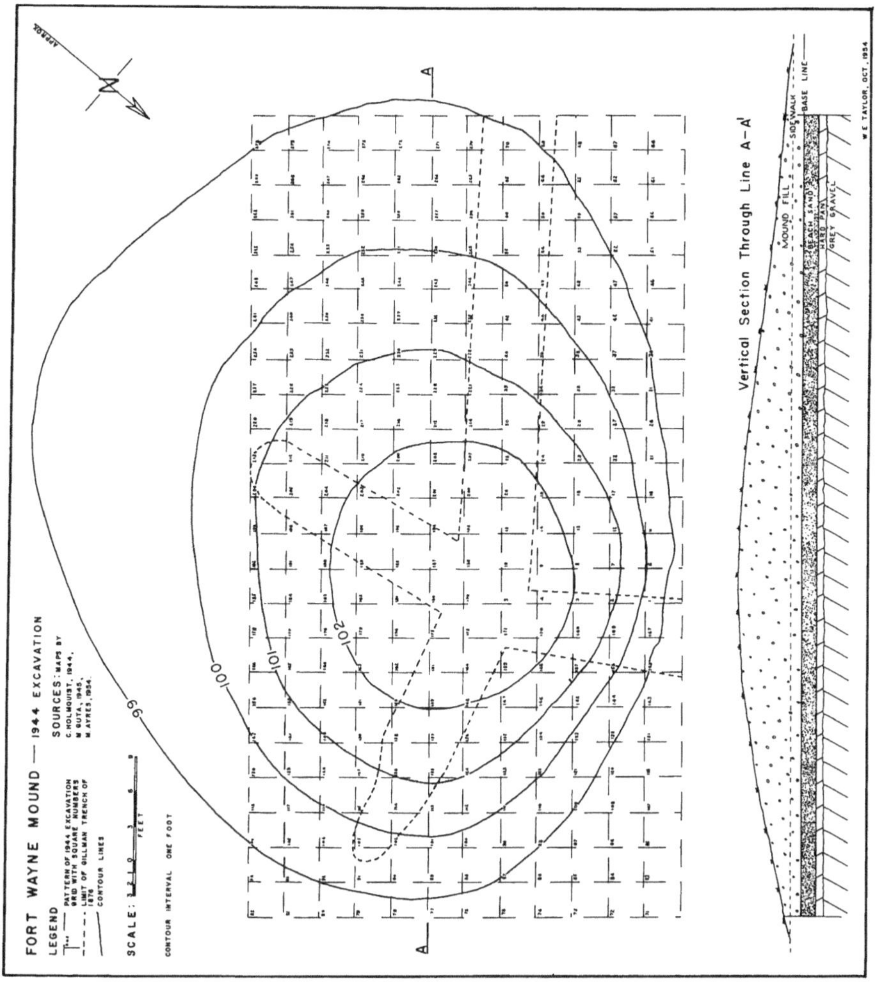
FORT WAYNE MOUND — 1944 EXCAVATION
LEGEND
PATTERN OF 1944 EXCAVATION GRID WITH SQUARE NUMBERS
LIMIT OF GILLMAN TRENCH OF 1876
CONTOUR LINES
SOURCES: MAPS BY C. HOLMQUIST, 1944. M. GUTA, 1945. M. AYRES, 1954.
SCALE:
FEET
CONTOUR INTERVAL ONE FOOT
N
APPROX.
99
100
101
102
A
A
Vertical Section Through Line A-A'
MOUND FILL
SIDEWALK
BASE LINE
BEACH SAND
HARD PAN
GREY GRAVEL
W. E. TAYLOR, OCT. 1954

FIG. 2

After the discovery of Burial 1 it was decided to start at the western end of the mound with a 6-foot trench. Immediately more mixed material was encountered. At this time a copy of Gillman's report was provided by Dr. Emerson F. Greenman of the University of Michigan Museum of Anthropology, and it was discovered that the areas of mixed material coincided with Gillman's trenches.

The original test trench was extended 15 feet back from the walk and continued to the west. The 2 feet paralleling the sidewalk were very disturbed because of grading and the 3 feet on the southern end of the strip contained part of the east-west trench of Gillman.

A grid consisting of 3- by 3-foot squares 1 foot in depth was established. These squares were numbered consecutively and lettered for elevation; A for the first foot above the base line, B for the second foot, etc. Below the base line the lettering was AS, AS-1, AS-2, and AS-3.

From the A level to the top of the mound there was no indication of stratification. Because the mound was made entirely of sand it would not support a good humus and, as Gillman noted, "The Structure . . . could hardly be supposed to present its original features" and "that at least in height the mound is much reduced" (Gillman, 1877:312).

BURIAL 1

Burial 1 is that of a small child of undetermined sex, between the ages of 1 and 2. This was a bundle burial near the present edge of the mound in Section 3-B.

In the bundle were 16 columella beads and a curved section of bone so modified as to defy identification. At its widest point the bone is 2.9 cm. wide and .2 cm. thick. On either side of the central curve is a design which looks like a disconnected *W*. From .4 cm. beyond the point of each *W* and around the edges is a band of short double-pecked dots (Figure 3; Plate I, A). It would

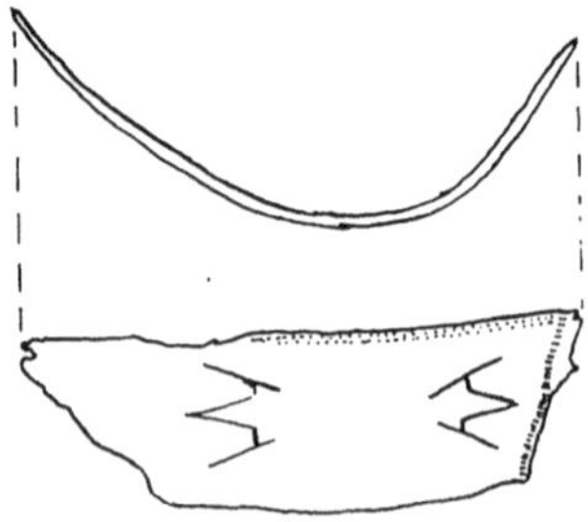

FIG. 3. Bone artifact with Burial 1.

seem that the means of attachment was probably holes drilled in the missing extremities of the artifact (cf. Ritchie, 1965:Plate 80, No. 9).

Burial Vessel

P-1 (Homquist's number)

Paste: Orange paste with angular crushed granite up to .7 cm.
Surface: Medium cord-marking on exterior. Interior smoothed.
Decoration: Cord-wrapped stick-impressions on the lip trend right.
Form: The vessel is so badly smashed that all that can be said is that the body was probably globular and the rim straight to slightly flaring.
Dimensions: Height—?
Rim height—?
Shoulder diameter—?
Rim diameter—?
Thickness at lip—.5 to 16 cm.
Thickness at shoulder—?
Thickness of body wall—.6 cm.
Thickness of base—.9 cm.
Type: Wayne Cord-marked

BURIAL 2

Burial 2 was located in Section 7-C. It was a bundle burial of a male over 40 years of age. Holmquist (1946:3) reports very distinct imprints of what appeared to be the whorls of some sort of fur. This is quite conceivable since the burial was a bundle and could easily have been covered with or wrapped in a fur.

Burial Vessel

P-2

Paste: Black with medium-size grit tempering. The exterior surface is yellow and the interior is gray and yellow.
Surface: Cord-marked exterior, smooth interior.
Decoration: Tool impressions on the lip.
Form: Squared, slightly outsloping lip. Nothing else could be ascertained.
Dimensions: Height—?
Rim height—?
Shoulder diameter—?
Rim diameter—?
Thickness at lip—.5 cm.
Thickness at shoulder—?
Thickness of body wall—.5 to .6 cm.
Type: Wayne Cord-marked

BURIAL 3

In Section 8, one foot below the base level, Burial 3 was discovered—a flexed female between the ages of 25 and 30. With this burial were 44 columella beads varying in length from .9 to 2.3 cm. They probably made up a graduated necklace (Plate I, B). An unretouched chip of gray and brown banded flint was found with the burial as well as a sharpening stone or whetstone of yellow sandstone with one long central groove (Plate I, C,D).

The head of the burial was oriented toward the east and the burial was covered with red ochre.

Burial Vessel (Plate IV)

P-3

Paste: The paste is black with angular crushed granite temper. The exterior surface is yellow to gray with some dark firing clouds.
Surface: Very slightly smoothed cord-marking on exterior. Interior smoothed.
Decoration: Cross-hatch incising forms irregularly sized diamonds. Diagonal cord-wrapped stick impressions on the lip usually .4 cm. apart.
Form: Slightly flaring rim with a flattened lip. The neck is slightly constricted. Body is globular and subconoidal with a rounded bottom.
Dimensions: Height—17.5 cm.
Rim height—2.5-3.0 cm.
Shoulder diameter—12.3 cm.
Rim diameter—11.5 cm.
Thickness at lip—.5 cm.
Thickness at shoulder—.7 cm.
Thickness of body wall—.5-.6 cm.
Type: Wayne Crosshatched.

BURIALS 4 AND 5

Burials 4 and 5 are both bundle burials and were located in Sections 13 B and C. Burial 4 was an adult female; Burial 5 was an individual approximately 16 years old, but of indeterminate sex. Both burials were extremely fragmentary.

Lying between these two burials was a badly crushed burial vessel that will be described below.

At a depth of .5 feet below and a distance of .6 feet east of this pot was located the most perplexing artifact in the mound. This is a birdstone of banded gray slate, 13.35 cm. in length, and with eyes of unequal size (Plate I, E).[3]

---

[3]Townsend (1959:204) cites Dr. James B. Griffin on the association of the birdstone with the pottery from this burial as follows:

The presence of this birdstone is further complicated by the presence of Marion Thick pottery in the fill. However, none of these sherds was within 10 feet of the birdstone and several were in the fill of Gillman's trench whereas the birdstone was in an undisturbed portion of the mound.

Several explanations have been put forward to account for the presence of this birdstone with a Late Woodland burial. One is that the birdstone is part of an occupation represented by the Marion Thick pottery.

Another theory would have birdstone surviving until this rather late date as an item in the cultural complex of the builders of this mound.

A slightly stronger position would be the idea that the birdstone was a curio or antique keepsake of the buried individual. I tend to exclude this possibility on the basis of the birdstone's position and depth in relation to the burials.

My personal choice of interpretation is that the birdstone is genuine, but that its inclusion with the burial—if, in fact, it was included—was purely accidental. The original resting place of this item was probably similar to that of the Marion Thick pottery, possibly a camp site on the sand knoll at Springwells that was later utilized for building the mound. Why the Indians overlooked such an artifact is difficult to explain, but artifacts as genuine and more useful have been discovered in the fill of other mounds.

Found near the birdstone was a rounded quartzite pebble 3.9 by 3.2 cm. It was originally believed that this pebble might have some special relationship to the birdstone, but the pebble is unworked and is probably just another random inclusion in the fill.

Burial Vessel (Plate V)

P-4

Paste: The color is dark gray to black with temper of medium crushed granite.

Surface: The surface treatment is coarse slightly smoothed cord-marking. The interior is smoothed.

"I have examined the pottery vessel from the Fort Wayne mound which is said to have been associated with the birdstone. The pottery vessel is a cord-marked jar with a cord wrapped stick impressed series of impressions around the lip of the vessel, and from its general shape, thickness and other features, I would think that it would belong to the Late Hopewell in the Detroit and southeastern Michigan area. I would think that its date would be somewhere around 1,000 to 1,500 years ago, and I do not believe that the birdstone form lasts until this period of time. I will say that there is considerably earlier pottery present in the fill or perhaps on the base of the mound, and it may well be that the birdstone became incorporated in a more recent burial. This is certainly in the realm of conjecture. My own feeling about the matter is that one should not take this association as a clear-cut and decisive one."

Decoration: The outside edge of the lip is impressed with broad (.5 cm.) deep cord-wrapped stick impressions. These are indented to such a degree that the lip appears as a narrow ridge.

Form: The rim is slightly flaring with minor neck constrictions. The body is subconoidal.

Dimensions: Height—20.3-.5 cm. (This vessel has been heavily and not very satisfactorily restored so all measurements except in the rim area are suspect.)
Rim height—4.5 cm.
Shoulder diameter—15.5 cm.
Thickness at lip—.5 cm.
Thickness at shoulder—.7 cm.
Thickness of body wall—.8-.9 cm.

Type: Wayne Cord-marked

BURIAL 6

Burial 6 was located in Sections 11-B and 12-B. Because this area is near the edge of the present mound there was a great deal of disturbance and the skull of this burial had apparently been eroded away. It was a bundle of an adult, probably a male. No definite age or sex criteria were present.

The only burial association was a Jack's Reef corner-notched point (Ritchie, 1961:26) 3.5 cm. long and 2.35 cm. wide. It is rather crudely made and one side has the remains of a flat cortical surface. The material is rather grainy purplish chert (Plate III, A).

BURIAL 7

Burial 7 in Section 11-A was a rather complete bundle burial of a female 17- to 18-years old. The skull was lying on its left side, facing north, with the mandible reversed in front of the maxilla. The rest of the bundle was underneath.

The only burial goods consisted of 22 *Anculosa* shell beads mixed in with the burial.

BURIAL 8

Burial 8, found in Sections 17-C and 18-C, was a badly crushed and scattered bundle burial of an adult of undetermined sex.

Burial Vessel (Plate VI)

P-5

Paste: The color is orange brown and temper is medium-sized hornblende and granitic grit.

Surface: Cord-marked roughly on the exterior and smoothed on the interior.
Decoration: Cord-wrapped stick impressions on the lip trend to the right.
Form: Semi-conoidal to globular body. The rim is flat and slightly thickened, and slightly flared.
Dimensions: Height—16.6 cm.
Rim height—3.3 cm.
Shoulder diameter—14.2 cm.
Rim diameter—12.3 cm.
Thickness at lip—1.0 cm.
Thickness at shoulder—.7 cm.
Thickness of body wall—.8 cm.
Volume—1775 cc.
Type: Wayne Cord-marked

BURIAL 9-X

Burial 9-X was in Sections 31-A and 32-A. This was a bundle burial of an adult female. The skull was face down and appears to have two holes punched in the right parietal, but this area of the skull is rather heavily eroded and we cannot be exactly sure about the nature of the holes.

BURIAL 10

Burial 10, located in Sections 17-AS and 22-AS, was flexed, face up with hands over the mouth. This was apparently a flesh burial as the small bones of the hands were in place (Holmquist, 1946:4). The individual was a female approximately 30 years old.

This burial was accompanied by four items; a broken section of deer tibia that does not appear to have been worked, a crescent-shaped knife or scraper of yellow-gray chert, a sharpening stone of fine-grained yellow sandstone, and a broken tabular piece of limestone that was not worked (Plate I, F-I). Also removed with this burial were 282 *Anculosa* shell beads.

Burial Vessel (Plate VII)

P-7

Paste: Paste is black with angular grit temper.
Surface: The surface is cord-marked rather coarsely and the interior is smoothed.
Decoration: The rim is marked with vertically incised lines.
Form: Flattened slightly thickened lip with a straight to slightly flaring rim. Globular body.
Dimensions: Height—19.8 cm.
Rim height—3.3 cm.
Shoulder diameter—14.0 cm.

Rim diameter—12.3 cm.
Thickness at lip—.8 cm.
Thickness of body wall—.7 cm.
Thickness at shoulder—.8 cm.

Type: Wayne Cord-marked

BURIAL 11

Burial 11, located in Sections 22-C and 23-C, was a bundle burial of a male over 40 years of age. The top of the skull was crushed because the burial was only .5 feet below the sod. The skull was facing north.

BURIAL 12

Burial 12, found in Sections 24-A and 29-B was the bundle burial of a female approximately 25 years old. The skull was lying on the occiput on top of the bundle. Both maxilla and mandible were missing.

Grave goods consisted of 12 flint chips, 2 of which showed usage retouch. These were of various types of smooth gray chert (Plate I, K). There was also a slate disc 6.7 by 6.2 cm. (Plate I, J). This disc is similar to that found with Burial 22.

BURIAL 13

Burials 13, from Section 23-AS, actually represents two individuals. The more complete skeleton of the two was partly flexed with the skull facing northeast. This person was an adult male of about 40 years. Holmquist (1946:5) reported that the burial appeared to have been made in the flesh, but was partially dismembered.

The fragmentary individual is represented by a right scapula, left clavicle, a left femur, both tibiae and fibulae, and a fragmentary cranium.

BURIAL 14

In the center of Gillman's trench in Sections 25-AS and 207-AS was evidence of a small fire and a heavy deposit of ochre. In this deposit 12 flakes of gray flint of different types (Plate I, O) and a sharpening stone of rust-colored and yellow sandstone were discovered (Plate I, N). A celt of laminar greenstone, possibly slate, with both ends broken, was also found in this fire bed. It is 2.5 cm. thick and 4.9 cm. wide (Plate I, P). South of this, Burial 14 was located; a female approximately 18 years old. The burial was a bundle with the skull lying face down. In a space between the skull and leg bones was P-62.

Burial Vessel (Plate VIII)

P-62

Paste: Temper is angular crushed granite. The color is black; however the exterior is yellow with a few dark firing clouds.
Surface: The exterior is cord-marked and the interior is smooth.
Decorations: Incised crosshatching on the neck. The lip has diagonal cord-wrapped stick impressions from .3 to .6 cm. apart. These trend to the right.
Form: The rim is straight with a flat lip. The body is rounded and subconoidal with a rounded bottom.
Dimensions: Height—17.2 cm.
Rim height—3.4-3.7 cm.
Shoulder diameter—13.9 cm.
Rim diameter—11.5 cm.
Thickness at lip—.7-.8 cm.
Thickness at shoulder—.7-.8 cm.
Thickness of body wall—.6-.8 cm.
Volume—1925 cc.
Type: Wayne Crosshatched

It is quite possible that the flint chips, celt, and whetstone do not belong with this burial and are in fact associated only with the fire bed. Nevertheless these are artifacts that do appear with burials elsewhere in the mound, in which case the fire bed may be interpreted as having some sort of ceremonial function. The pot may have been "killed" since a hole was knocked in the bottom.

BURIAL 15

Burial 15, in Sections 34-AS-3 and 35-AS-3 was a tightly flexed male over 40 years old. The burial pit went through the hardpan and extended into the gravel to a depth of 3 feet. The skull was uppermost, facing west, with the vertebrae, ribs, etc. all in their proper anatomical positions (Holmquist, 1946:5). This was the most tightly flexed of the burials and was entirely lacking in grave goods.

BURIAL 16

This was a badly crushed bundle in Sections 151-C and 152-C with the skull lying on its right side, facing north. The burial was that of a male at least 45 years old. Again there were no burial goods.

BURIAL 17

Burial 17 was a bundle burial facing southwest, located in Sections 163-A and 163-B. The mandible was pushed to the right with the teeth at the lower edge of the right orbit and the maxilla was shifted to the left (Holmquist, 1946:7).

The burial is that of a female more than 40 years old. Two right femurs were found with this female indicating that two individuals were present. The absence of any long bones other than those of the legs prevents any other speculation about this second individual.

There were no burial goods except for the vessel described below.

Burial Vessel (Plate IX)

P-39

Paste: The color of the paste is orange and the temper is crushed angular granite up to .4 cm.
Surface: The exterior is cord-marked and the interior is smoothed.
Decoration: There are short cord-wrapped stick impressions on the exterior edge of the lip with longer ones on the interior of the rim. There is a continuous cord impression around the top of the squared, slightly outsloping lip.
Form: The rim is straight to slightly flaring. The body is subconoidal with a rounded bottom.
Dimensions: Height—15.7 cm.
Rim height—3.4 cm.
Shoulder diameter—12.5 cm.
Rim diameter—12.0 cm.
Thickness at lip—.7-.8 cm.
Thickness at shoulder—.7-.9 cm.
Thickness of body wall—.8-.9 cm.
Volume—1690 cc.
Type: Wayne Cord-marked

BURIAL 18

Burial 18 was found in Sections 181-AS and 182-AS. This was another bundle burial consisting of an individual 16- to 18-years old, but sex was indeterminable. The skull was facing north.

A single large columella shell bead 2.7 cm. long and 2.9 cm. wide was recovered with the burial (Plate I, M). There was also a crudely whittled awl or punch 14.25 cm. long made of deer bone (Plate I, L).

Burial 18 must receive a slightly different interpretation than the rest because of the large number of sherds found in the fill.

In one case sherds from a vessel found in Burial 18 fit those found in Pits 1 and 4. In the case of two other vessels, sherds fit with several found in Pit 5, and Pit 4. It is thus evident that Burial 18 is a much later intrusive burial related to the occupation represented by the pottery of the pits than to the rest of the burials. Unfortunately the skeletal material was in such poor condition that no physical separation could be made.

BURIAL 20

Burial 20 is a fragmentary burial of a young adult, found in Sections 195-C, 201-C-D, and 202-C-D. The sex of the skeleton was indeterminable.

The location of this skeleton appears to place it in the west extension of Gillman's south trench and it might be the remains of one of Gillman's burials 8, 9, and 10.

BURIAL 21

Burial 21, a male over 40 years old, was located in Sections 197-B, 196-A, and 197-A and presents a unique mode of burial. This was a flesh burial in a supine position, with legs widely spread and flexed on each side. The right hand was covering the pelvic region. The upper part of the body was turned with the right shoulder at a 30 degree angle and the head was facing north (Holmquist, 1946:8).

There were no burial goods.

BURIAL 22

Burial 22 was located in Sections 195-A and 195-AS. It was a flesh burial in a flexed, or what Holmquist called "seated" position (1946:8). The skull was upright facing northwest with arms crossed over the breast--the right arm over the left with the left hand at the right shoulder. The legs were flexed to the right. The individual is a female approximately 35 years old.

Grouped behind the right pelvic in a deposit of ochre was a fairly elaborate set of artifacts. There were 3 slate disks measuring 7.2 by 5.0 cm., 8.7 by 5.0 cm., and 7.75 by 9.45 cm. respectively (Plate I, Q). All of these are chipped and battered around the edges. They would have made serviceable knives or scrapers.

There were 3 triangular chert kinves in this cache also. One is quite crude with secondary retouch on one exterior face only. The other 2 knives have flaking on all three sides. Each knife is made from a different variety of gray chert (Plate I, R).

One blue flint drill was in the cache. It is side-notched with a length of 3.35 cm. a width of 2.05 cm. and a minimum stem diameter of 1.4 cm. (Plate I, S).

Thirteen unretouched flint chips were also found in the cache.

Burial Vessel (Plate X)

P-55

Paste: Color is grayish yellow and the temper is finely crushed hornblende. The exterior color is gray.

Surface: The surface is finely cord-marked and the interior is smooth.

Decoration: The lip is marked with diagonal cord-wrapped stick impressions which trend to the left. At the beginning of the shoulder is a cord impression around the whole circumference of the pot. Below this impression are 73 punctates .3 cm. in diameter circling the shoulder, and beneath these another single cord impression. The width of this design complex is 1.4 cm. Below this is a zig-zag pattern of .3 cm. punctates; there are 102 of these punctates. The average width of this band is 2.0 cm.

Form: The rim is straight with a flat and slightly thickened lip. The body is subconoidal with a rounded bottom.

Dimensions: Height—21.3 cm.
Rim height—3.4 cm.
Shoulder diameter—13.1 cm.
Rim diameter—12.3 cm.
Thickness at lip—.6-.7 cm.
Thickness at shoulder—.7 cm.
Thickness of body wall—.6-.7 cm.
Volume—2425 cc.

Type: Wayne Punctate

BURIAL 23

In Sections 201-A and 202-A was found a bundle burial—Burial 23. The very fragmentary remains are those of a female about 25 years old.

BURIAL 24

Burial 24, a female 25 to 30 years old, was extremely fragmentary even for a bundle. It was located in Sections 216-A and 216-B. The top of the skull was down and faced west.

BURIAL 19

Burial 19 was an extended burial of a dog and was located in Sections 190-A and 191-A.

Several very important facets of burial practices of the Fort Wayne Mound are concealed in the straight-forward listing of Holmquist burials I have just presented. The most striking is the fact that of the burials of identifiable sex, only women were buried with burial goods of any type. (Burial 18 is excluded from the following discussion for reasons explained in the description of that burial.) If the descriptions are checked carefully the reader will note that I have apparently contradicted myself by describing a Wayne Ware vessel with Burial 2, a male over 40 years old. In Holmquist's original report, this vessel is not described with the burial nor is it shown in the drawing of the burial. The only connection established between the burial and the pot is in the ceramic catalogue. Because the vessel was located near the edge of the mound and near the surface it may have been associated with a totally eroded burial.

In the case of Burial 6, I do not believe the association of one projectile point demonstrably below the burial, should be interpreted as a burial offering.

Eight of the 11 female burials are accompanied by some form of burial goods. There is no apparent reason for the other 3 women not having burial goods.

It would seem, therefore, that women enjoyed a favored position in this society at least in death and are associated with what may be considered female goods. The problem of the 4 indeterminate sex burials might be brought up at this point. Burial 20 is very suspect in that it is located in the fill of Gillman's south trench extension and if it is, as is suggested in the burial description, a disturbed burial of Gillman association with burial goods would be difficult to prove. Gillman, however, does state that a pot was found in this area.

Burial 1, being a child, was impossible to sex. The favored position of children in many primitive societies may account for the relative wealth of material found with this burial. On the other hand we may extrapolate from the data provided by other burials and interpret this as the burial of a little girl.

Burial 5 was too fragmentary to sex and any further conjecture here can only be to note that the youngest male buried in the Fort Wayne Mound was 40 years old while females cover a range of ages of possibly 1 or 2 or 40. It would seem likely that this too is a female.

Burial 8 accompanied by a pot would also appear to be a female.

Gillman's data does nothing to help these theses and if anything seems to provide evidence to the opposite. In at least two cases, Skull No. 2 (page 87) and Cranium No. 5 (page 88), the description of the skeletal material would seem to indicate males. Skull No. 3 (page 88), a burial accompanied by 5 projectile points, would also appear to be a male if only on the inclusion of these points, a type of burial good not found with any other burials.

The flexed burial posture in particular has a limited distribution among the burials recovered by Holmquist, being found only below the A level of the mound. Five, possibly 6, individuals were recovered in this posture. Three or 4 females and 2 males make up this count. All 3 sandstone abraders are also found below the A level.

Turning to Gillman's account for confirmation we once again are disappointed on two counts. The first is that Gillman found no burials below the "hard pan" described by Holmquist and in fact none below 4 feet, the mound having been 5 feet high at the time of Gillman's excavation. The second is that Gillman describes 4 flexed burials (page 87) at a depth of only 2.5 feet, probably not deep enough to support any thesis of flexed burials being a strictly submound feature.

As for picking out *the* individual or group of burials for whom the mound was built, we are faced with the problem of 50 individuals and data gathered by two expeditions 70 years apart. I cannot concur with Gillman's interpretation of the cremation in the pot as being the individual in whose honor the mound was erected. Burials below the A level of the mound were certainly among the first burials in the area beneath the mound. These may have been relatively shallow burials which when covered would leave slight mounds that were later augmented and consolidated by burials in the mound. Gillman's group of 4 flexed burials near the center may have been the catalyst for erecting a mound of some size into which later burials were intruded.

It is impossible to determine the number of burials in the mound after the burials with Wayne Ware ceramics. We have only one, Burial 18, which is demonstrably later because of the contents of the pit fill. There are indications in Gillman's articles that the historic tribes also made use of the mound for burial purposes. It is quite conceivable that the bones of recent Indians were those that covered the Springwells mounds in the time of McKenney and Blois.

ARTIFACTS NOT ASSOCIATED WITH BURIALS

Ground Stone

Gorget (Plate II, A)

In Section 150-A a small unfinished gorget of a gray slate was recovered. It is 7.7 cm. long and 3.4 cm. wide. The slate is of rather low quality. There are no visible marks of attempts to drill holes in it. Section 150-A is one of the sections included in the Gillman trench and it is likely that this gorget is from a disturbed burial, possibly Gillman's burial No. 5.

Celts and Adzes (Plate II, B)

A small greenstone adze was recovered from Section 10-D. It is heavily stained with ochre. It is 6.3 cm. long, 2.4 cm. wide at the butt and 3.5 cm. wide at the bit. The surface is moderately well-finished everywhere but on the butt. There are several raw areas on the broad faces.

A greenstone celt was described with the account of Burial 14.

Slate (Plate II, C, D, E, F)

There are 3 fragments of slate representing at least 2 implements. One is evidently a large knife or axe although it is too badly broken to tell. One side has been ground down with striations running parallel to this side to form a rather keen edge. There are striations that run perpendicular to this edge indicating it was used for chopping or scraping rather than cutting.

The second tool is represented by only a fragment of the blade of a highly ground fine-grained slate. The blade has the shape of a plane and on the bottom side deep scars are observed trending perpendicular to the edge. There are some minor scars on the top. There is a strong possibility that this was a scraper. Two slate scrapers or discs were recovered from the mound fill. These differ in no way from those found with Burial 22. They both display use on all edges. One measures 6.5 by 6.4 cm. and the other 6.4 by 4.7 cm. It seems likely that these were burial goods ignored by Gillman.

Hammerstones (Plate II, G)

A large gabbro cobble was found in Section 234-B. Its status as a *bona fide* artifact is dubious, but it could have been utilized in its present state as a hammerstone. It weighs 3.25 pounds.

Marbles (Plate II, H-J)

Three "marbles" were recovered in the Fort Wayne Mound. Two of these are limestone and 1 is clay. One of the limestone specimens is quite hard; it is 1.5 cm. in diameter. The second is of gray limestone and is 1.65 cm. in diameter. Both of these are quite round and perfectly formed. The clay specimen is slightly elongated, being 1.4 by 1.6 cm.

There is historic material present in the mound (see page 135). However, if these marbles are to be considered historic, they would constitute no less than 25 per cent of the entire historic sample. Since this is very unlikely, and considering the fact that marbles unearthed in the 1965 University of Michigan Museum of Anthropology excavations at the Central Mound were glass, it would appear that the stone and clay specimens are of Indian manufacture. However none of them were associated with burials nor with Gillman's trench and we can only assume that they became incorporated in the mound fill during its construction. Their original purpose and/or function remains unknown.

Bone (Plate II, K-M)

In Pit 1, Section 24-B a very fine bone needle 10.1 cm. long was discovered. It is made on a splinter of deer bone that is highly ground and polished. On the proximal end along the top are 7 notches. On the top are 4 more notches. It does seem likely that these notches were involved with the tool's function. Holmquist's suggestion (1946:4) that these were for engaging threads in sewing seems likely. However, 3 of the notches on top are located too far forward to be functional but in any case only 2 notches, 1 on top and 1 on the bottom, and a knot in the thread would suffice to secure the thread to the needle.

In Pit 4, Section 231-AS, a bone awl (A-74) made from a splinter of deer bone was discovered. It is ground and polished on the edges and upper surface and sides, and to a lesser degree on the bottom interior surface of the bone. This is apparently the original size of the tool since there is some polish on the broken proximal end.

The awl or punch found with Burial 18 is very crudely made and the only working is the whittling of one end into a point. This is also of deer bone.

There is also a sternal rib of a deer which may have been pointed on the distal end. This was located in Section 244-C in Pit 6.

Pipes (Plate II, N-Q)

Four aboriginal pipe fragments were recovered. In each case the fragment is part of the bowl.

The first is a crumbly clay with pieces of grit temper up to .4 cm. The bowl is cylindrical and smoothed on the inside and outside. The lip is smoothed and slightly outsloping.

The second has a very dark paste with grit temper, size reaching .2 cm. The bowl is curved in toward the base and then flares out again to form a pedestal-like projection.

The third pipe is of untempered clay. The base is keel-shaped. The stem hole and the bowl are the same size--.7 cm.

The last pipe fragment is a section of the rim of the bowl. The exterior of the bowl is covered with semicircular punctates arranged in rows with each row going in the opposite direction of the row above it. The lip has similar punctates. Thickness at the lip is .45 cm. The tempering agent is a medium grit.

Chipped Stone

Projectile Points (Plate III, A-I)

The projectile points from the Fort Wayne Mound are just 9 in number and only 1 was found in association with a burial (Burial 6). Seven of these points (A-G) fall into the Jack's Reef Corner-notched range. Each one of these 7 points is made on a different type of chert or flint. The form of the points is "ovoid or pentagonal in outline, and flat or nearly so in cross section. Edges excurvate or are angular. Stem corner-notched and basally flaring, barbs small to large, thin and sharp. Base straight and occasionally slightly smoothed" (Ritchie, 1961:26). The flint types are dark solid blue, dark blue with white mottling, banded gray and light gray, and four other shades of gray.

The 2 other points (H, I) are not in the Jack's Reef category. These are both side-notched but differ from each other. One (A-51, Plate III, I) is bevelled on alternate edges with a moderate amount of secondary retouch on the blade. The basal element has squared sides and a straight base. The notches are medium in size. This point is made on mottled gray flint.

The second point (A-46, Plate III, H) is made on a fine homogeneous gray flint. The notches are very shallow and were chipped from opposite sides. The edges exhibit rather steep coarse retouch. The base is straight.

It becomes apparent after seeing these artifacts plotted on a graphed layout of the mound that all but 2 of the projectile points

(A-4 with Burial 6 and A-37 from Section 145-D) come from the intensively dug area near the original center of the mound. It is quite likely that these accompanied burials, perhaps Gillman's Burials 3, 5, or 6. It is possible that A-37 belongs with Gillman's Burial 7 because the artifact was found so near the surface and the burial was only 20 inches deep.

TABLE 2

METRIC ATTRIBUTES OF FORT WAYNE MOUND PROJECTILE POINTS

Point	Length	Width	Min. Stem Diam.	B-MSD	Thick.	Base Width
Side-notched						
A-46	3.35	1.425	1.025	.60	.40	1.15
A-51	3.30	1.65	.95	.75	.55	1.7
Jack's Reef						
A-4	3.50	2.125	1.30	.75	.70	1.4
A-37	3.25	2.70	1.30	1.0	.45	1.7
A-38	3.50	...	...	...	.65	...
A-41	3.40	2.40	1.4	.95	.5	2.0
A-42	...	2.25	...	...	.5	...
A-45	3.35	2.65	1.65	.7	.4	2.3
A-54	3.1	2.7	1.55	.8	.5	1.95

It is possible that the 2 side-notched specimens are inclusions from an earlier period--like the Marion Thick pottery and the birdstone--because they are typologically similar to Late Archaic points.

Drills (Plate III, J, K)

There are 2 specimens in this category. One (A-39) is made from good gray flint with a few blue-white inclusions. It is T-shaped with a lozenge cross section. The base is wide and well finished, but one side was apparently finished as cortex and this has since rotted off. The total length is 4.0 cm. and the bit length is 2.7 cm.

The second drill (A-49) is rather crudely made from the blue flint of nonlocal derivation. This specimen is of the expanding base variety, in other words there is no sharp juncture between the base and the bit. There is no secondary working on the edges. The tip is broken off and the projected length of 5.2 cm. is somewhat in doubt.

A third drill was described with Burial 22.

Knives (Plate III, L-N)

Although any flint chip is a potential knife, there are 3 definite knives in addition to those described with Burials 10 and 22. One of a mottled gray and white chert is crescent-shaped, but not so well formed as that with Burial 10.

Another is represented by 2 badly broken fragments that may have been part of a triangular knife or blade. The flaking is flat and very well done.

A third knife is made on good blue flint with white streaks, and the edges are slightly retouched. It is entirely possible that this is a blank or preform for some other tool like an expanding base drill.

End Scrapers (Plate III, O-Q)

There are 3 end scrapers of diverse quality made from 3 different chert types. One is worked on all 3 sides and is made on a fine quality light gray chert.

The second is made on very poor mottled gray chert with various inclusions, some of which have dropped out giving the scraper the appearance of being notched. There is no retouch along the working edge.

The third scraper is broken and is made from very poor quality gray chert. Half of the remaining piece is cortex. There is no secondary retouch.

Side Scrapers (Plate III, R-S)

One specimen shows retouch on one side of one edge. The total configuration of the artifact is much like that of the knife found with Burial 22.

There is a block flake of very high quality dark blue flint provisionally included in this category because it has usage marks on the 90 degree-angled sides. It also has a very sharp point that was not used.

Ceramics

Marion Thick (Plate XII, A, B; Fig. 4, A)

The amount of Marion Thick pottery in the Fort Wayne Mound is rather surprising. Marion Thick ware is an Early Woodland type, and among the earliest pottery to be found in the northeastern United States. "It is quite thick, from 1 to 1.5 cm., and has large tempering particles of crushed rock, and sometimes of flint.

The vessel bases are either flat or rounded. The rim area is vertical and the side walls contract toward a rounded lip. . . . Most of this type has impressions on the exterior surface made by a paddle around which cords have been wrapped so that the clay has preserved the imprints of the individual cords. In addition, there are horizontal cord impressions on the interior surface" (Griffin, 1952:97).

Twenty-four Marion Thick sherds belonging to at least 2 vessels were found in the Fort Wayne Mound. One vessel is represented by a single body sherd only. This sherd differs from the standard type of Marion Thick pottery because it has no cord-marking at all on the interior. This variety however, is not rare at the Schultz Site in Saginaw County (F. W. Fischer, personal communication). This sherd is 1.3 cm. thick.

The other 23 sherds are from 1 vessel and they include 2 rim sherds. Interior cord-marking is horizontal and exterior cord-marking is oblique. The thickness at the rim is .8-1.1 cm. and body wall thickness is 1.1-1.3 cm.

Wayne Ware

At least 29 vessels of this type were found in the Fort Wayne Mound. (A complete type description may be found in Fitting, 1965:158.) Nine of these vessels are described with the burials and all but 2 of them are complete or entirely restored. The other 20 vessels (number based on rim sherds and there may be several more vessels represented by body sherds only) were found mostly in the fill of Gillman's trench. These divided among the variants Wayne Crosshatched, Wayne Corded Punctate, Wayne Punctate, and Wayne Cord-marked.

Wayne Crosshatched (Plate XII, C-F; Fig. 4, B-E)

"The rim has been decorated with criss-cross incisions on this variant. Lip decoration, which is relatively rare, takes the form of cord-wrapped stick or paddle edge impressions . . . and parallel to oblique or criss-cross tool impressions. Occasionally a single cord is impressed into the lip around the circumference of the vessel opening" (Fitting, 1965:158-59).

This variant has at least three recognizable subtypes:

1) Interior and exterior crosshatching, producing diamonds of the same size. Oblique cord-wrapped stick impressions on the lip. Only one example (Plate XII, C; Fig. 4, B).

2) Interior crosshatching only. The exterior is cord-marked

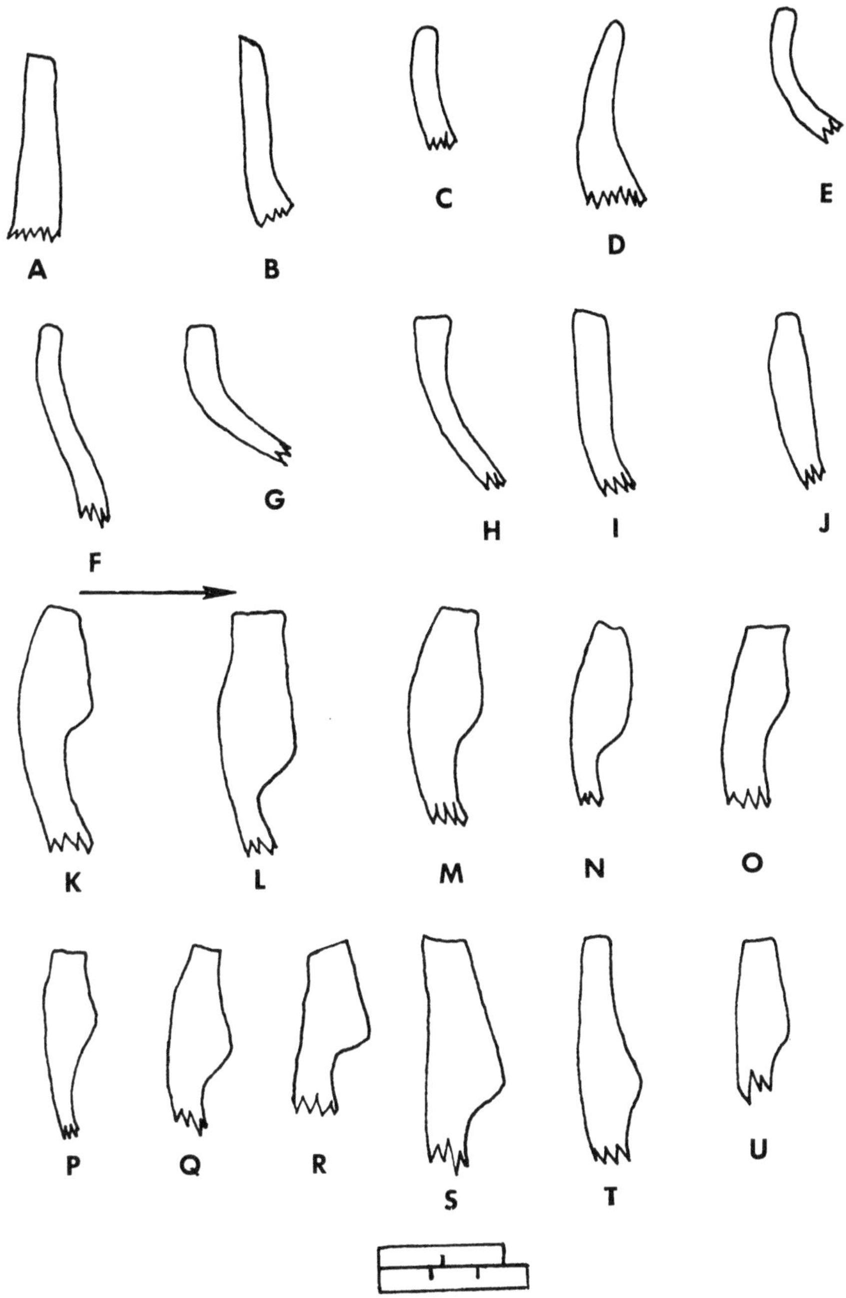

FIG. 4. Marion Thick, Wayne Ware, Springwells, and Vase Tool-impressed rim profiles.

up to the lip which has straight cord-wrapped stick impressions. Again, only one example (Plate XII, D; Fig. 4, C).

3) Exterior crosshatching only. These incisions extend varying degrees down the rim. Straight and oblique cord-wrapped stick impressions are found on the lip. There are 5 vessels of this subtype represented (Plate XII, E, F; Fig. 4, D, E).

Wayne Corded Punctate (Plate XII, G; Fig. 4, F)

There are 2 divergent examples of this type. One specimen has a single row of irregularly spaced punctates 2.1 cm. below a flared rim. These punctations were made with a cord-wrapped stick. There are oblique cord-wrapped stick impressions on the lip which trend to the left.

The other vessel is a little more elaborate, with 4 rows of cord-wrapped stick punctates closely spaced. Immediately beneath the bottom row of punctates is a single cord impression encircling the vessel at the shoulder.

Wayne Cord-impressed (Plate XI; XII, I; Fig. 4, G)

A subtype of this variant has 4 cord impressions on the shoulder instead of only 1 which is usually the case. Oblique cord impressions on the lip trend to the left.

A second subtype has 3 cord impressions on the neck and cord impressions on the lip.

Wayne Punctate (Plate XII, J)

Two of the Wayne Ware vessels were punctated. One of these was described with Burial 22 (Plate X).

The other vessel has a cord-impressed and cord-marked exterior with circular punctates on the interior rim. The decorating tool appears to have had an indentation in the end.

Wayne Cord-marked (Plate XII, K, L; Fig. 4, H, I)

Fifteen Wayne Cord-marked vessels were recovered. "This is the most common form with cord-marking up to the lip" (Fitting, 1965:158). However, 14 of the 15 vessels also have lip decoration in the form of cord-wrapped stick impressions.

Miscellaneous Wayne Ware Sherds

There were a total of 538 Wayne Ware sherds. Two body sherds were incised and these cannot be definitely associated with other vessels (Plate XII).

By examining the locations of the various sherds, it becomes quite evident that almost every one is to be found in Gillman's trench. There is almost no Wayne village occupation represented in the mound fill.

Riviere Ware

Springwells Net-impressed (Plate XIII; Fig. 4, K-R)

Sixteen vessels of this type were found, only in the pits. The rim form is what Fitting calls "Type A." It is straight to slightly outsloping (Fig. 4). The type name is derived from impressions on the rim and lip which appear to have been made with a net of loosely woven fabric. In 5 cases the interior rim is net-impressed. In another 4 the interior rim bears fingernail impressions rather than net impressions.

Both castellated and uncastellated forms are found. All forms are collared. Lip forms noted are flat in all cases but one, and are either horizontal, insloping, or outsloping.

Temper size is quite variable and particles of crushed granite up to .8 cm. in length are not rare. The paste is laminated and friable.

Surface treatment consists of smoothed cord-marking. Cord-marking is generally almost entirely obliterated near the neck while further down the sides it again becomes visible.

The thinnest portion of the body wall is in the neck area. The neck area is also slightly constricted, while the body appears to be elongated. The size of body sherds suggests that several of the vessels approach a height of from 45 to 60 cm. The basal form of this type is unknown but was probably rounded.

Vase Tool-impressed (Plate XIV, A-C; Fig. 4, S, T)

This type is represented by 4 vessels. The decorative technique consists of oblique tool impressions along the rim. One vessel has a herringbone design. Tool impressions are generally found on the lip of this type, and on the herringbone specimen they are also seen on the interior rim. The decorating tool is usually wide (.3 cm.) although the tool that produced the herringbone design was only 1 cm. wide.

All of the observed rims of this type in the Fort Wayne Mound are castellated and collared (Fitting's Type A). They are straight to slightly outsloping (Fig. 4).

Temper is composed of crushed granite; the size is variable and ranges up to .5 cm. The paste is gray and although friable is more likely to crumble.

Body surfaces were roughened or smoothed, and cord-marked. The over-all shape and basal form of this type are not known from this mound, but Fitting says that they are probably elongated with a rounded to semiconoidal base (1965:155).

Vase Dentate (Plate XIV, D; Fig. 4, U)

Only one vessel of this type is represented. A single rim sherd bears oblique dentate stamping along the top centimeter. Below this is an irregular row of circular punctates and then more oblique dentating down over the collar to an undetermined point on the body.

The lip is flattened with a single cord impression about the circumference of the mouth. The rim is collared, but rather weakly, and is straight (Fig. 4).

The crushed granite temper averages .3 cm. in diameter. The paste is laminated and friable. Body form is unknown and the surface treatment is assumed to be cord-marking or textile-impression.

Vase Corded (Plate XIV, E-J; Fig. 5, A-E)

Fourteen vessels fell into this type in which the dominant decorative motif is oblique to vertical cord impressions on the rim. The rim is always collared and usually castellated (Fig. 5). Lips are always decorated, usually with cord-wrapped sticks, but there are 2 cases of what appear to be massed fingernail impressions. On these same 2 vessels the oblique cord impressions are interrupted by horizontal cord impressions.

Lips are flattened and are either horizontal or outsloping with tool impressions, cord-marking and cord-wrapped stick impressions on the interior rim. The lips are thickened in some cases.

The grit tempering is large with pieces approaching .5 cm. The paste is laminated and friable.

Surface treatment is cord-marking and smoothed-over cord-marking. Bodies are elongated to greatly elongated.

Macomb Linear (Plate XIV, K-N; Fig. 5, F-H)

There are 5 vessels of this type from the Fort Wayne Mound. They are characterized by horizontal cord impressions on castellated and collared rims. Cord-wrapped stick impressions are often found on the lip which is flattened horizontally or outsloping (Fig. 5).

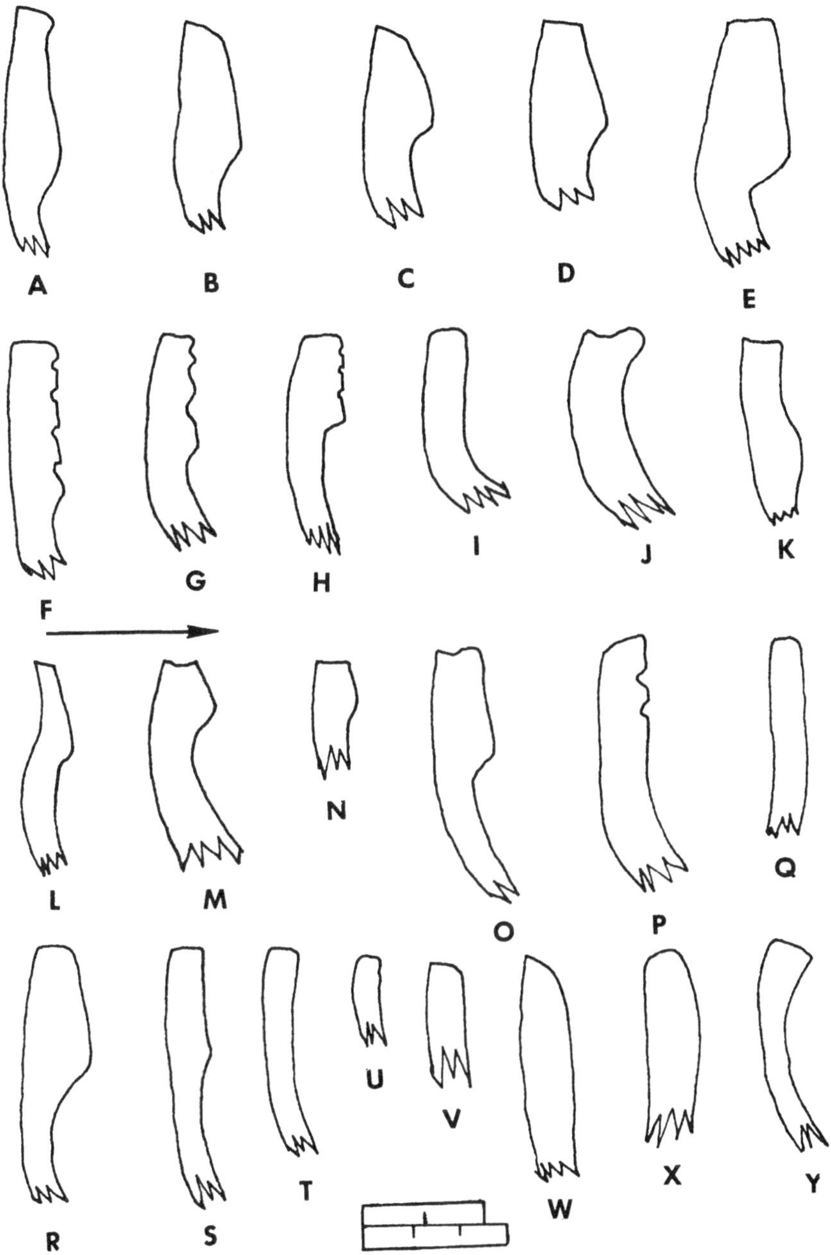

FIG. 5. Vase-corded, Macomb Linear, and miscellaneous rim profiles.

The paste again is laminated and friable and the temper is crushed granite, frequently including pieces .8 cm. in length.

Surface treatment appears to have been smoothed-over cord-marking at least in the vicinity of the slightly constricted neck. The bodies were probably elongate.

One specimen of the subtype Macomb Interrupted Linear was present.

Miscellaneous Ceramics

As in any site, there are numerous vessels from the Fort Wayne Mound that are not easily accomodated in any recognized type. Each will be described individually.

1) One is a small vessel with a globular body. The lip is rounded and slightly thickened. Beneath the lip are five incised horizontal lines interrupted at irregular intervals by groups of three or four vertically incised lines. Lip thickness is 1 cm. The rim is slightly flaring. The base is rounded (Plate XV, A; Fig. 5, I).

The surface treatment is difficult to determine but appears to be plain or smoothed cord-marking.

Temper is grit and in size ranges up to .5 cm. The paste is very crumbly and exfoliates freely.

2) Two rim sherds belong apparently to a cultural expression found further south in Ohio (Greenman, 1935*a*, Fig. 27, B; and Greenman, 1935*b*, Fig. 7, O). These vessels have scalloped rims caused by finger impressions. One rim flares a good deal and there is not enough of the other one to say. They are neither collared nor castellated. The granitic temper ranges up to .8 cm. The orange paste is laminated. The surface treatment is smoothed or smoothed cord-marking. Body and basal form are unknown (Plate XV, B-C; Fig. 5, J-K).

3) A third vessel is collared and castellated and in many ways resembles Springwells Net-impressed. The castellations are of two different sizes and the decorative motif consists of inverted *V*s (2) incised on each castellation. On the larger castellations, two short incisions are placed inside the *V*s on the edge of the collar. On the smaller castellations only one incision is seen. The collar itself is net-impressed and these impressions are also found on the flattened lip and the channeled inner rim. On the edge of the collar short cord-wrapped stick impressions were placed.

The body and rim are fairly thin (.7 cm.). The surface treatment is brushed cord-marking. The grit temper approaches

.5 cm. in size in a few isolated instances and the paste, though laminated, is cohesive. Body and basal forms are unknown (Plate XV, D; Fig. 4, L).

4) Another vessel also bears close resemblance to Springwells Net-impressed. It is castellated with a rather short collar. The lip is indented with what appears to be a knotted cord. The interior rim bears net impressions. The external collar however, has been smoothed and the body brushed with striations running vertically. The rim flares slightly and the neck is moderately constricted.

The grit-tempering is rather coarse, averaging .3 cm. with a few grains about .5 cm. The paste is laminated and friable.

Body form was probably elongate; basal form unknown (Plate XV, E; Fig. 5, M).

5) This vessel is similar to the preceding one except that it has knot impressions on the interior rim as well as on the lip. The collar is weak and there are no apparent castellations. It is rather thin.

The grit temper averages .3 cm. in diameter. The paste is laminated. Nothing else could be determined (Plate XV, F; Fig. 5, N).

6) We have seven sherds from another vessel that display a decidedly bizarre decorative mode. The castellated and collared rim has been impressed with a thin broken sherd. Experiments with modeling clay and a Wayne Ware sherd produced very similar examples. These sherd impressions are also found on the flattened horizontal lip with the long axis of most impressions following the circumference of the vessel.

The surface treatment of the body is smoothed over textile impressions. The grit-tempering is coarse, the paste laminated and friable. The rim flares slightly and the neck is moderately constricted. The body appears to have been elongated but this shape is largely conjectural (Plate XV, G; Fig. 5, O).

7) Another vessel represented is uncollared and uncastellated. The slightly thickened lip bears random tool impressions while on the rim immediately below the lip are two incised lines .3 cm. around the circumference of the vessel. Tool impressions are also found on the exterior of the rim. The rim flares slightly. The interior of the rim appears to be smoothed brushing. Temper is moderately sized with a few pieces .6 cm. long. Body form appears to be globular (Plate XV, A; Fig. 5, P).

8) Two rim sherds remain from a rather anonymous little vessel that is crudely smoothed all over. Although the exterior is yellow, the core color of the paste is black. There is a small

amount of grit temper in the .2 cm. size class. The lip is flattened, the body walls straight-sided and elongate.

9) This vessel is rather large and very crudely made. The rim is collared and has many castellations of different sizes on it. On the rim and flattened lip are parenthetical punctates.

Below the collar the cord-marking on the body is largely smoothed over, although not to such a great degree on the collar.

The grit temper size is enormous, the average being .4 cm. with pieces up to .8 and .9 cm. In addition to being so large, the temper is also very abundant. The orange paste is laminated and friable.

The rim flares slightly and the neck is constricted. Body form is presumed to be elongated rather than globular (Plate XV, J; Fig. 5, R).

10) The vessel represented by this section of rim sherds is very weakly collared with oblique rows of punctates on the collar. Similar punctates are found on the lip. The rim flares very slightly. The body is cord-marked.

Temper is crushed granite and the paste while laminated is not particularly friable. The assumed body shape is globular (Plate XV, K; Fig. 5, S).

11) Two fairly thin uncollared noncastellated vessels are represented by rim sherds which are punctated on the interior rim, the lip, and the exterior rim. Surface treatment consists of smoothed-over cord-marking. Temper is medium grit, and the paste is laminated (Plate XV, L, M; Fig. 5, T, V).

Another vessel represented by a punctated rim sherd has the "stab and drag" style of punctation and incising on the exterior, with knot impressions on the lip, and rather amorphous punctations on the interior rim. The paste is remarkable because it is nonlaminated. Temper size ranges between .1 and .4 cm. (Plate XV, N; Fig. 5, V).

12) Another vessel is represented by a single castellated sherd that is not collared. The rim and lip are heavily and crudely incised or tool-impressed. The majority of the incisions trend obliquely to the right; however there are two long curving parallel incisions that are similar to those of Vessel No. 3 in this group of miscellaneous sherds.

Temper is grit and in size is in the .3 to .4 cm. range. The paste is laminated and friable (Plate XV, O; Fig. 5, W).

13) A plain vessel is represented by a section of rim. The lip has oblique punctations but the surface of the body is only roughened. The lip is slightly thickened. Temper size does not exceed .3 cm. (Plate XV, P; Fig. 5, X).

14) Another castellated vessel is represented by a single rim sherd. The rounded lip is undecorated. The exterior surface is roughened and the interior is plain. It does not appear to be collared. Temper size does not exceed .4 cm. The paste is laminated and friable.

15) One very interesting vessel is represented by 3 rim sherds. It is uncollared and uncastellated with a slightly thickened lip. The exterior and interior rim and lip are net-impressed. As has been noted previously, Springwells Net-impressed vessels are usually collared. The temper size is .2-.3 cm. and the paste is laminated. These sherds were found in Pit 3. The rim flares more than that of any other vessel in the pits (Plate XV, Q-R; Fig. 5, Y).

There were 9 other rim sherds too small or fragmentary to provide much useful information. They represent 4 cord-marked vessels, 4 punctate or tool-impressed vessels, and 1 plain vessel.

Body Sherds

There were 1938 body sherds in the mound fill and in the pits. Two types were readily discernible, the Wayne Ware and the Marion Thick; the former because of its distinctive thinness and the latter because of its interior and exterior cord-marking. It should also be noted that neither of these types were found in the pits. The pits were filled entirely with Riviere Ware and miscellaneous aberrant vessels.

Surface treatment of the various types was noted previously with the type descriptions. Unfortunately each type contains a variety of body treatments--textile impressions, cord-marking, etc.--and one vessel, for example, may show plain, smoothed cord-marking and unaltered cord-marking on different areas of the body. The Riviere body sherd must then be treated as a whole, divisible into only a minimal number of categories and nearly impossible to isolate as to individual vessels.

The legitimate question arises as to how and why I have set up the Wayne Ware body sherds in a different category from the rest of the cord-marked sherds. The answer has several parts.

1) Fitting's type definition and illustrations of Wayne Ware are rather (too?) broad, but the Wayne Ware vessels observed from the Fort Wayne Mound conform to this type and are, I think, the standard by which Wayne Ware should be judged.

2) The thinness of vessel walls and the quality of cord-marking observed in Wayne Ware are not found among the Riviere sherds.

3) The distribution and function (such as burial goods) of Wayne

Ware in the Fort Wayne Mound do not in any case coincide with that of Riviere Ware.

Both ware types had utilitarian function as witnessed by the carbonaceous cooking crust observed on vessels of each type.

David Brose, in "The Valley Sweets Site," proposes a second type of Wayne Ware which he calls Wayne Textile-marked. Aside from the fact that several of the vessels that Brose calls Wayne Textile-marked are castellated, when the type definition says they should not be, I am willing to accept this type with the proviso that it be placed at the end of the Wayne sequence. In the Fort Wayne Mound there was no Wayne Textile-impressed, but in other sites such as Gibraltar, south of Detroit, and the Bussinger site in Saginaw, there are vessels that could be considered Wayne Textile-marked.

Textile-marking appears as a late trait in southeastern Michigan and textile-marked body sherds account for 611 or 31.5 per cent of the body sherds in the Fort Wayne Mound. But it should be noted that the textile-marking is associated with the Riviere Ware vessels which are generally later in time than the Wayne Ware. I think Brose erred in attempting to make Wayne Textile-impressed contemporary with Wayne Cord-marked. The textile-impressed vessels should be later.

FAUNAL REMAINS

The only faunal remains from the Fort Wayne Mound aside from the burial of the dog were found in the pits. Table 5 lists these faunal remains.

A few things must be explained about this faunal listing. First of all, unless we propose cannibalism, it is clear that the presence of human bone in these pits is due to disturbance of burials when the pits were dug. Second, all of the turtle material is worked carapace. There are no plastron or other skeletal fragments. These carapace were most likely dishes and their appearance with the broken pots in these pits would be expected.

Holmquist stated that he believed Pit 1 was a type of altar or central feeding place for the dead. In its contents, however, it does not differ significantly from any of the other pits. In fact Pits 1, 4, 5 and 6 are virtually contemporaneous, containing sherds from the same vessels. Pits 2 and 3 are also ceramically related. Evidently Holmquist's only criterion was its position on top of the mound and the presence of animal bone. He interpreted the pits uncovered beneath the mound as evidence of pre-mound village occupation, but the interconnection demonstrated above between the pits shows them to be intrusive and of a considerably later time period.

HISTORIC ARTIFACTS

Metal

Expanded Cartridges

Three cartridge casings were recovered in the fill of the mound. One is a .30-.40 used in a Krag Jorgenson rifle, a type that was in service from 1894 to 1903 and after that was used as a training rifle in World War I (Logan, 1959:116). The second is a .45-.60 used in a model 1876 Winchester (Logan, 1959:141).

There is no cut-off date given for this type. The third is a .45-.70 Rabbeth's Patent cartridge manufactured by Winchester after 1896.

It would thus appear that these cartridges were incorporated in the mound only after Gillman's excavation. Gillman's back dirt pile was still open and visible in 1882 and 1919, and it would have been easy for someone to throw a few empty cartridges into this pile of dirt.

Miscellaneous

Other metal artifacts include a military button, a brass hook with two rivets and some leather attached, and a silver earring or nose bangle from Section 187-C in Gillman's trench. This item raises the possibility of a historic or contact burial in the top of the mound that was disturbed by Gillman, who did not recognize it as such.

Ceramics

There is one piece of brown raised glaze on a white underglaze. The form was probably a bowl.

Kaolin Pipes

One kaolin pipe stem with the word HENDERSON stamped on it was recovered. Henderson pipes were manufactured in Montreal and were a popular type throughout this area in the second half of the nineteenth century (Fitting, 1965:68; Halsey n.d.).

TABLE 3

TOTAL VESSELS

Type	Total	Percentage of Total
Wayne Cord-marked	15	15.2
Wayne Crosshatched	7	7.1
Wayne Corded Punctate	2	2.0
Wayne Punctate	2	2.0
Wayne Cord-impressed	2	2.0
Wayne Smoothed	1	1.0
Other Wayne	2	2.0
Marion Thick	2	2.0
Vase Corded	14	14.0
Vase Dentate	1	1.0
Vase Tool-impressed	4	4.0
Macomb Linear	5	5.1
Springwells Net-impressed	16	16.2
Miscellaneous	26	26.3
	99	100.0

TABLE 4

RIM AND BODY SHERD COUNTS AND PERCENTAGES

Rim Sherds			
Type	Number	Per Cent RS	Per Cent TS
Wayne Ware	53	23.9	2.5
Marion Thick	2	.9	.1
Vase Corded	26	11.7	1.2
Vase Dentate	1	.5	.05
Vase Tool-impressed	7	3.1	.3
Macomb Linear	24	10.8	1.1
Springwells Net-impressed	43	19.4	2.0
Miscellaneous	66	29.7	3.05
	222	100.0	10.3
Body Sherds			
Type	Number	Per Cent RS	Per Cent TS
Wayne Ware	485	25.0	22.5
Marion Thick	22	1.1	1.0
Cord-marked	149	7.7	6.9
Smooth Cord-marking	325	16.8	15.0
Textile-impressed	225	11.6	10.4
Smoothed Textile	386	19.9	17.9
Roughened	282	14.6	13.1
Plain or smoothed	53	2.7	2.4
Incised	11	.6	.5
	1716	100.0	89.7
Total	1938		

TABLE 4 (Cont'd.)

Riviere Ware	Number of Vessels	Per Cent RWRS	Per Cent RWV
Vase Corded	14	25.7	35.0
Vase Dentate.	1	1.0	2.5
Vase Tool-impressed	4	6.9	10.0
Macomb Linear	5	23.8	12.5
Springwells Net-impressed .	16	42.6	40.0
	40	100.0	100.0
Wayne Ware		Per Cent WWRS	Per Cent WWV
Wayne Cord-marked.	15	43.4	48.4
Wayne Crosshatched.	7	26.4	22.6
Wayne Corded Punctate. . . .	22	20.7	6.4
Wayne Punctate	2	3.8	6.4
Wayne Cord-impressed. . . .	2	1.9	6.4
Wayne Smoothed	2	3.8	3.2
Other Wayne	2	-1	6.4
	31	100.0	100.0

TABLE 5

FAUNAL REMAINS FROM FORT WAYNE MOUND PITS

Pit Number	Species	Individuals	Pieces
1.	Raccoon (*Procyon lotor*)	1	3
	Deer (*Odocoileus virginianus*)	1	62
	Sauger (*Stizostedion canadense*)	1	1
	Turtle ?	1	1
2.	Raccoon (*P. lotor*)	1	11
	Muskrat (*Ondatra zibethicus*)	1	1
	Deer (*O. virginianus*)	3	305
	Turtle (*Emys blandingii*)	3	25
	Sauger (*S. canadense*)	1	1
	Largemouth Bass (*Micropterus salmoides*)	1	1
	Human (*Homo sapiens*)	1	4
3.	Raccoon (*P. lotor*)	1	7
	Deer (*O. virginianus*)	1	16
4.	Deer (*O. virginianus*)	2	65
	Human (*H. sapiens*)	1	1
5.	Deer (*O. virginianus*)	1	24
	Human (*H. sapiens*)	1	2
6.	Muskrat (*O. zibethicus*)	1	4
	Deer (*O. virginianus*)	2	50
	Largemouth Bass (*M. salmoides*)	1	1
	Turtle (*E. blandingii*)	1	2

TABLE 5 (Cont'd.)

Pit Number	Species	Individuals	Pieces
8.	Deer (*O. virginianus*)	1	4
	Spike or Lady Finger (*Elliptio delatatus*)	4	7
	Human (*H. sapiens*)	1	60
No provenience	Raccoon (*P. lotor*)	2	9
	Deer (*O. virginianus*)	?	142
	Fish ?	?	69
	Turtle ?	2	4
	Spike (*E. delatatus*)	6	13
	Human (*H. sapiens*)	2	11

Totals

Species	Percentage of Remains	Percentage of Individuals	Individuals	Pieces
Deer	.8077	.2500	11	668
Raccoon	.0362	.1136	5	30
Muskrat	.0060	.0454	2	5
Turtle	.0362	.1363	6	30
Fish	.0870	.2272	10	72
Clam	.0241	.2272	10	20
			44	827
Human	.0861	.1200	6	78
			50	905

IV

THE CENTRAL MOUND

The intriguing accounts of John Blois and the fact that no one ostensibly had dug into the Central Mound at Fort Wayne since Blois, made re-excavation of this mound seem worth while. Despite the fact that a map dating from 1848 noted that "this mound has been removed," there was a slight chance that the mound, instead of being leveled, had been incorporated into the north glacis of the military fort.

In early May of 1965, David Brose and I visited the site with a Gossen Geohn and carried out a preliminary soil resistivity survey (see Ford 1964 for details of this process). Results were inconclusive; the mound itself could not be located.

A University of Michigan Museum of Anthropology field crew assisted by Mr. George Miller of Wayne State University commenced clearing a 5- by 40-foot unit. A shallow humus of recent age was encountered for the first .2 of a foot. Below this in the eastern 30 feet there was a wedge of loosely packed sand and gravel. Below the sandy gravel there was a brown humus zone of varying thickness resting on a coarse orange clayey gravel that tended to be more sandy toward the western end of the trench. The sandy fill and the brown humus contained the historic material described below. A provenience level was closed at a depth of 1.3 feet.

The first aboriginal artifact, a greenstone celt, was recovered at a depth of 1.9 feet in the eastern half of the 5 by 40. In the western half of the trench there was a sandy gravel zone beneath the heavy orange clay and gravel. Under this was a relatively pure gray-brown sand showing a bedding in some places. A slump in the north wall brought forth a human calcaneus.

A north-south trench 500E515 was now opened. At a depth of .5 feet a second greenstone celt was uncovered. It was deeply stained with an ochreous substance. Excavation in the west wall revealed an iron pipe that proved to be part of the old fort water supply system installed in 1886.

To trace the path of this water pipe (because it passed directly through the area where we now believed the mound was) a

15- by 15-foot excavation unit 505E520 was opened. The pipe angled down through the glacis and no artifactual material was recovered except for one small sherd.

Another 5- by 10-foot excavation was opened westward from 500E515 but nothing was found and excavations on the site were closed.

It now appears certain that the mound was leveled in the construction of the glacis in 1845. This accounts for the scattered nature of the artifacts and bone. When the pipe was laid in 1886, anything that might have been left of the mound was destroyed.

The artifacts recovered in the 1965 excavations are described below. The historic material is all from the second half of the nineteenth century.

Summary

The 1965 excavations confirmed the statement that the mound had been leveled. Profiles showed no evidence of any remaining mound structure. The presence of artifactual material and bone in the fill of the glacis would seem to indicate that the razed mound was used in the construction of the glacis.

ARTIFACTS FROM THE CENTRAL MOUND AT FORT WAYNE

Historic Material

Bottle Necks

A. Number of specimens: 1
   Color: Blue-green
   Wire rim: Absent
   Inside diameter of mouth: 2.1 cm.
   Neck diameter below the thickened area: 2.45 cm.
   Neck height below the thickened area: 2.8 cm.
   Diameter of the thickened area: 3.3 cm.
   General configuration of the thickened area: It is hand finished with horizontal striations and swirls. It is slightly uneven along the base.
   General configuration of the neck: Vertical striations. The neck and thickened area are quite similar to my description of a Group III whole bottle from the Bussinger site (n.d.). (Plate XVI, A)

B. Number of specimens: 1
   Color: Nearly opaque yellow
   Wire rim: Absent
   Inside diameter of mouth: 2.1 cm.
   Neck diameter below appliqué strip: 2.9 cm.
   General configuration: The appliqué strip was applied while still molten

and the top was sheared off. The neck appears to be hand finished (Plate XVI, B).

C. Number of specimens: 1
Color: Brown-orange
Wire rim: ?
Inside diameter of mouth: ?
Neck diameter below the thickened area: ?
Neck height below the thickened area: ?
Diameter of the thickened area: ?
General configuration of the thickened area: Truncated cone variety very slightly concave. Striations are horizontal and hand finished (Plate XVI, C).

Miscellaneous Bottle Bottoms

A. Number of specimens: 1
Color: Blue-green
Description: Shallow depressed bottom with no markings visible on this sherd. Foot ring not as sharply defined as some (Plate XVI, D).

B. Number of specimens: 1
Color: Clear
Description: No basal mark. Circular central depression sharply demarcated by the square interior wall of the foot ring. Foot ring is 1.1 cm. wide and the outer edge is beveled (Plate XVI, E).

C. Number of specimens: 1
Color: Light green
Description: This is apparently a panel bottle bottom but is quite different from the others noted. Each corner has a facet so that the bottom actually has eight sides. There is a depressed ring above the base and above this an inward sloping surface .6 cm. wide surmounted by a raised ridge. The side then curves back out and takes a straight face with ridge corners. The bottom itself is only slightly depressed (Plate XVI, F).

Miscellaneous Marked Glass

A. Number of specimens: 1
Color: Blue-green (painted)
Description: Flow swirl marks very prominent.

. . .ONK'S
JA WATE
DETROIT
MICH

B. Number of specimens: 1 (Plate XVI, I)
Color: Blue-green
Description: . .CI. . . .

Miscellaneous Glass

Bottles: 2 blue-green, 1 clear
Fluted: 1 clear

Yellow: 1
Window: 2
Very thick: 2 (.75 cm.)
Thick: 1 (.6 cm.)

Marbles

There were two marbles. One was opaque green, white, and red. The other was translucent green and gray-green (Plate XVI, J).

Kaolin Pipes

Stem portions of three kaolin pipes were recovered. None was marked and there were no bowl fragments. Two are oval in cross section. The round one appears to have been lacquered (Plate XVI, K).

Ceramics

Print

Blue Edge - Two vessels represented by two sherds (Plate XVI, L).
Blue Transfer - Three sherds represent one plate (Plate XVI, M).

Plain

Common yellow - Four sherds representing one vessel of unknown shape (Plate XV, N).
Plain white - Forty-six sherds representing at least three vessels.

Metal

A flattened circular iron ring.
A trapezoidal sheet of iron with the edges folded back.
A bolt 9.3 cm. long with a hexagonal slotted head.
Five wire nails.
A large piece of plate iron, cut.

Miscellaneous

A broken carbon rod from a dry cell.

Bone

Human

That the mound had been where we were digging is evidenced by the recovery of three human bones—the shaft of a right humerus, a left talus or ankle bone, and an end of a metatarsal.

Animal

There were six fragments of cow bone and one of deer. Three other pieces of animal bone were unidentifiable.

Aboriginal Material (Artifacts of Native Significance)

Ceramics

Two very small sherds were recovered from the Central Mound area. These fitted together making one sherd. This sherd is large enough to show that it is Wayne Ware, but unfortunately it is not a rim sherd.

Ground Stone

Two adzes were recovered from the Central Mound area. The first is 11.1 cm. long, 5.1 cm. wide at the bit, and 2.5 cm. wide at the poll or butt. The material is greenstone or diorite. Under magnification the convex face of the adze shows striations which trend slightly to the left. Both sides of the bit are polished. The concave face shows no real definite striae and it would appear that the bit was sharpened from this side by abrasion perpendicular to the blade. The dorsal side of the celt is almost unfinished on the upper third. The ventral surface is worked down to within 2 cm. of the butt.

The second greenstone adze is 8.1 cm. long, 4.5 cm. wide at the bit, and 2.8 cm. wide at the butt. The bit is heavily worn with striations again trending to the left, but the majority of these are obscured by a heavy layer of iron oxide. The grinding on the convex face is lateral while that on the concave face appears to be perpendicular to the bit.

CONCLUSIONS

The Springwells mound group, and in particular the Fort Wayne Mound, may now be viewed in a much broader context of time and space than was possible 20 or 120 years ago. The burials and grave goods represented in the mounds, excluding the Great Mound, are no longer unique when compared with material from the nearby Riviere au Vase and Gibraltar Sites and with material from the Bussinger site near Saginaw. There also appear to be strong similarities with the Intrusive Mound Culture of Ohio and the Kipp Island Phase in New York.

The ceramic relationships between the Fort Wayne Mound, Gibraltar, Bussinger and Riviere au Vase sites are very strong and other artifactual material such as *Anculosa* beads, columella shell beads, bone ornaments and slate scrapers as burial goods extended the relationships to the south and northeast. The Fort Wayne Mound is actually rather poor in burial goods when seen amidst the relative wealth and diversity that this apparently widespread burial complex exhibits elsewhere.

At the present time there are two dates available on the Fort Wayne Mound material. A sample of bone from Burial 14 was dated at 750 A.D. ± 120 A.D. (M-1843). This would be in agreement with Ritchie's published date of 630 A.D. for the Kipp Island Phase (1965:228).

The date on Pit 5 in Section 40-A of 1159 ± 75 A.D. (M-741) dates the Springwells Phase of the Younge Tradition at Fort Wayne. (The Younge Tradition is described by Fitting as being the dominant sequence in southeastern Michigan in the Late Woodland period [Fitting, 1965:151]. In a more recent article Fitting gives radiocarbon dates and suggested time intervals for the phases of the Younge tradition [1966:738]).

Phase	Radiocarbon Date	Suggested Time Interval
Wolf	A.D. 1320 ±100 (M-1520)	After A.D. 1250
Springwells	A.D. 1159 ±75 (M-741)	A.D. 1100 to A.D. 1250
Younge	A.D. 1085 ±100 (M-1431)	A.D. 900 to A.D. 1100
Riviere aux Vase	A.D. 700 ±120 (M-1519)	A.D. 600 to A.D. 900

The Wayne Ware thus appears to be early in the Late Woodland sequence and is possibly the remnant of a terminal Middle Woodland tradition of mortuary elaboration.

REFERENCES

Blois, John T.
1838 Gazetteer of Michigan. Detroit: Sydney L. Rod & Co.; and New York: Robinson, Pratt and Co.

Brose, David S.
1966 The Valley Sweets Site. The Michigan Archaeologist, Vol. 12, No. 1, pp. 1-21. Ann Arbor.

Brown, Samuel R.
1817 The Western Gazateer; or Emigrant's Directory,. . . . Auburn, N. Y.: H. C. Southwick.

Crane, H. R. and Griffin, J. B.
1960 University of Michigan Radiocarbon Dates. American Journal of Science Radiocarbon Supplement Vol. 2, 1960, pp. 31-48.
1968 University of Michigan Radiocarbon Dates XII. Radiocarbon, Vol. 10. New Haven, Conn.

Farmer, Silas
1884 The History of Detroit and Michigan. Detroit: Silas Farmer & Co.

Fitting, James E.
1965 Late Woodland Cultures of Southeastern Michigan. Museum of Anthropology, University of Michigan, Anthropological Papers, No. 24. Ann Arbor.
1966*a* Radiocarbon Dating the Younge Tradition. American Antiquity, Vol. 31, No. 5, Pt. 1, p. 738. Salt Lake City.
1966*b* The Archaeology Explosion in Michigan. Michigan History, Vol. 50, No. 3, pp. 219-27. Lansing.

Ford, Richard I.
1964 A Preliminary Report of the 1964 Resistivity Survey at the Schultz Site (20SA2). The Michigan Archaeologist, Vol. 10, No. 3, pp. 54-58. Ann Arbor.

Gillman, Henry
1874 The Mound Builders and Platycnemism in Michigan. Smithsonian Institution, Annual Report for 1873, pp. 364-90. Washington, D.C.
1876*a* Certain Characteristics Pertaining to Ancient Man in Michigan. Smithsonian Institution Annual Report for 1875, pp. 234-45. Washington, D.C.
1876*b* The Ancient Men of the Great Lakes. Proceedings of the American Association for the Advancement of Science, 24th Meeting, held at Detroit, August, 1875, pp. 316-31. Salem, Mass.
1877 Investigation of the Burial Mound at Fort Wayne, on the Detroit River, Michigan. Proceedings of the American Association for the Advancement of Science, 25th Meeting, held at Buffalo, August, 1876, pp. 311-25. Salem, Mass.
1880 The Mound-builders in Michigan. Report of the Pioneer Society of the State of Michigan, Vol. 2 (1877-78), pp. 40-52. Detroit: Wm. Graham's Presses.

Greenman, Emerson F.
1935*a* Excavations of the Reeve Village Site, Lake County, Ohio. The Ohio State Archaeological and Historical Quarterly, Vol. 44, No. 4, pp. 3-64. Columbus.
1935*b* Seven Prehistoric Sites in Northern Ohio. The Ohio State Archaeological and Historical Quarterly, Vol. 44, No. 2, pp. 220-37. Columbus.
1937*a* Two Prehistoric Villages near Cleveland, Ohio. *Ibid*., Vol. 46, No. 4, pp. 305-66. Columbus.
1937*b* The Younge Site. Occasional Contributions from the Museum of Anthropology of the University of Michigan, No. 6. Ann Arbor.
1939 The Wolf and Furton Sites, Macomb County, Michigan. *Ibid*., No. 8. Ann Arbor.
1945 The Hopewellian in the Detroit-Windsor Area. Papers of the Michigan Academy of Science, Arts, and Letters, Vol. XXX (1944), pp. 457-64. Ann Arbor
1958 Prehistoric Detroit. The Michigan Archaeologist, Vol. 4, No. 4, pp. 81-98. Ann Arbor.

Griffin, James B.
1952 Some Early and Middle Woodland Pottery Types in Illinois. *In* Hopewellian Communities in Illinois, Thorne Deuel, editor. Illinois State Museum. Scientific Papers, Vol. V, No. 3, pp. 93-129. Springfield.

Halsey, John R.
n.d. Two Historic Occupations in the Saginaw Valley. Unpublished manuscript on file at the Museum of Anthropology, University of Michigan.

Harper, Victoria G.
1945 A Ceramic Study of the Riviere au Vase Site in southeastern Michigan. Papers of the Michigan Academy of Science, Arts, and Letters, Vol. XXX (1944), pp. 479-91. Ann Arbor.

Hinsdale, Wilbert B.
1925 Primitive Man in Michigan. University of Michigan, University Museum, Michigan Handbook Series, No. 1. Ann Arbor.

Hinsdale, W. B. and E. F. Greenman
1936 Perforated Indian Crania in Michigan. Occasional Contributions from the Museum of Anthropology of the University of Michigan, No. 5. Ann Arbor.

Holmquist, Carl E.
1946 The Fort Wayne Mound. Aboriginal Research Club Bulletin. Detroit.

Howard, Ruth
1950 Preliminary Report on the Fort Wayne Mound, Detroit, Michigan. Papers of the Michigan Academy of Science, Arts, and Letters, Vol. XXXIV (1948), pp. 261-66.

Hubbard, Bela
1880 Relics in Michigan. The American Antiquarian, Vol. 2, No. 3. Chicago: Jameson and More, 1879-80, pp. 233-35.

Hubbard, Bela
1887 Memorials of a Half-Century. New York and London: G. P. Putnam's Sons.

Logan, H. C.
1959 Cartridges: A Pictorial Digest of Small Arms Ammunition. New York: Bonanza Books.

McKenney, Thomas L.
1827 Sketches of a Tour to the Lakes. Baltimore: Fielding Lucas, Jun'r. Of the Character and Customs of the Chippeway Indians, and of Incidents connected with the Treaty of Fond de Lac.

Peabody Museum of American Archaeology and Ethnology
1873 Sixth Annual Report. Cambridge.

Pilling, Arnold R.
1961*a* Six Archaeological Sites in the Detroit Area I. The Michigan Archaeologist, Vol. 7, No. 3, pp. 13-30.
1961*b* Six Archaeological Sites in the Detroit Area II. *Ibid.*, No. 4, pp. 33-54.

Priest, Josiah
1833 American Antiquities and Discoveries in the West. . . . Albany: Packard, Hoffman and White.

Riley, Henry H.
1881 The Mound-builders and their Work in Michigan. Report of the Pioneer Society of the State of Michigan, Vol. 3 (1879-1880) pp. 41-48. Lansing: W. S. George & Co.

Ritchie, William A.
1961 A Typology and Nomenclature for New York Projectile Points. New York State Museum and Science Service, Bulletin Number 384. Albany.
1965 The Archaeology of New York State. Garden City, New York: The Natural History Press.

Townsend, Earl C. Jr.
1959 Birdstones of the North American Indian. Indianapolis: Privately published.

Witherell, Benjamin F. H.
1884 Mounds of the Dead on Springwells Sand Hill. Address of President J. C. Holmes at Annual Meeting, January 7th, 1882. Report of the Pioneer Society of the State of Michigan. Vol. V (1882), pp. 4-6. Lansing: W. S. George & Co.

PLATE I

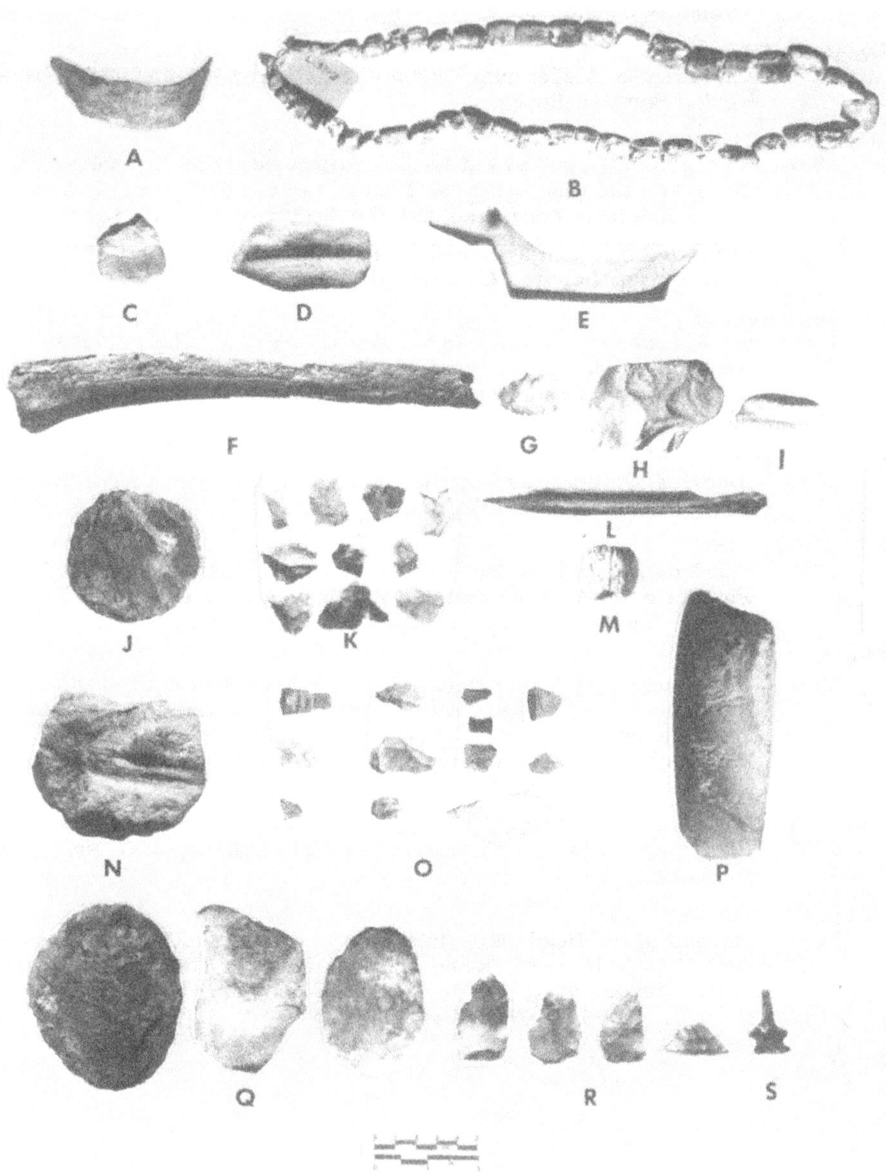

Burial artifacts.

PLATE II

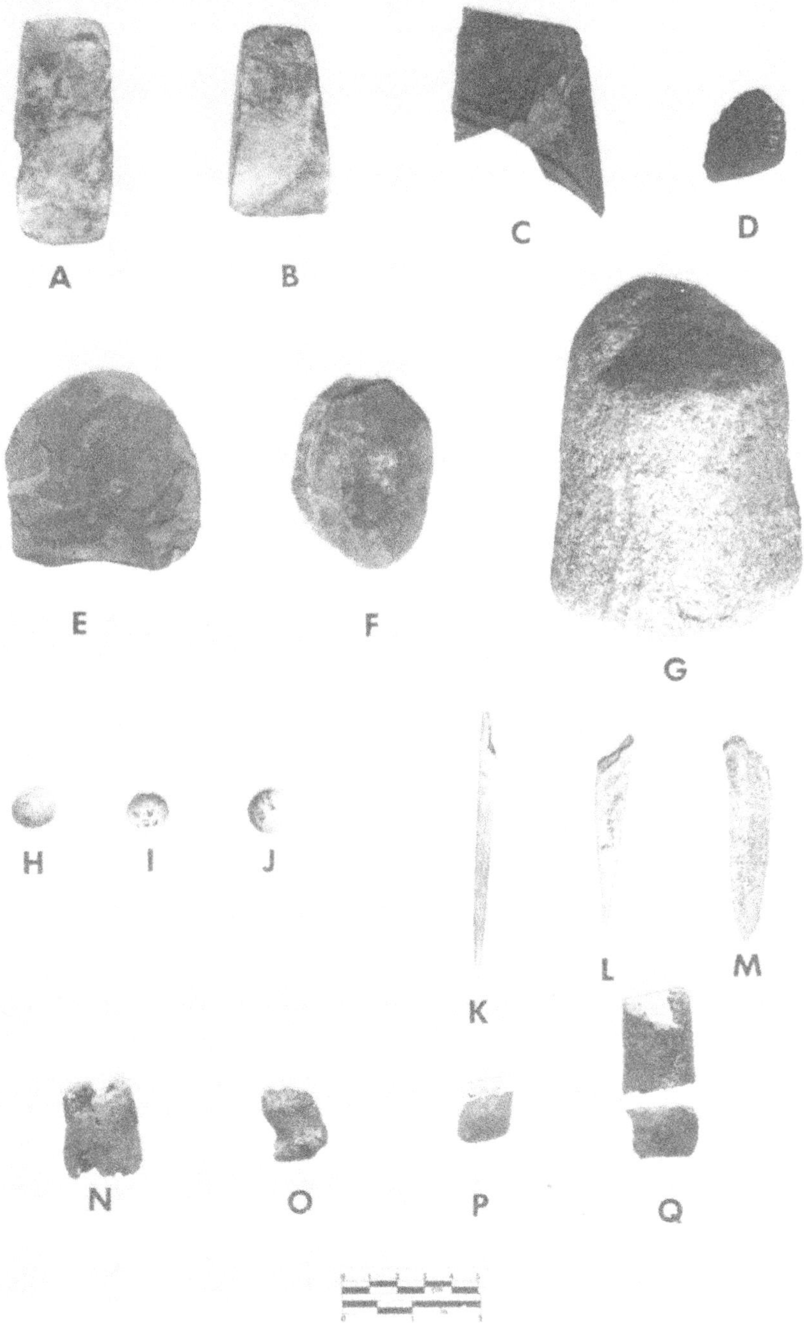

Worked slate, bone, and pipes.

PLATE III

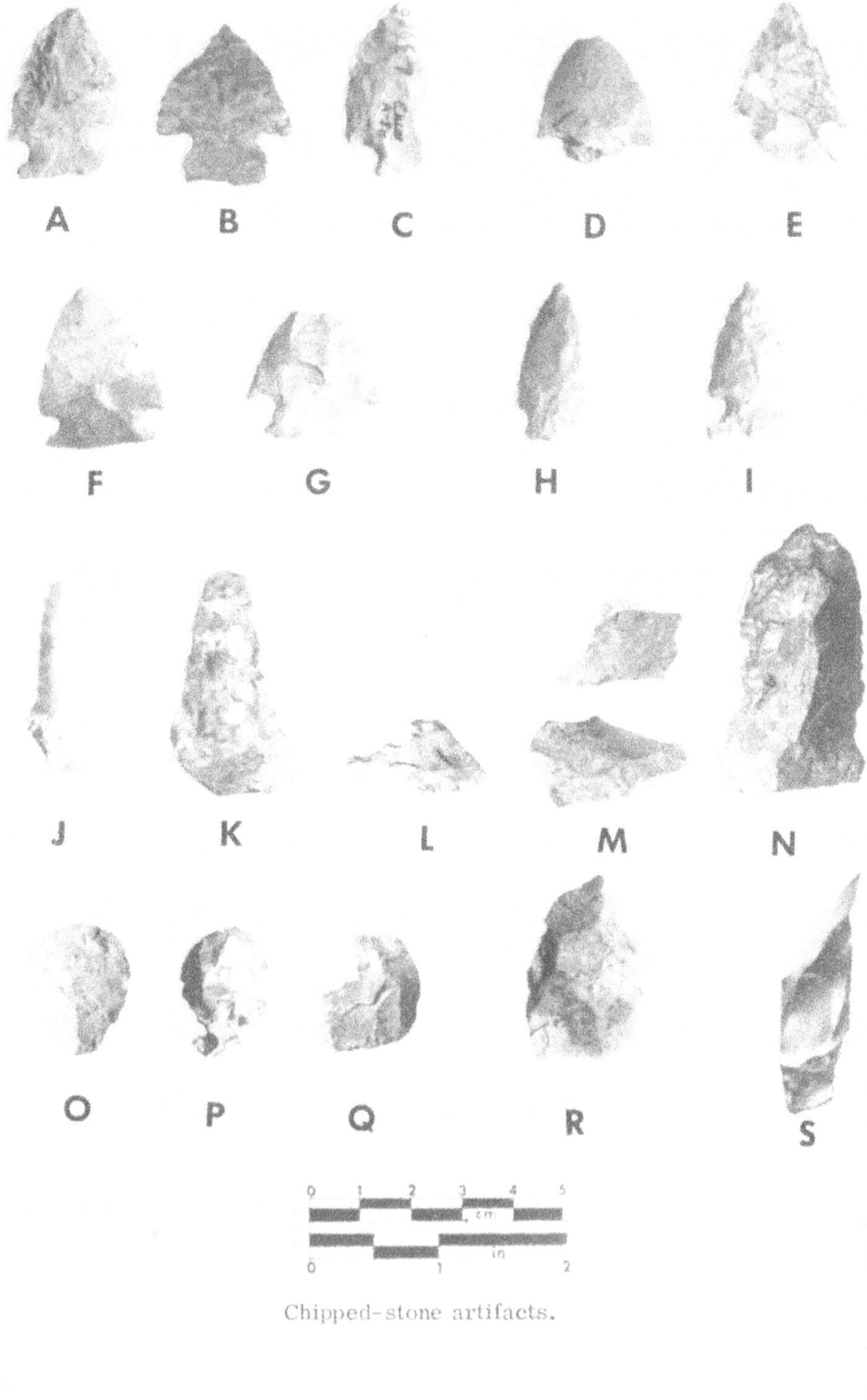

Chipped-stone artifacts.

PLATE IV

Wayne Crosshatched vessel—Burial 3.

PLATE V

Wayne Cord-marked vessel—Burials 4 and 5.

PLATE VI

Wayne Cord-marked vessel—Burial 8.

PLATE VII

Wayne Cord-marked vessel—Burial 10.

PLATE VIII

Wayne Crosshatched vessel—Burial 14.

PLATE IX

Wayne Cord-marked vessel—Burial 17.

PLATE X

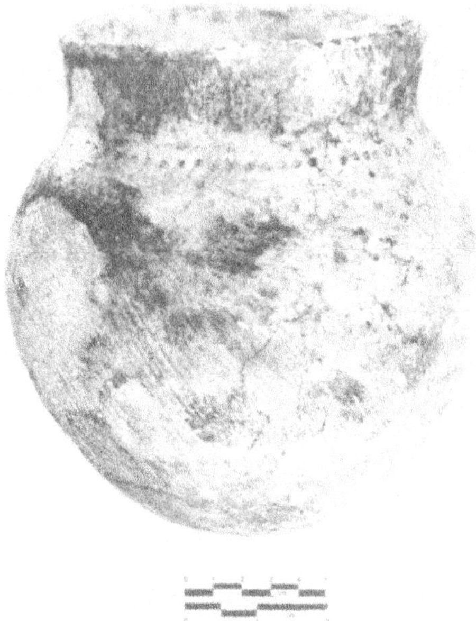

Wayne Punctate vessel—Burial 22.

PLATE XI

Wayne Cord-impressed vessel.

PLATE XII

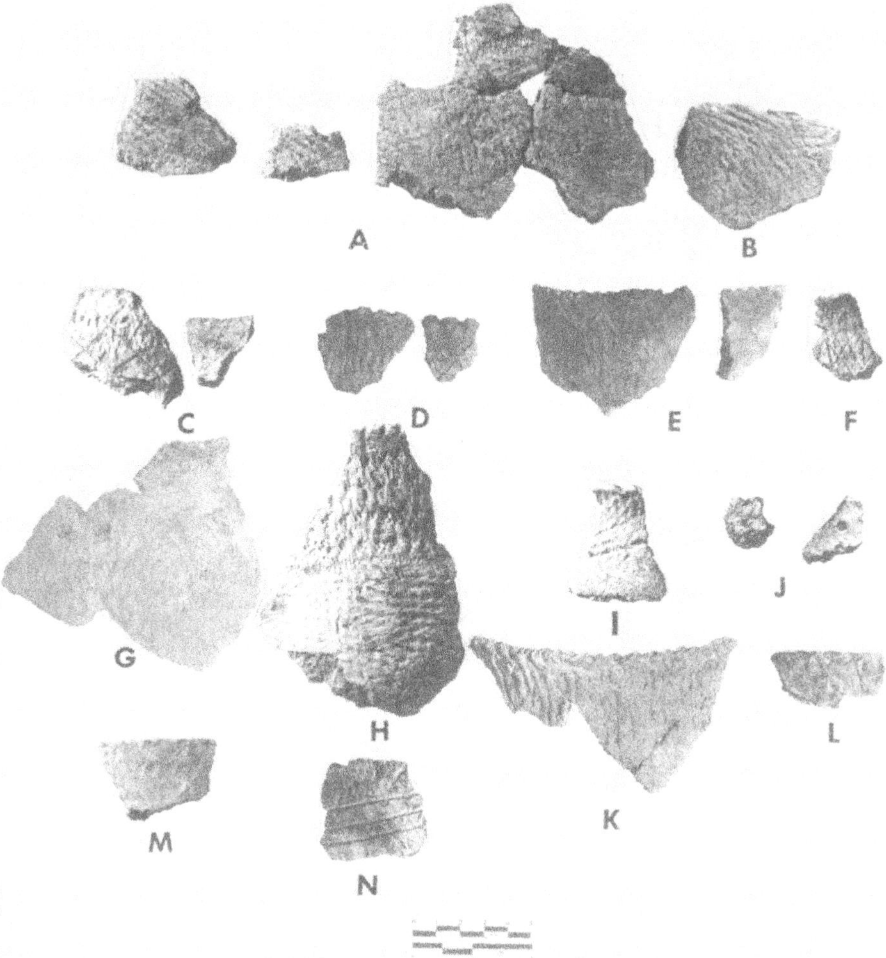

Marion Thick and Wayne ware sherds.

PLATE XIII

Springwells Net-impressed sherds.

PLATE XIV

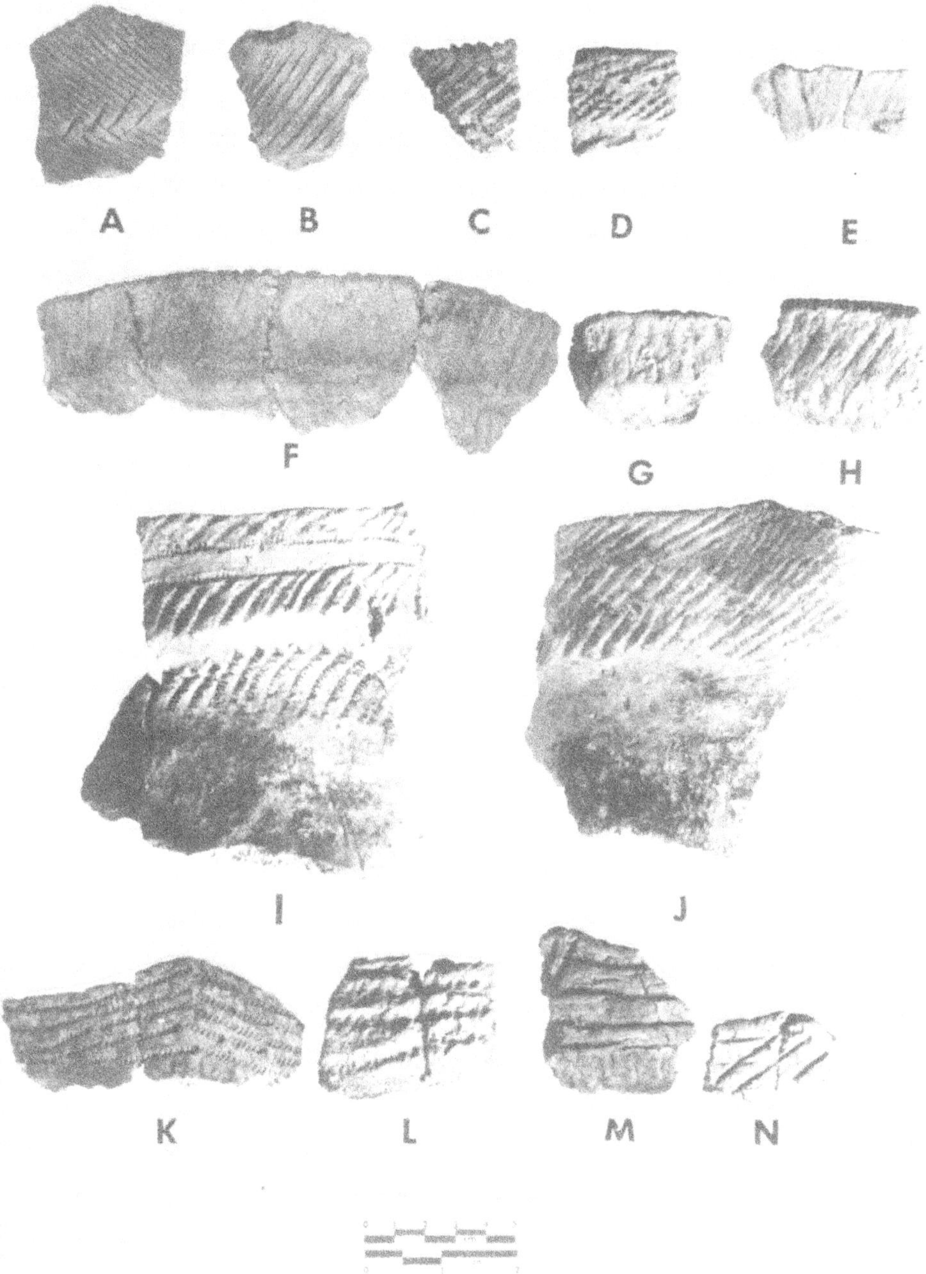

Vase Tool-impressed Vase Dentate, Vase-corded and Macomb Linear sherds.

PLATE XV

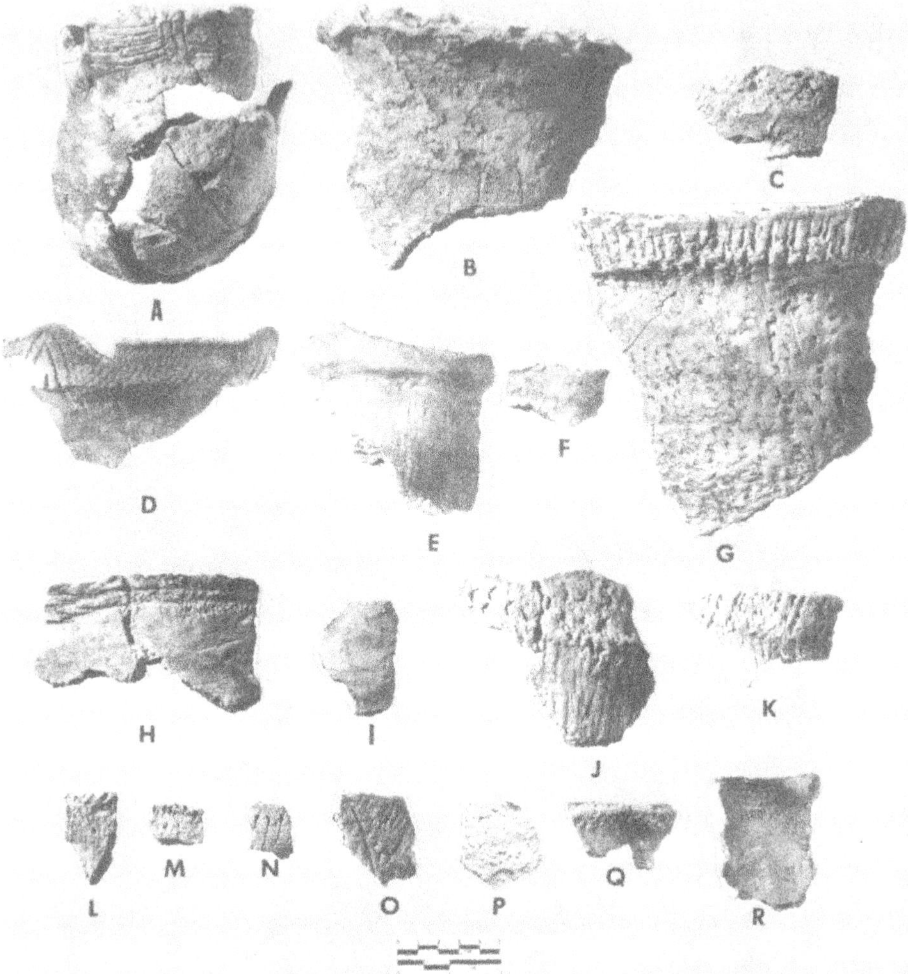

Miscellaneous sherds.

PLATE XVI

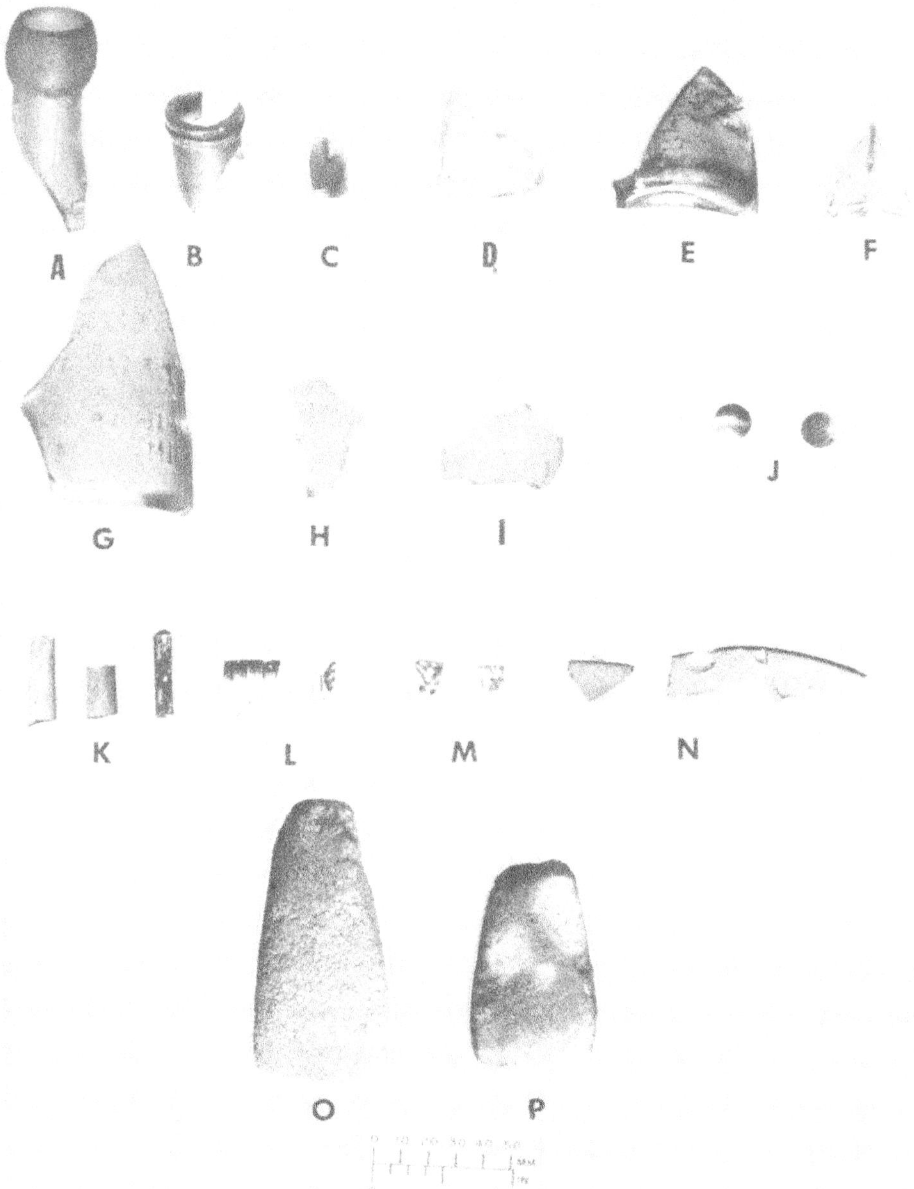

Material from the Central Mound.

ANALYSIS OF THE FORT WAYNE MOUND SKELETAL REMAINS

Richard G. Wilkinson

The skeletal material upon which this report is based was recovered from the Fort Wayne Mound in the summers of 1944 and 1945 by Carl E. Holmquist. This excavation yielded 24 distinct burials and scattered human remains from eight refuse pits (Holmquist, 1946); the 16 burials recovered in 1876 by Henry Gillman bring the total number of individuals buried in the mound to approximately 50.

This report is to serve as an appendix, and as such contains no cultural information; it is only necessary to state here that the mound is considered early Late Woodland. It is the purpose of this paper to describe the population of the Fort Wayne Mound as evidenced by the skeletal material, and to compare this population with other spatially related populations.

BURIAL FORM AND DISTRIBUTION

Figure 2 represents the burials from the Fort Wayne Mound, including both those recovered by Gillman, as well as those of Holmquist. The majority of the burials are bundles, and there are at least 7 flexed burials; from Gillman's report it would appear that there are an additional 4 flexed burials a few feet west of the center of the mound, which would bring the total of flexed burials to 11. Holmquist also uncovered an extended burial under Gillman's south trench, and Gillman reports a cremated burial found in a pot at the approximate center of the mound. There are no skull burials as were reported from the Riviere au Vase site (Fitting, 1965), the Bussinger site (Wilkinson, ms.), the Juntunen site (Eyman and Bettarel, ms. 1965) and the Younge site (Greenman, 1937) all of which have Late Woodland cultural affinities. The Riviere au Vase site is located in Macomb County, Michigan, the Bussinger site is in Saginaw County, the Juntunen site is on Blois Blanc Island, Mackinaw County, and the Younge site is in Lapeer County.

The burials are more or less randomly distributed, with no significant clustering apparent, although most of the burials and all of the pits are to the west of the center of the mound. This lack of distinctive burial patterns differs significantly from some of the Middle Woodland mounds, such as Mound M of the Norton Mounds in Grand Rapids, Michigan (Wilkinson, 1965), and is similar to the random distribution of burials observed at the Bussinger and Juntunen sites.

Sex and Age Distribution

The distribution of sex and age of the 24 burials recovered by Holmquist is represented in Table 1, below. Sexing was accomplished by nonmetric observations of the crania and postcranial skeletons, and when possible, was reinforced by a discriminant function analysis based on metric observations of the crania (Giles and Elliot, 1963). Age determination was based on epiphyseal union (Stevenson, 1924), tooth eruption (Kronfeld, 1934; Meredith, 1946), endocranial suture closure (Todd and Lyon, 1924) and on tooth wear and pathologies associated with aging. As age estimation from skeletal material is quite subject to error, especially among adults, large age categories were employed: children, 0-10; adolescents, 10-20; adults, 20-40; old adults, 40+.

TABLE 1

AGE AND SEX DISTRIBUTION

Sex	Age				
	0-10 years	10-20 years	20-40 years	40+ years	Total
Male	. . .	. . .	1	6	7
Female	. . .	2	8	1	11
Indeterminant . . .	2	4	. . .	. . .	6
Total	2	6	9	7	24

As can be seen from Table 1, the distribution of age and sex is somewhat peculiar. In primitive populations we could normally expect the mortality rate to be expressed by a simple S-curve, with the greatest number of deaths occurring among the very young and the middle-aged adults. At Fort Wayne, however, there is a steady increase in mortality from 0 to 40 years, with only a slight decrease among the adults. The mortality rates at the Juntunen site and the Bussinger site tend to reflect a more normal distribution. The most likely explanation for the Fort Wayne distribution would seem to be a preferential burial ritual which tended to favor older people while restricting the number of children

The sex distribution is perhaps more striking, in that there are 8 adult females to one male, but 6 old adult males to 1 female. If we can assume an absence of warfare in this population, then the discrepancies in the proportions of sexes might be explained by the greater burden placed on women by sexual division of labor and the dangers inherent in childbirth. If the 2 females in the 10 to 20 year group, who are both in their late teens, are added to the other adult females of reproductive age, then the female-male proportion becomes 10 to 1, which makes our assumption even more plausible. Very similar sex proportions were seen in the Bussinger burials, although the dichotomy was not as marked as among those of the Fort Wayne Mound.

Cranial Pathologies and Anomalies

Most prevalent among the Fort Wayne crania were pathologies of the dentition, occurring in 50 per cent of the observed burials. Dental pathologies are especially frequent among the males, as 87.5 per cent are affected to some degree. Such a frequency is not approached in other populations of the Great Lakes Area, neither in Middle nor Late Woodland times. Premortem tooth loss accounts for most of the dental pathology among the males and occurs, interestingly enough, only in the males.

Caries have an over-all frequency of 20.8 per cent, being slightly more frequent among the females, but not significantly so. Such an incidence of caries conforms fairly closely to that of the Bussinger site, but is slightly lower than that observed among Hopewellian populations of Michigan, Ohio and Illinois (Eyman, 1965). Congenital absence of teeth, especially the third molars, is quite common in human populations, but none was observed among the Fort Wayne burials.

Two of the burials, both adult females, bear post-mortem plaque removals. On one of the crania there are two perforations on either side of the sagittal suture near bregma, 12 and 14 mm. in diameter, another in the right occiput 35 mm. in diameter and possibly a fourth in the right temporal. The second cranium has two perforations in the right parietal, about 15 mm. in diameter. These small perforations are very similar to those observed in an adult male and two sub-adults from the Mallon mound group in Newaygo County, Michigan. In two of these burials the perforations occurred in the frontal bone just above the orbits, while a third bore two plaque removals along the coronal suture. The perforations of the Newaygo County burials range in size from 10 to 17 mm., and the burials are thought to have Late Woodland cultural affiliations. Post-mortem plaque removal is completely absent from the crania of the Bussinger site, but is quite frequent among the Hopewellian burials of the Norton Mounds. In the latter case, however, the plaque removal is of a totally different type, occurring only in the occiput, the perforations being much larger and more irregular in shape than those of the Fort Wayne and Newaygo burials. Cranial perforation and plaque removal similar to that found at Fort Wayne have also been described for the Younge site (Greenman, 1937) and Riviere aux Vase (Fitting, 1965; Greenman, 1957). A more complete description of the distribution of perforated crania in eastern Michigan and southwestern Ontario is given by Hinsdale and Greenman (1936).

There is no indication of artificial cranial deformation among the Fort Wayne burials, nor was it observed in Late Woodland burials from the Bussinger and Juntunen sites. Such cranial alteration, generally in the form of lambdoid flattening, occurs with varying frequencies in all of the Hopewellian populations observed by Eyman.

Auditory meatus exostosis is the most frequent single anomaly, occurring in 37.5 per cent of the observable burials, and being represented equally among males and females. Of interest because of its low frequency is the occurrence of wormian bones. Two females and one indeterminant burial bear wormian bones in the occipital sutures; none appeared among the males. This low frequency of occurrence contrasts sharply to the frequencies

TABLE 2

TYPES OF CRANIAL PATHOLOGIES AND THEIR DISTRIBUTION BY SEX

Pathology	Male	Female	Indet.	Total	Frequency (Per Cent)
Auditory meatus exostosis . .	4	4	1	9	37.5
Alveolar abcess	3	1	...	4	16.7
Wormian bones	...	2	1	3	12.5
Temperomandibular fossa pitting	2	...	...	2	8.3
Plaque removal	...	2	...	2	8.3
Inca bones	...	...	1	1	4.2
General dental pathology . . .	7	4	1	12	50.0
Caries	2	3	...	5	20.8
Premortem tooth loss	5	...	...	5	20.8
Dental abcess	2	2	...	4	16.7
Alveolar absorption	1	2	...	3	12.5
Malocclusion-crowding	1	1	...	2	8.3
Anomalous teeth	1	...	1	2	8.3

observed for certain Hopewellian populations of the lower Great Lakes region, where the frequencies ranged from 50 per cent to 75 per cent (Eyman, ms. 1965). Only one of Holmquist's burials, Burial 5, has an "inca" bone; Gillman also reported one from his Burial II. A summary of the types of cranial pathologies and their distribution by sex is given in Table 2.

Postcranial Pathologies and Anomalies

The presence of condylar lipping and spondylolisthesis, combined with temperomandibular fossa pitting gives an indication of the presence of osteoarthritis. It is interesting to note that these pathologies are somewhat more prevalent in males than in females. The most frequent postcranial anomaly is the presence of septal apertures of the distal humeri. They occur in 37.5 per cent of the burials, being three times more frequent in females than in males, while showing no preference for occurrence on right or left side; two of the females had bilateral apertures. Gillman also noted the presence of septal apertures, but gives no information other than an approximate frequency of 50 per cent. In white and Negro samples, septal apertures have been found to be more frequent in females, and show a tendency towards the left side (Trotter, 1934). The most recent study of septal apertures (Benfer and McKern, 1966) indicates that apertures are positively correlated with the degree of humeral robusticity, which would account for the higher frequencies among females. Benfer and McKern also refute the occurrence of apertures on one side of the body in opposition to the other.

The rather high frequency of vertebral osteoporosis may be associated with the dental pathologies, especially abcesses. Such an association has been made by Ingelmark *et al.* (1959). In general, the

TABLE 3

POSTCRANIAL PATHOLOGIES

Pathology	Male	Female	Indet.	Total	Frequency (Per Cent)
Septal aperture	2	6	1	9	37.5
Vertebral osteoporosis	3	1	...	4	16.7
Condylar lipping	3	1	...	4	16.7
Spondylolisthesis	4	2	...	6	25.0
Femoral shaft bowing	1	2	...	3	12.5
Crushed vertebral centra.	2	1	...	3	12.5
General exostoses	1	1	...	2	8.3
Squatting facets	...	1	...	1	4.2
Lumbar-sacralization	...	1	...	1	4.2

postcranial pathologies, represented in Table 3, are reminiscent of those of the Bussinger site in types and frequencies. This is especially true of the septal apertures, the occurrence of which is considerably less in earlier Middle Woodland populations, and show even a greater difference from white populations, in which the frequency of septal apertures is less than 5 per cent (Trotter, 1934).

Metrics

The cranial metrics are represented in Table 4, and the indices derived from these measurements appear in Table 5. The osteometric techniques employed in this study are those of Hrdlička (Stewart, 1952). The conversion of Gillman's measurements from inches to millimeters reveals that the crania he measured were somewhat larger than the current sample. This is probably a reflection of different measuring techniques, and it should further be said that the Gillman measurements fall within one standard deviation of those listed in Table 4.

From the cranial indices, the crania fall within the mesocranic classification, as did the crania from the Bussinger, Juntunen, and Younge sites. The crania can be further characterized as having rather short faces, rectangular orbits, and the nasal index is classified as mesorrhine. The crania are high in relation to their length and breadth, resulting in a slightly vaulted appearance. The over-all morphology of the Fort Wayne crania resembles closely that of the Bussinger site, as revealed by the cranial indices.

From measurements of the few available long bones, the stature of the Fort Wayne burials was calculated at 172.9 cm (68.1 in.) for males, and 168.8 cm. (66.5 in.) for females. Gillman reports that Burial V was "of simian proportions," and calculated the stature at 5 feet, 10.5 inches. Using Gillman's long bones measurements for this burial, and applying the Trotter and Gleser (1958) formulae for stature, our stature estimate is 70.47 inches, or exactly the same as Gillman's.

Gillman was extremely interested in platycnemism among the various populations he studied, and found the mean index of platycnemism of the Fort Wayne burials to be 67.6 per cent; the same index for the Holmquist burials has a mean value of 67.8 per cent. Such values are similar to those of Ohio, Michigan and Illinois Hopewellian populations (Eyman, 1965), and which, furthermore, are classified as mesocnemic, or moderately flattened. Due to the small sample size, a table of the post-cranial measurements and indices has not been included in this report.

TABLE 4

CRANIAL METRICS

Measurement	Males		Females		Total		S.D.
	N	x̄	N	x̄	N	x̄	
Maximum length	3	173.7	2	178.5	5	175.6	6.26
Maximum breadth	3	135.0	1	130.0	4	133.7	4.79
Minimum frontal	4	91.5	4	90.3	9	91.0	3.32
Basion-bregma height	3	131.0	...	...	3	131.0	6.25
Auricular height	3	115.3	...	...	3	115.3	6.82
Endobasion-nasion length	2	98.0	...	...	2	98.0	2.94
Endobasion-prosthion length	2	92.5	...	...	2	92.5	1.00
Bizygomatic diameter	1	127.0	...	...	1	127.0	...
Nasion-prosthion height	3	73.0	3	64.7	6	68.8	5.20
Nasion-menton height	1	121.0	2	110.5	3	114.0	6.25
Nasion height	3	56.0	3	48.0	6	52.0	4.73
Nasal width	3	25.3	3	23.7	6	24.5	2.14
L. Orbital height	2	36.0	3	35.0	6	35.4	1.32
R. Orbital height	2	37.5	1	32.0	3	35.7	3.39
L. Orbital length	2	40.5	3	38.7	5	39.4	1.32
R. Orbital length	2	42.0	1	39.0	3	41.0	1.73
External palatal length	3	50.0	3	48.7	6	49.3	2.32
External palatal width	4	65.3	3	58.0	7	62.1	5.15
Internal palatal height	2	15.0	1	10.0	3	13.3	3.08
Symphsis height	3	37.0	4	32.3	8	34.3	3.18
Mandibular body length	3	90.7	4	92.3	8	92.4	2.73
Body thickness	3	15.0	4	14.0	8	15.0	2.67
Bigonial width	2	98.5	1	91.0	3	96.0	4.58
Bicondylar width	1	123.0	...	...	1	123.0	...
L. ramus height	2	66.0	2	51.5	4	58.7	9.71
L. ramus minimum width	2	34.5	2	33.0	5	34.0	1.00

TABLE 5

INDICES

Index	Males		Females		Total	
	N	x̄	N	x̄	N	x̄
Cranial	2	78.5	2	75.4	4	76.9
Height-length	2	76.1	1	74.1	3	75.4
Height-breadth	2	97.2	1	97.0	3	97.1
Auricular height-length	2	66.4	1	66.5	3	66.4
Fronto-parietal	2	68.7	2	67.3	4	68.0
Cranial module	2	148.9	1	142.0	3	146.6
Mean orbital	1	87.9	1	84.5	2	86.2
Nasal	2	45.3	4	48.4	6	47.3
Upper facial	...	...	1	48.0	1	48.0
Fronto-gonial	2	104.8	1	100.0	3	103.2
Zygo-frontal	...	...	1	70.1	1	70.1
External palatal	2	91.6	5	120.2	7	114.9
Gnathic	1	92.0	...	...	1	92.9

Summary

A Late Woodland burial mound, now located within the confines of Fort Wayne, in Detroit, Michigan, was originally excavated in 1876 by Henry Gillman. This first excavation, consisting of two intersecting trenches, uncovered 16 burials. In 1944 and 1945 Carl Holmquist excavated the mound for the second time, recovering 24 distinct burials and scattered human remains in eight pits, bringing the total number of individuals to approximately 50. This report was based on mainly the 24 burials excavated by Holmquist; Gillman's burials have been lost or destroyed, but some of the information from his report is still pertinent, and has thus been employed.

The burials were found to be distributed randomly throughout the mound, although most were located to the west of the center of the mound. Eleven of the burials were flexed, one was extended, and there was a cremation in a pot near the center of the mound. The remainder of the burials were bundled or scattered.

Of Holmquist's 24 burials, there were 7 males, 11 females, and 6 of indeterminant sex. The sex ratio, when correlated with the age categories, shows a marked discrepancy, as there are 10 females of reproductive age to only one male. Among the old adults, this ratio is reversed, there being 6 males and 1 female. Sexual division of labor and childbirth trauma were suggested as possible explanations for these inequalities. The age distribution also was somewhat unexpected, as the mortality rate is represented by a straight line instead of the expected S-curve.

Among the cranial pathologies, those of the dentition were most frequent, especially among males, 87.5 per cent exhibiting some form of dental pathology. Post-mortem plaque removal was observed in two adult female crania, being very similar in size and shape to the perforations observed in three Late Woodland burials from Newaygo County, Michigan. Artificial cranial deformation was absent from the Fort Wayne crania, as it was from the Juntunen and Bussinger sites, both having Late Woodland affinities. In contrast to some earlier Hopewellian populations, the frequency of wormian bones among the Fort Wayne crania was quite low, having a frequency similar to that of the Bussinger crania. Osteoarthritis and a high occurrence of septal apertures were also noted among the Fort Wayne burials.

The metric observations and the indices tended to reinforce the similarities observed between the Fort Wayne burials and other Late Woodland burials from Michigan. This similarity was demonstrated by such characteristics as wormian bones and morphological features, all thought to bear genetic relationships. Further similarity among the selected Late Woodland populations was illustrated by cultural mechanisms as they are expressed in the skeletal material, such as the lack of cranial deformation and the presence of postmortem plaque removal. Finally, the population of the Fort Wayne Mound, known previously only by its material products, has been brought to light, and generic and cultural relationships existing between this and other temporally and spatially related populations have been suggested. It is hoped that more information concerning the relationship of the Fort Wayne population to other spatially related populations will be found pending the analysis of the skeletal material from the Riviere aux Vase site and the re-evaluation of the osteology of the Younge site, both of which are currently in progress.

REFERENCES

Benfer, Robert A. and McKern T. W.
1966 The Correlation of Bone Robusticity with the Perforation of the Coronoid-Olecranon Septum in Man. American Journal of Physical Anthropology, 24, pp. 247-52.

Eyman, Charles E.
1965 A Comparison of Michigan and Other Hopewellian Skeletal Remains. Paper presented at 69th Annual Meeting, Michigan Academy of Science, Arts, and Letters.

Eyman, Charles E. and Bettarel, Robert L.
1965 Physical Anthropology of the Juntunen Site, 20 MK 1, Blois Blanc Island, Michigan. Paper presented at 69th Annual Meeting, Michigan Academy of Science, Arts and Letters.

Fitting, James E.
1965 Late Woodland Cultures of Southeastern Michigan. Museum of Anthropology, University of Michigan, Anthropological Papers, No. 24. Ann Arbor.

Giles, Eugene and Elliot, Orville
1963 Sex Determination by Discriminant Function Analysis of Crania. American Journal of Physical Anthropology, Vol. 21, No. 1, pp. 299-307.

Gillman, Henry
1876 Investigation of the Burial Mound at Fort Wayne, on the Detroit River, Michigan. Proceedings of the American Association for the Advancement of Science, pp. 311-25. Buffalo.

Greenman, E. F.
1937 The Younge Site: An Archaeological Record from Michigan. Occasional Contributions from the Museum of Anthropology of the University of Michigan, No. 6, Ann Arbor.
1957 Riviere aux Vase Site: A Preliminary Report. The Michigan Archaeologist, Vol. 3, No. 1, pp. 9-11.

Hinsdale, W. B. and Greenman, E. F.
1936 Perforated Indian Crania in Michigan. Occasional Contributions from the Museum of Anthropology of the University of Michigan, No. 5. Ann Arbor.

Holmquist, Carl E.
1946 The Fort Wayne Mound. Detroit Aboriginal Research Club Bulletin.

Ingelmark, B. E., Møller-Christensen, V. and Brinch, O.
1959 Spinal Joint Changes and Dental Infections. Acta Anatomica, Supplement 36-1 to Vol. 38.

Kronfeld, Rudolf
1935 Development and Calcification of the Human Deciduous and Permanent Dentition. The Bur, Vol. 35, No. 1, pp. 18-25.

Meredith, Howard V.
1946 Order and Age of Eruption of the Deciduous Dentition. Journal of Dental Research, Vol. 25, No. 1, pp. 43-66.

Stevenson, Paul H.
1924 Age Order of Epiphyseal Union in Man. American Journal of Physical Anthropology, Vol. 7, No. 1, pp. 53-93.

Stewart, T. Dale (Editor)
1952 Hrdlička's Practical Anthropometry, Wistar Institute of Anatomy and Biology, Philadelphia.

Todd, T. W. and Lyon, D. W., Jr.
1924 Endocranial Suture Closure. American Journal of Physical Anthropology, Vol. 7, No. 3, pp. 326-84.

Trotter, Mildred
1934 Septal Apertures in the Humerus of American Whites and Negroes. American Journal of Physical Anthropology, Vol. 19, No. 2, pp. 213-27.

Trotter, Mildred and Gleser, Goldine C.
1958 A Re-evaluation of Estimation of Stature Based on Measurements of Stature Taken During Life and of Long Bones After Death. American Journal of Physical Anthropology, Vol. 16, No. 1, pp. 70-123.

Wilkinson, Richard G.
1965 Skeletal Analysis of the Norton Mounds. Paper presented at 69th Annual Meeting, Michigan Academy of Science, Arts, and Letters. Skeletal Remains from the Bussinger Site, 20-SA-194,
n.d. Skeletal Remains from the Bussinger Site, 20-SA-194. Ms. on file at The University of Michigan Museum of Anthropology.

Part III

THE BUTTERFIELD SITE, 20 BY 29, BAY COUNTY, MICHIGAN

H. Martin Wobst

I

INTRODUCTION

ONE day in the early part of this century Mr. Walter Schmidt, an amateur archaeologist devoted to the prehistory of Bay County, extended his collecting trip to a newly plowed sand ridge east of Pinconning. Chips and ceramics strewn about the surface attracted Mr. Schmidt's attention and since that time, now nearly fifty years ago, collections from the site have filled drawer upon drawer in Walter Schmidt's cabinet. He informed the University of Michigan Museum of Anthropology of his finds, but no work was done on the site until 1965 when Schmidt had reached the age of seventy-five. During more than fifty years of his life Schmidt has accumulated an unequaled knowledge of the area's archaeology. This site report is dedicated to Walter Schmidt as the pioneer of Bay County prehistory.

I wish to thank my coworker, Pete Carruthers, now at the University of Alberta, for sharing three weeks of field work in Pinconning and life in the University of Michigan truck. The thorough discussions with him contributed much to my understanding of the site. Gary A. Wright and Carruthers' survey of the area (Wright, 1966) helped to place the site in its ecological context. Students who participated include Carole Crumley, Mary Hrones, Don Janzen, Squire Jaros, and Linda Wood. I am indebted to the owner of the site, Mr. Ira M. Butterfield, for his interest and co-operation. Last but not least I would like to thank the Carstens family for their hospitality, contributing so much to the well-being of the field crew, and Casey Carstens in particular for his participation in the excavation. Finally, I would like to express my appreciation to Dr. James E. Fitting and Dr. James B. Griffin for their guidance and advice on my research program.

Work on the site and in the laboratory was supported by NSF Undergraduate Science Education Program Grant GE-6226 (Dr. James B. Griffin, Director, and Dr. James E. Fitting, Program Supervisor) as well as a graduate research assistantship in the Museum of Anthropology.

II

THE SITE

The Butterfield site is located to the east of Pinconning on the north side of the Pinconning River in Bay County, Michigan (Pinconning Township, northeast and northwest quarters, Section 25, T 17N, R 5E). It is located approximately 30 miles to the south of the Central Michigan High Plains, part of the Canadian Biotic Province, and some 60 miles to the north of Saginaw as the center of the Saginaw Valley, the most prominent cultural area to the south. The site is only a few minutes from the shore of Lake Huron with which it is connected by the Pinconning River. The river is now only a trickle of water but formerly was of larger dimensions and probably navigable by canoe. The Pinconning River has only a small drainage area and no physical feature to separate its valley from that of the Kawkawlin to the south and the Pine River to the north. The site (20 BY 29) follows the rim of a sand ridge, running parallel to the river at the point of the major concentration of cultural material. At this point the site reaches an altitude of 590 feet above sea level. To the north of this point the sand ridge merges into another set of ridges and can be traced for a long distance along the river. To the south it is crosscut by the river and continues due south. These sand ridges are vestiges of the time when Lake Huron was higher than the present altitude of the site.

Now the site is demarcated to the south by the meandering river while the northern edge is defined by the Pinconning Road; the east is bounded by a residential area; and the west again by the river. The present vegetation on the site consists of grasses and brush. At the time the site was first visited by Walter Schmidt, pine stumps were still visible. The area of the site entered written records when three Chippewa Indians acquired a deed to the property around 1850. Since then the site has seen many owners. Ira M. Butterfield, the present owner acquired title in 1961. For some thirty years the site was plowed and seeded, and it was during this time that Walter Schmidt acquired most of his surface collections from the site.

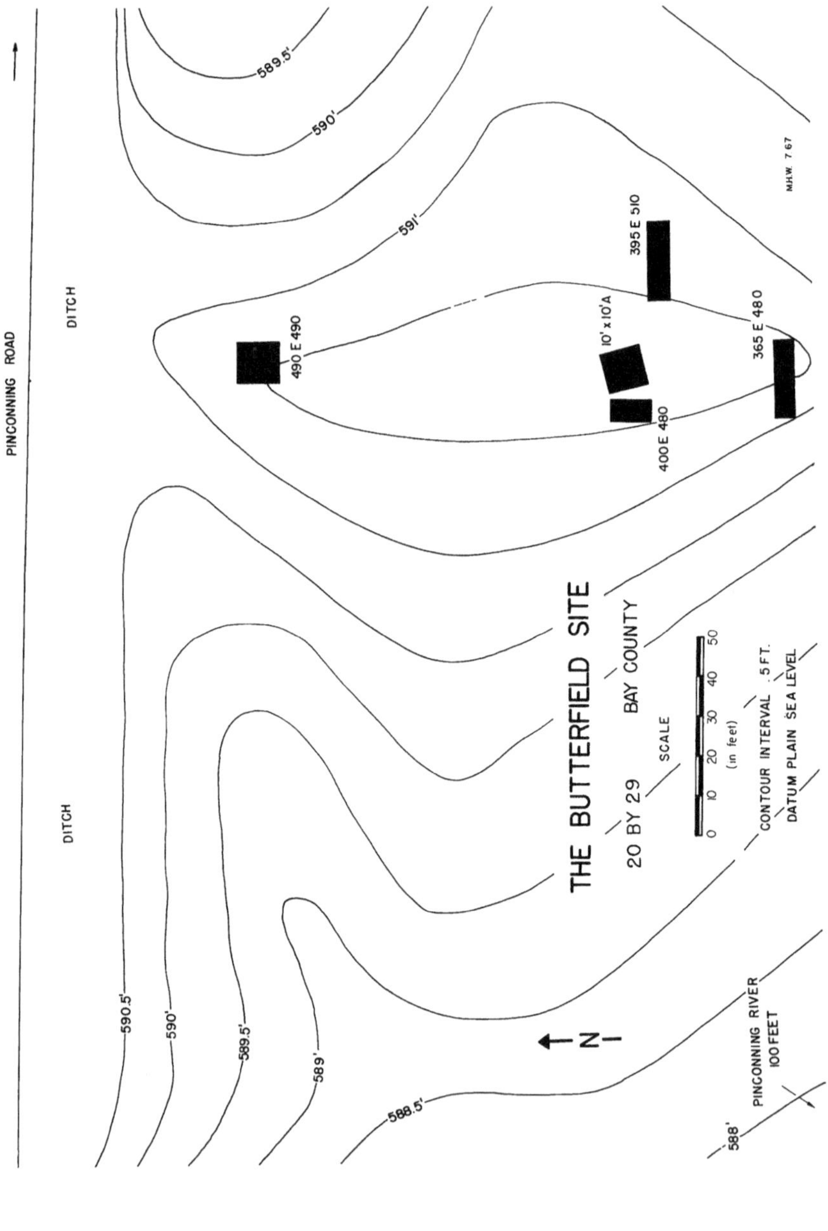

FIG. 1. Contour map of the Butterfield site.

As far as can be determined cultural material is found both to the north and to the south of the excavated area within a range of 1 mile. This material covers a cultural sequence from Late Archaic to Late Woodland times. On the site itself only the Terminal Archaic and the Early Late Woodland periods are found in stratigraphic context. For this reason, an evaluation of Walter Schmidt's collections has to be postponed until a more complete stratigraphic sequence has been established in the area.

Nature and Extent of Excavations

Gary A. Wright and Pete Carruthers of the University of Michigan Northeastern Edge Survey visited the site in June, 1965, on the advice of Walter Schmidt, Pinconning (Wright, 1966). The wealth of cultural material in surface collections from the site and from its six test pits clearly recommended further excavation. During the last weeks of the 1965 field season Pete Carruthers and the author tested the site in order to define its stratigraphy and chronology and to determine its relationship to the Carolinian-Canadian edge. Actual excavation began on June 29, 1965, and lasted until July 14. During this time five units were excavated for a total of 450 square feet (Table 1).

TABLE 1

Unit	Size	Area
1) 10 x 10 A	10' x 10'	100 ft^2
2) 400 E 480	5' x 10'	50 ft^2
3) 490 E 490	10' x 10'	100 ft^2
4) 365 E 480	5' x 20'	100 ft^2
5) 395 E 510	5' x 20'	100 ft^2
Total		450 ft^2

Units 1, 2, and 3 were placed into the central ridge rim, while units 365 E 480 and 395 E 510 were sunk into the southern margins at right angles to the occupation zone to provide a stratigraphic cross section between the deposits. In order to explain the relationship between cultural levels and geologic history of the area, a geological test pit was dug through the sterile subsoil reaching down to the water table. The elevation of the site was determined from the nearest bench mark. In March, 1966, the site was again visited by the author to trace the extent of the sand ridge.

Techniques of Excavation

Throughout our fieldwork we relied on standard University of Michigan excavation techniques. Every bit of dirt removed from the excavation units was screened except for the sod which was carefully shaken out by hand above a screen. The plow zone was removed and screened with one-fourth-inch mesh screen while cultural deposits below the plow zone were taken out in 5- by 5-foot squares and sifted through a one-eighth-inch mesh screen. Where it was not possible to follow the natural stratigraphy, artificial levels were taken at 3-inch intervals. Within such levels it was usually possible to distinguish areas of different occupations and the material was bagged and labelled accordingly. By shovel-skimming the floor of the excavation units we were able to pick up most artifacts in their original position and their exact co-ordinates could be recorded. Others, discovered in the screen, could usually be placed within the 5- by 5-foot by 3-inch unit from which they came. Features were excavated with trowel, brush, and if necessary, dental picks. This material was fine-screened. Thus, practically all cultural material including vegetal and faunal remains could be returned for laboratory analysis. In addition soil samples were taken from all layers. Fire-cracked rocks were counted, weighed, and discarded on the site.

Stratigraphy

The stratigraphy of the site was complex. Irregularities caused by ground water fluctuations, windblow, and small scale erosion were frequent, while tree stumps, rodents, and interdigitating cultural features added to our problem. The ideal profile outlined below presents the conclusions derived from approximately forty profiles and a laboratory analysis of some fifty soil samples. A geological test pit down to the groundwater table helped to clarify the stratigraphical sequence below the cultural horizons. Two sequences of soil development were recognized on the site. The upper one (I), fairly complete in most places, includes the cultural material of the Woodland occupations, while the lower soil profile (II), highly incomplete, contained the Terminal Archaic assemblage.

I). Upper sequence: The A horizon (IA) is made up of loam, sands, and humus. Its Munsell color readings range from 10 YR 2/1 to 10 YR 4/3, while the pH is slightly to medium acid. On the County Soil Survey chart it is described as Newton Loamy Sand

and covers 4.3 per cent of Bay County. This soil, as opposed to the Eastport Sand, which is found on the recent sand ridges along Saginaw Bay, occupies an intermediate position between the high and low paleobeaches.

The upper 2 or 3 inches of our profiles consisted of a dense network of grass roots and of decaying or decomposed organic matter (IA_0) and a disturbed layer of sand loam and humus mottled by rodents, roots, and plows (IA_{1a}). The uniform distribution of charcoal, charred wood, and ash throughout the 4 to 8 inches of this horizon suggests that the surface has been repeatedly burned prior to cultivation. Occasionally where the plow shares did not reach the bottom of the top soil, A_{1a}, the horizon showed more homogeneity and a less dark brown hue, partly due to the absence of charcoal from the surface burning (A_{1b}). The bottom of the plow zone was usually reached between 6- to 9-inches depth.

A .5- to 1.5-inch thick alluvial horizon (IB_h) enriched with minerals and humus from the topsoil underlies the A horizon. The color ranges from whitish- to blackish-gray with widely varying Munsell readings, and medium acidity.

The parent material of the A and B horizons is a layer of windblown sand of varying thickness and fine to medium grain size (C_1). The Munsell color readings from this layer cluster around 10 YR 7/2, so that it is easily distinguished from over- and underlying horizons. Since the accumulation of the sand was accompanied by occasional occupation of the site, it is frequently of a mottled character, and roots of rodents have contributed to the disturbance of this horizon. In general it is of medium acidity and contains little organic material.

II). Lower sequences: The C_1 horizon of the upper soil sequence fills all of the surface irregularities of the lower soil horizon. This paleosoil (IIA) is of strong acidity, while its color ranges from 10 YR 4/1 to 10 YR 5/6, clustering around 10 YR 5/2. It consists of medium- to large-size sands and contains a fair amount of organic material. The cultural material contained in it is usually found in the lower part. It is highly truncated and eroded, and in some units has been completely removed. Color and pH set it off from over- and underlying deposits.

Only occasionally an incipient B horizon (IIB_a) can be recognized as a thin band of lighter color and decreased acidity, which is usually void of cultural material.

The paleosoil IIA_1 is derived from a sterile sand (IIC_1) of medium- to coarse-grain size with additional windblown material of smaller grade. The color of this horizon is light yellow to whitish with Munsell readings approaching 10 YR 8/1. The pH is very slightly acid, and organic material is generally absent.

Only the geologic test pit revealed the underlying deposits of a receding shoreline (II C_2, D_1, D_2). Although they consist of several markedly different horizons, only a general sequence could be worked out since their character was often disturbed by groundwater action. Below IIC_1 a layer of finegrained sand (IIC_2) followed, of 4- to 7-inch thickness, underlain by silty sand (D_1) and silt (D_2). The groundwater table was reached at an altitude of 586 feet, or 6 feet below the surface. Despite decreasing grain size toward the bottom, the lower deposits became increasingly more alkaline and surpass a pH of 7 just above the water table.

In addition to the general sequence outlined above, many geological features of small scale were encountered, such as small iron oxide horizons (Fe). Their presence, however, does not add to the information obtained from the soil sequence outlined above, and was of no influence on the cultural sequence. The cultural sequence on the site is contained in the deposits IIA_1 to IA_0 at an altitude of between 588 to 592 feet above present sea level, or up to 4 feet below the present surface.

Chronology and Stratigraphic Column

The bipartition of the stratigraphic column is reflected in the bipartition of the archaeological assemblage from the site. The archaeological material, on, in, and below the paleosoil horizon consists of projectile points, heavy cutting tools, backed blades, and preforms, a high percentage of flakes of bifacial retouch and other debitage. Pottery is entirely absent. This material forms a homogenous assemblage both vertically and horizontally. Stratigraphic subdivision of the material beyond that observed among the features (cf. below) was impossible. No occupational nor sedimentological hiatus could be observed.

Overlying this assemblage, beginning within the windblown sand stratum, the material consists of scraping tools, light blades, pottery and core-derived flakes, and other debitage. This assemblage in turn is internally consistent and homogeneous. Evidence of stratgraphic breaks is absent, and no occupational hiatus is indicated by the archaeological material.

In the absence of datable radiocarbon from the site, we have to determine its chronology by correlation to geological and archaeological events that have been dated elsewhere. Thus, the archaeological assemblage from the upper soil sequence can be dated into a relatively narrow time range from 600 to 900 A.D. and assigned to an early Late Woodland culture on the basis of the pottery types present. The evidence for this is outlined in succeeding chapters.

Here we shall deal only with the age of the lower soil sequence. Its age estimate can be based on three factors: 1) subsurface geology, 2) elevation and morphology of the site, and 3) the archaeological record. The subsurface of the lower soil horizon consists of lake bottom and near shore deposits such as fine grained sand (IIC_2), silty sand (D_1), and silt (D_2). The elevation of the excavated area's surface ranges from 590 to 592 feet; the lower archaeological assemblage is contained in deposits usually more than 2 feet below the surface. The elevation of the site, therefore, ranged from 588 to 590 feet when these layers were deposited, disregarding any post depositional uplift of the area, The upper time limit for the archaeological assemblage in the lower soil horizon is indicated by the complete absence of pottery from the assemblage and by the lack of Early Woodland ceramics from the site surface and from plow-disturbed horizons, suggesting a pre-Woodland age for this assemblage. The earliest dated Woodland horizons in the neighborhood of the Butterfield site are found at the Schultz site in Saginaw County, where thick exterior and interior cord-marked pottery has been radiocarbon dated at 530 ± 150 B.C. (M-1525), and 540 ± 130 B.C. (M-1524). This provides us with a minimum age for the lower archaeological horizons at the Butterfield site of around 600 B.C.

The maximum age limit of this horizon is determined by the elevation of the site at the time of occupation, ranging from 588 to 590 feet above main sea level. This requires that the recession of the lake shore, as evidenced in the sub-surface, must have progressed below 588 feet before the site could have been occupied. The Algoma beach line in the area of the site has a mean altitude of 595 feet a.m.s. (Leverett and Taylor, 1915). This lake level was attained approximately around 1100 B.C. (Griffin, 1961, 1966). Allowing some time for the lake level to drop below 588 feet one must conclude that the date of the lower occupation horizon on the Butterfield site should be around 600 B.C., bringing its Terminal Archaic cultural assemblage within very close chronological proximity, or possibly even to overlap the Early Woodland occupation sites in the Saginaw Valley. Similar Terminal Archaic assemblages have been reported from the Andrews, Stroebel, Frazier and Pomranky sites in the Saginaw Valley. All of these occur on, or slightly below the Lake Algoma level (Griffin, 1966).

Why, then, is the assemblage at the Butterfield site still

lacking ceramics at a time that we find a rich Early Woodland ceramic assemblage at the Schultz site? A possible explanation might be found in the marginal position of the site in relation to the main centers of the Saginaw Valley Woodland culture. If we assume that ideal conditions permitted the diffusion of agriculture into the Saginaw Valley around 600 B.C., it should have taken a considerable time before this new adaptation would spread to the margins of the valley. Even today conditions are far from ideal for agriculture in Pinconning Township. The county soil survey suggests that the sandy soils should not be farmed at all. Only during periods of population pressure in the Saginaw Valley as might have existed during Middle and Late Woodland times, can we expect Woodland culture to extend its range into the margins, as is evidenced from the site by the intense Early Late Woodland occupation. Thus, it is not disturbing to find a Terminal Archaic adaptation at this site persisting at the same time that an Early Woodland adaptation was making inroads in the Saginaw Valley.

The Features

Within the excavated 450 square feet more than 30 loci were designated as features and treated separately. This number might seem very large considering the small size of the excavation units. Judged against the wealth of cultural material from the site, however, a large number of occupational disturbances would seem only natural. After an initial period of trial and error, we were soon able to distinguish cultural features from "natural" disturbances such as root molds, historic pits, and rodent burrows of which there was an ample supply.

Unfortunately, the prehistoric inhabitants of our site during repeated occupations frequently chose the same locations for their hearths and trash pits. Instead of distributing them neatly over the excavated area, they many times put them right on top of the hearth of their predecessors, thus cross-cutting or destroying it. The same choice spots appealed to the historic occupants. By digging large-sized pits, they managed to damage or destroy many of our most interesting features.

We took great care to separate feature fill of later periods from the material contemporaneous with the use of the pits. Due to the lack of characteristic cultural material in many of the features, chronological correlations are often based on stratigraphic position only.

Of the 33 features, 4 are of historic origin (Table 2). Nine features could be assigned to Late Woodland proveniences, representing

TABLE 2

VERTICAL DISTRIBUTION OF OCCUPATIONAL DISTURBANCES

Age	Horizon	Feature Number	Amount	Per Cent
Historic	within IA_1	6;11;25;31	4	11.7
Late Woodland.	within IC_1	2B;3B;4;7; 9B;10;17;24; 29	9	26.4
Terminal Archaic I . .	on or slightly below IIA_1	1;2A;3A;5;8; 9A;14;15;30	9	26.4
Terminal Archaic II . .	within IIA_1	13;16;18;26; 27;28	6	17.6
Terminal Archaic III. .	below IIB	19	1	2.9
Questionable	?	12;20;21;22; 23	5	14.7
Total			34	99.7

little or no vertical separation. The Terminal Archaic features seem to belong to three occupation floors, one below the IIB horizon, another within the paleosoil, and a third on top of the paleosoil. Most of the features in both time horizons served as fire pits as indicated by charcoal, heat spalled rocks, flint chips and fire-reddened sand. Because of the lack of characteristic cultural material in the features belonging to the Terminal Archaic horizon, a vertical bipartition of the Terminal Archaic assemblage could not be obtained. The three occupation floors very likely belong to a relatively short time span.

From Table 2 it becomes apparent that most of the occupational disturbances stem from the Terminal Archaic site occupation. Most of these again have to be attributed to the youngest of its occupation floors. Although not too much importance should be attached to this distribution on the basis of such a small excavated area, it seems as though the Terminal Archaic occupation increased in intensity as time progressed. This is to be expected from the geologic evidence, since after the retreat of the lake water from the area, it must have taken some time before the sand ridge and the surrounding area became inviting enough for occupation. As time progressed the value for such occupation must have increased. The increasing horizontal spread of the Terminal Archaic occupation (Table 3) should be explained in the same terms.

On the following pages are recorded the characteristics of the individual features:

TABLE 3

HORIZONTAL DISTRIBUTION OF OCCUPATIONAL DISTURBANCES

(Prehistoric features with defined stratigraphy only)

	Late Woodland	Terminal Archaic I	Terminal Archaic II	Terminal Archaic III	Total
10 X 10A . .	2B;3B;4	1;2A;3A;5	...	...	7
400 E 480. .	7;9B;10	8;9A	...	...	5
490 E 490. .	...	14;15	13;16	...	4
395 E 510. .	17	...	18	19	3
365 E 480. .	24;29	30	26;27;28	...	6

Feature Number 1--SW-corner, SW 1/4, 10 x 10A

The top of this shallow rectangular pit (4 X 2 ft.) was discovered at a depth of 1.5 feet as a dark discoloration within the lighter colored paleosoil. Its symmetrically inclined wall gives it the appearance of a trough. Although containing little cultural material (9 flint chips), the 43 fire-cracked rocks, burnt wood, bark, and bone, leave no doubt about its use as a hearth. Nine different tree species were identified in the charcoal (cf. Table 38, p. 271).

Feature Number 2--NW-corner, NW 1/4, 10 x 10A

This number includes 2 pits belonging to 2 different occupation horizons. Due to their irregular outline and complexity, it was impossible to distinguish between them before their profile was drawn.

Feature 2A is a rectangular flat bottomed and shallow pit (5 X 2 ft.), in shape and stratigraphic position comparable to Feature 1. Burnt bone, fire-burned sand and 262 fire-cracked rocks (2.6 kg.) point to its use as a fire pit. The highly acidic pH accounts for the absence of vegetal material. Among the charcoal pieces, seven different tree species were identified (Table 38).

Feature 2B was in use after the blown sand began to accumulate and crosscut part of Feature 2A. It is marked by many fire-cracked rocks (534, 10 kg.). Compared to Features 1 and 2A it is of irregular, roughly circular outline, and very shallow (10 inches). The associated pottery consists largely of plain body sherds. The 126 flint chips derive from use chipping and/or resharpening tools, although there were a few decortication flakes and large amorphous nodule fragments. Surrounding the hearth rim, a piece of ground slate of unknown function was unearthed. The extreme heat and the prolonged use of the hearth is reflected by the disintegration of wood-charcoal, the absence of bone, and the thorough coloring of the surrounding IC_1 sands.

Feature Number 3--N/SW 1/4 of 10 x 10A

When the survey crew tested the site, Feature 3 was discovered by chance. It prompted us to begin our excavation in the adjoining 10 X 10 (A). It turned out to consist of 2 distinct pits, the younger one crosscutting the older hearth.

Not much was left of the older feature (No. 3A). Apparently of circular shape with a round bottom it's contents include a few flint chips (27) from use and resharpening of bifacial tools, 2 small pieces of calcined bone and 9 fire-cracked rocks. Three tree species were identified in the wood-charcoal (Table 38). Like Features 1 and 2A, Feature 3A served for a short time as fire pit.

Feature 3B was a large, amorphous, dark discoloration, roughly 6 by 3 feet, of trench-like appearance and seems to have been used as a hearth and trash pit. Parts of it were obstructed by Feature 6, test pit Number 1, the west wall of the unit and an elaborate design of rodent burrows. Flat-bottomed and of shallow depth, it yielded a wealth of cultural material, although all vegetal information was destroyed by the heat of it's fire. The fire colored the surrounding C_1 sand pink or orangish, while it left the wood in the form of unidentifiable cinders or ash. The pit contained about one hundred fire-cracked rocks of small size. The chipped-stone assemblage of this feature consisted of a side-notched projectile point, a simple convex flake scraper, and 80 small retouch chips and waste flakes. In addition the hearth yielded 15 unidentifiable sherdlets (14 body, 1 rim) and two small pieces of calcined bone. The hearth belongs to the Early Late Woodland occupation of the site (cf. Feature 2B).

Feature Number 4--N 1/2 of SE 5 x 5, 10 x 10A

This roughly circular, quite shallow, and flat-bottomed fire pit (3 ft.Ø) dates from the same occupation as Features 2B and 3B, being covered by and partly crosscutting the wind-blown sand IC_1. Its cultural inventory is poor: 8 flint chips, 5 sherdlets, and 2 textile-impressed sherds, except for 99 fire-cracked rocks. There were 10 small unidentifiable bone fragments (1.6 g.) of which 5 were calcined. The charcoal included wood from 2 different tree species (Table 38). The feature in turn is crosscut by Feature 6 on the north and borders on Feature 5 on the south side.

Feature Number 5--SE corner of SE 5 x 5, 10 x 10A

This is another feature of the paleosoil occupation level. Having become suspicious of a concentration of cultural material in this corner of the unit, we excavated the wind-blown sand with special care. On the 5th square sheet we picked up the outlines of a rectangular fire pit (4 by 2 ft.) with a shallow round bottom. The cultural material within the hearth itself was poor: 8 small flint chips, 49 fire-cracked rocks, and the charcoal containing wood from 3 tree species (Table 38). This gave us, however, a clue to the concentration of cultural material above. After short-time use, Number 5 was abandoned. Later occupants (i.e., the people of Features 2B, 3B, and 4) used the shallow depression in the sand to discard their trash (pot sherds, flint chips, and fire-cracked rock).

Feature Number 7--E side, S 5 x 5, 400 E 480

First in short time use as a fire pit after the sand had begun to accumulate: [charcoal from 6 tree species (Table 38), 152 fire-cracked rocks, slight discoloration of surrounding soil] the feature took over trash pit functions at the time Feature 3B was in use. This accounts for the large number of flint chips (68) and pottery (6 rim, 157 body sherds) in the small circular pit. According to the rim sherds, the minimum vessel count for this Early Late Woodland trash pit should be 3, but the many different kinds of surface treatments among the body sherds suggest a much higher number. The ceramics are closely related t[o] those in Feature 3B, occasionally permitting a perfect fit of 2 o[r] more sherds. Unfortunately, the very high acidity of the feature removed any organic traces except for a few tiny calcined bone fragments. Unidentifiable seeds discovered slightly above the feature must be written off to some parsimonious rodent.

Feature Number 8--NE corner, N 5 x 5, 400 E 480

Damaged on one side by the historical pit Number 11 and on th[e] other withdrawing into the wall, the round-bottomed circular pit of Feature 8 (4 ft. diameter, 1.3 ft. deep) can only be interprete[d] as a trash pit, belonging to the same occupation level as Features 1, 2A, 3A, and 5. The pit showed up first on square sheet below the wind-blown sand and reached fairly deeply into the sterile IIC_1. The cultural material is not very revealing, consisting of 20 flint chips of small size and 20 fire-cracked rocks. As in the case of Feature 7, very high pH destroyed unburnt bones and vegetal material.

Feature Number 9--S 1/2, S 5 x 5, 400 E 480

The feature consists of two non-contemporaneous hearths, the boundary between which has been obscured by rodents who seem to have freely communicated between them in the upper levels. Since we were not able to separate the cultural material of Features 9A and 9B above square sheet Number 4 due to the lack of a clear boundary above this level, only the material from the profile and below this square sheet can be associated with either one of the pits. On square sheet 4 they both appeared as clearly distinct, circular, dark discolorations within the sterile subsoil, while the profiles separated them according to their respective occupation floors.

Feature 9A turned out to be a fire pit of the paleosoil occupation level, a dark-colored round-bottomed pit of roughly circular shape, 5 feet in diameter and 1 foot deep, within the IIA_1 horizon. It is partly crosscut by the younger Feature 9B, while its west part is obscured by the west wall of the unit. After the pit served its function as a hearth (fire-cracked rocks, reddened sand, and ash), it slowly filled with the wind-blown sand and cultural debris of a later occupation, possibly from the time Feature 9B was in use.

Feature 9B is a Late Woodland fire pit of the same occupation as Features 2B, B, 4 and 7, flat-bottomed and of cylindrical shape, five feet in diameter. It contains a small amount of core fragments and large waste flakes, a few fire-cracked rocks and some pottery (1 rim, 4 body sherds). None of the uncharred remains survived due to the very high acidity of the features.

Feature Number 10—Middle, N 1/2, 400 E 480

Because of its poor cultural inventory (10 flint chips, 18 fire-cracked rocks), this irregular-shaped, round-bottomed feature seems to have served only for a short time as a hearth during the paleosoil occupation: concentration of fire-cracked rock in the bottom, some wood charcoal (Table 38), and discolored surrounding sands. Afterwards the depression of the pit filled with sand and cultural debris of the Late Woodland occupation. The outlines of the depression above square sheet 4 are not recognizable except as a concentration of cultural debris within the windblown sand. The high acidity of the ashy soil of the hearth prevented preservation of uncharred organic materials. The feature is partly crosscut by Feature 11.

Feature Number 11—NW 1/2, N 5 x 5, 400 E 480

The farmer went to the root of his problems again by excavating this large-sized pit (maximum dimensions within unit: 7 ft. long, 3 ft. wide, 4 ft. deep) around a pine stump in the west part of our unit. After burning the stump thoroughly, he added some branches to the debris on the pit bottom. Some of this buried wood was still undecayed. Then he systematically refilled it, as evidenced by shovel bedding, without disturbing much of the surrounding stratigraphy.

Feature Number 12—SW 1/2, S 5 x 5, 400 E 480

Except for a concentration of fire-cracked rocks, this dark discoloration within the IIC_1 sand is sterile. It might be the oldest fire pit in the units 400 E 480 and 10 X 10A. However, the historical pit Number 11 destroyed most of it forever, and the profiles remained inconclusive about its stratigraphic position.

Feature Number 13—S 5 x 10, 400 E 480

A hearth of the second Terminal Archaic horizon belongs to the same occupation level as Feature 16 to the northeast, and might actually be contemporary with it. It is a roughly circular flat bottom pit with a 2-foot diameter, rich in cultural material and organic matter. It shows up clearly as a dark discoloration within the IIC_1 horizon. The majority of the 159 flint chips within the feature are small use and retouch chips and larger flakes of bifacial retouch although there is a strong minority of core fragments and core-struck flakes. Six hundred and fifty fire-cracked rocks (15 lbs.) of all sizes attest to the function of the feature. The charcoal is made up of wood from 7 tree species, besides bark, acorns, and a few unidentifiable charred seeds (Table 38). Among the 5 pieces of tiny calcined bone, some fish bone can be recognized. On the feature rim, made up of reddish stained sand, a drill was discovered. The post mold slightly to the north of the feature might be part of some structure, related to Features 13 and 16.

Feature Number 14—SW 5 x 5, 490 E 490

This is a hearth belonging to the Terminal Archaic I occupation floor. It is irregular in shape with a flat bottom 3 feet in diameter, that slopes from northeast to southwest. The 48 flint chips in the feature are characterized by a high percentage of flakes of bifacial retouch. Exotic flint is absent and cortex is rare. Five pounds of fire-cracked rocks filled the bottom of the hearth, while the charcoal contained wood from 9 different tree species (Table 38).

Feature Number 15—W 1/2, NW 5 x 5, 490 E 490

In the same stratigraphical position as Feature 14, Feature 15 is a deep circular hearth with a round bottom (4 ft. diameter), dug into the IIA horizon. One half of the pit is contained in the west wall of the unit. It was relatively poor in cultural material, and contained 12 flint chips and 3.5 pounds of heat spalled rock. Devoid of charred bone, 6 tree species could be singled out in the charcoal (Table 38). Considerable heat must have been generated by its fire as can be seen in the discoloring of the surrounding soil and the cindering of much of the wood charcoal. A post mold just beneath the pit should be related to Feature 16.

Feature Number 16—largely NE 5 x 5, 490 E 490

This feature is the most interesting and enigmatic of our series. It is a circular, roughly conical, flat-bottomed pit of large size, 5.6 feet in diameter and 1.5 feet deep. Its presence was first suspected when we noted a concentration of cultural waste in the northeast part of this unit. Finally we discovered the top of the hearth, below the top of the paleosoil, as a dark discoloration of ashy character. The bottom of this ash concentration was made up of a mixture of red ochre, tiny cindered bone fragments (250), fire-cracked rocks, charcoal, and bark. The red ochre was also traceable in dense concentration around the margins of the bottom, where again it was intermixed with bone. This matrix included a first or second molar, not yet erupted, of a young individual, leading to the suspicion that the whole pit might represent a red ochre cremation burial. Although fitting chronologically, many supporting data would have to be collected from the site before such a guess could be validated. Conditions for the preservation of bone in the feature were extremely poor, due to very high acidity and intensely hot fire that caused the surrounding sands to become mottled, and cindered much of the charcoal and bone. The heat of the fire is also evident in the flint assemblage: high percentage of core pieces, block fracture flakes, and heat spalls. Together with hearth number 13, this is the only feature in the unit containing exotic flint, including a medial fragment of a projectile point. A total of 820 fire-cracked rocks was found above, within, and below the red ochre, while the charcoal yielded wood from 11 different tree species, bark, and a few unidentifiable seeds (Table 38). The 2 post molds mentioned above (cf. Features 13 and 15) seem to point to some associated structure. After the feature had served its function, debris accumulated in the remaining depression from the subsequent occupation (Features 14, 15). We hope that future analysis of this area of the site will solve some of the enigma around Feature 16.

Feature Number 17—396.5 E 515

The youngest feature of the unit, Feature 17 is a small flat lense of circular shape, slightly below the A_1 horizon 3 feet in diameter. Its cultural inventory includes 219 flint chips of high mean weight (1.2 g.) and some very large flakes (8 per cent). The lense contained 1 textile-impressed sherd and 40 fire-cracked rocks. Charcoal in Feature 17 consisted entirely of burnt bark.

Feature Number 18—5 x 5 B+C, 395 E 510

This trenchlike pit crosscuts the unit in a north-south direction, lensing out toward the south and expanding in depth to the north. Its top is covered by several inches of paleosoil. Eight hundred sixty-two fire-cracked rocks (32 lbs.), charcoal from 4 tree species, (Table 38), and 17 small pieces of calcined bone, as well as large areas of soil discolored by fire, indicate that the pit served for a long time as a hearth. One thousand thirty-six chips in the feature derive from use-chipping, marginal, and bifacial retouch. The mean weight of the chips is low (0.6 g.), and the percentage of large flakes is very small (2.4 per cent).

Feature Number 19—S 1/4, 5 x 5 C, 395 E 510

Located below horizon IIB, this hearth should be the oldest feature on the site. It contains some 8.6 pounds of fire-cracked rock and 111 flint chips, the mean weight of which is low (0.7 g). Some sheet mica pieces were discovered in the feature's ash. The soil is of low pH. Burnt bone, bark, and charcoal from 7 tree species (Table 38) make up the rest of the assemblage.

Feature Numbers 20-23—5 x 5 D, 395 E 510

The ultimate nature of these 4 dark discolorations in the east part of this excavation unit could not be determined with certainty. They were covered by several inches of paleosoil IIA_1.

The disturbances are clearly cultural in nature as can be seen from their content of cultural material. The flint assemblage of these pits (235 flakes) is marked by a high percentage of large flakes. A Pomranky-like point (Plate VII*a*) was associated with Feature 20. No charcoal was discovered in the pits and the prohibitively low pH removed any organic material. Most likely these discolorations are only trash lenses associated with Feature 19. A large number of fire-cracked rocks were strewn about (820-10.8 lbs.).

Feature Number 24—NE corner, 5 x 5 D, 365 E 480

A hearth rich in cultural material, Feature 24 belongs to the early Late Woodland occupation level within IC_1. It is a large, circular, round bottomed pit 5 feet in diameter and of 2 feet average depth. Lacking any pottery, the feature is rich in fire-cracked rocks (1,179-15 lbs.) and flint chips (364). As in Feature 17, average weight per chip is 1.2 grams and the percentage of large flint chips is high (13.5 per cent). We also observed a high percentage of nodule fragments and core-derived flakes together with a large number of flakes retaining part of their cortex. Probably this feature was associated with a flint workshop area. Within the charcoal, wood from 4 different tree species was observed (Table 38), innumerable pieces of bark, and 29 burnt bone fragments. The pH of the feature is very slightly acid.

Feature Number 25—west of Feature Number 24, 5 x 5D, 365 E 480

A burned out tree stump of *Carya* sp., containing charcoal and bark.

Feature Number 26—near south wall, 5 x 5 D, 365 E 480

This feature is a small ashy lense within the IIA_1 horizon. It contained 4 small colored bone pieces, 50 fire-cracked rocks of small size, 6 flint chips from use or marginal retouch, and some cindered charcoal fragments. The pH is very low.

Feature Number 27—in north wall, 5 x 5 C, 365 E 480

Feature 27 is a relatively small circular lense 2 feet in diameter and 8 inches deep, which is partly obscured by the north wall of the unit. It has been assigned to the Terminal Archaic II occupation floor. The flint assemblage is largely derived from bifacial retouch (67 per cent) of low mean weight and small mean size. The charcoal, mostly cindered, yielded wood from 2 tree species (Table 38), much bark and 3 small pieces of charred bone.

Feature Number 28—5 x 5 B + C, north wall, 365 E 480

On the same level with Feature 27 is the hearth Feature 28, a deep circular pit 3 feet in diameter with a round bottom. It contains a rich cultural assemblage, including 506 fire-cracked rocks (16.7 lbs.) and 258 flint chips. Among the latter, flakes of bifacial retouch are dominant (67 per cent). Very likely the living floor surrounding the feature served as a workshop area. For this same reason, the mean weight of chips is higher than in other Terminal Archaic features. Two tree species (Table 38) and bark, as well as 16 small pieces of burned bone make up the charcoal. The pH is very acid.

Feature Number 29—central 5 x 5 B, 365 E 480

This has a large dark discoloration within the wind-blown sand. Culturally sterile, it might have served as a trash pit.

Feature Number 30—S side, 5 x 5 B, 365 E 480

For a change this circular pit with flat bottom belongs to the Terminal Archaic living floor on top of the paleosoil horizon. Its rim overlaps that of Feature 28. Relatively poor in cultural material, its flint assemblage (29) resembles that of Feature 19. One hundred sixty-one fire-cracked rocks, cindered charcoal, and 14 pieces of charred bone attest to use as a hearth. It is a low pH in ashy soil.

Feature Number 31—test pit number 4

This is another pine stump with which a former farmer tried to trap us. He managed to remove most of its roots before refilling the pit but apparently missed a few. Only after we had encountered Features 6 and 11 were we able to account for the pieces of undecayed wood left on the bottom of this large-sized pit.

III

LITHIC INDUSTRIES

DEBITAGE

Introduction

Next to the fire-cracked rocks, the chipped-stone assemblage represents the largest category of cultural material from the site. Within an excavated area of 450 square feet, some 27,000 pieces of chipped stone were uncovered with a total weight of 19.5 kilograms. This concentration indicates a density of cultural material that is unequaled by other sites in Michigan, where similar recovery procedures have been employed. It corroborates the intense occupation of the site, suggested on the basis of the high number of occupational disturbances. At first glance such dense concentrations of chippage might be interpreted as a chipping station. A close analysis of the assemblage shows this interpretation is not warranted. Instead the distribution and character of the assemblage suggest that through time and space different cultural causes contributed to its accumulation. In fact, the specific assemblages of certain areas within the site allow the construction of models which will help us to predict the nature of the cultural activities which went on at the time of their deposition.

Nature of the Sample

Raw Material (Bayport Chert)

To a much larger degree than at other sites in this area, the Indians at the Butterfield site relied on Bayport chert. Of the total of 27,000 flint chips, more than 99 per cent are derived from Bayport chert nodules (Table 4). The Upper Grand Rapids series crops out a few miles to the north of Pinconning in Arenac County within easy reach of the site. These outcrops are rich in nodular Bayport chert. Compared to the other exotic cherts found at the site, Bayport chert is of poor quality. Its color ranges from whitish-gray to dirty blue with intermediate shades

TABLE 4

CHARACTERISTICS OF DIFFERENT PARTS OF BAYPORT CHERT NODULES

(Measurements determined on fifty flakes in each case)

	Color Range	Specific Gravity	Diaphaneity	Luster	Texture	Impurities	Banding
Cortex	10 YR 6-8/1-3; 2.5 YR 7-8/0-2	2.25	Dull	Dull	very rough	impure	absent
Intermediate . .	2.5 YR 4-5/0; 7.5 YR 3.5-5/0	2.46	Dull	Dull to shiny	rough to smooth	small impure	rare
Center	10 YR 5-7/1-1.5; 10 YR 3.5-5/0	2.56	Dull to translucent	Shiny	smooth	small impure	absent

occurring in varying frequencies throughout the site. The cortex color varies between dirty white and dirty yellowish-brown with frequent greyish patina. It is of very rough texture and contains cavities which sometimes exceed one-fourth inch in depth. The luster of Bayport chert is dull while diaphaneity is low or absent. Although fossils and large inclusions are absent, the raw material is rich in small impurities. Banding is rare. When present the bands are concentric and do not exceed a few millimeters in diameter. The specific gravity varies from 2.1 to 2.5 depending on the part of the cortex (Table 4). Irregular and impure texture as well as frequent "microfacies" changes within the nodules make Bayport chert relatively hard to work with compared with the exotic flint. Many tool fragments on the site can be explained simply by some irregularity in the selected raw material which caused a break before the tool was finished. This disadvantage, however, was easily balanced for the aboriginal inhabitants by the easy availability of the outcrops in Arenac County.

Dustin already noted that Bayport nodules were small in size—never exceeding 8 inches in diameter and usually being not larger than 6 inches across. At the Butterfield site this was nicely demonstrated by the determination of nodule sizes from the cortex of decortication flakes. An analysis of 150 large decortication flakes by stratigraphic levels showed that the size of the nodules stayed well below the upper limit, the mean size being 2.51 inches across. In our data we were able to observe that during Terminal Archaic times the knappers selected for smaller nodules while this selection seems to have been relaxed during Late Woodland times. The metrical data of our Bayport nodule size are presented below (Table 5).

TABLE 5

	N	ΣX	ΣX^2	$\bar{X}$	S
Plow Zone	50	130.5	342.4	2.61	.26
Late Woodland	50	141.2	399.6	2.82	.20
Terminal Archaic	50	106.1	226.0	2.12	.19

x = Nodule diameter

We attempted to use flakes from different nodules to get more valid means for the respective nodule sizes. This was accomplished on the basis of differences in cortex characteristics such as texture and color.

We attempted to break down the total Bayport assemblage into several descriptive categories. Thus, the flint was sorted into types on the basis of color, luster, diaphaneity, texture, impurities, cortex appearance, and specific gravity. This was only possible by eliminating borderline cases between two type groups thus making the type appear more typical than it really was. Subjective decisions were involved in more than 50 per cent of the cases, and at the end it turned out that more than 30 per cent of our sample consisted of borderline cases. When the remaining 70 per cent were checked against pieces containing more than one descriptive attribute within a single category, it was found that these cases were quite common. In addition we recognized that different parts of the same tool found in adjacent areas of the same stratigraphic unit had assumed quite distinctive attributes due to differential soil action. Finally the analysis of cores and nodule fragments convinced us that all our types were present in different parts of the same nodule. What other Bayport types were present could be assigned to specific soil activity: pinkish flint was found mostly in fire-burned sand and brownish flint was found in areas of the site with ground water activity. Thus, it was impossible to use the distribution of different grades of Bayport chert at the Butterfield site for reconstructing the vertical and horizontal stratigraphy, such as has been done by Fitting at the Holcombe site (Fitting, 1966). Significant differences, however, were found to occur between flint chips from different parts of the nodule (Table 4).

The best quality Bayport chert stems from the center and the area immediately surrounding the center of the nodule, while the poorest is found around the cortex. The Indians at the Butterfield site, however, were not very discriminating and selected flakes more for their shape and size than for the quality of the material. Apparently the aboriginal occupants carried the chert in nodular form to the site and worked it there, whenever it was needed. The absence of unexhausted cores and nodules, and the small average size of flakes suggest the utilization of all parts of the nodule. The Terminal Archaic and Late Woodland people used the same source for their raw material. This is astonishing since right across the river from the Butterfield site there is a Dustin site where the people relied on quite a different source: chert of high quality, smooth texture, translucent diaphaneity, and shiny luster.

Exotic Chipped-Stone Raw Material (Table 6A and B)

Numbering only .85 per cent by number and .68 per cent by weight of the total assemblage, the exotic chipped stone raw material on the site does not tell us much about the flint industry of the Butterfield site inhabitants. However, it can be utilized to delineate the extent of occupational units and to support hypotheses about the cultural development on the site. The absence of decortication flakes, nodules, and core fragments of exotic chipped-stone material suggests that much of it was imported to the site in the form of blanks or finished tools. The majority of the exotic chipped stone consisted of resharpening and use chips and finished tools. The group of 237 pieces can be broken down into several types, the sources of which are unknown.

Type A.--A highly colored flint of high luster, translucent diaphaneity, and smooth surface; this type accounts for more than 59 per cent of the exotic chipped stone assemblage (Table 7). The color, always mottled, ranges from greyish-yellow to dark red, banding usually being absent. On the site, the distribution of this type is limited to the Terminal Archaic horizons and the plow zone. The same kind of flint makes up most of the raw material of the adjacent Dustin site and it is suggested that what is found on the site derives from that source.

Type B.--This type is found in Late Woodland levels and loci with disturbed stratigraphy. It is characterized by its dark gray color and intensive banding. The luster is high and the diaphaneity slightly translucent to dull. It accounts for 15 per cent of the assemblage (Table 7).

The remaining 26 per cent of the exotic chipped-stone consist of chipped slate, shale, quartzite, diorite, and a variety of

TABLE 6

A. EXOTIC FLINT DEBITAGE DISTRIBUTION - GENERAL SITE
(Weights in Grams)

Unit	Late Woodland				Terminal Archaic				Plow Zone				Total	
	No.	Per Cent	Wt.	Per Cent	No.	Per Cent	Wt.	Per Cent	No.	Per Cent	Wt.	Per Cent	No.	Wt.
10 X 10A . .	5	0.19	0.6	0.48	10	1.96	4.1	0.73	43	2.21	11.9	1.14	58	16.6
400 E 480 . .	6	1.10	2.3	0.03	7	1.88	2.4	1.91	31	2.03	8.6	0.60	44	13.3
490 E 490 . .	2	1.07	0.5	0.30	10	3.16	10.7	6.06	10	0.81	6.7	0.80	22	17.9
395 E 510 . .	7	0.81	10.7	1.70	9	0.50	8.3	0.64	27	0.78	14.2	0.54	43	33.2
365 E 480 . .	5	0.43	1.5	0.16	7	0.24	10.8	0.62	44	1.04	32.7	1.36	56	45.0
Total . . .	25	0.47	15.6	0.38	43	0.73	36.3	1.00	155	1.25	74.1	0.88	233	126.0
													.85 per cent	.68 per cent

B. EXOTIC FLINT DEBITAGE DISTRIBUTION - FEATURES ONLY
(Weights in Grams)

	Late Woodland		Terminal Archaic	
	Number	Weight	Number	Weight
10 X 10A . . .	2	0.2	...	...
400 E 480 . . .	...	...	...	...
490 E 490 . . .	...	...	5	3.6
395 E 410 . . .	...	...	7	6.3
365 E 480 . . .	...	...	...	...
Total	2 (0.29 per cent)	0.2 (0.03 per cent)	12 (0.56 per cent)	9.9 (0.64 per cent)

TABLE 7

DISTRIBUTION BY TYPE OF EXOTIC CHIPPED STONE

(Feature and Nonfeature)

	A		B		N-(A+B)		Total
	Number	Per Cent	Number	Per Cent	Number	Per Cent	
Plow Zone	97	63	15	10	43	27	155
Late Woodland.	1	4	18	66	8	30	27
Terminal Archaic . . .	41	74	2	3	12	23	55
Total.	139	59	35	15	63	26	237

colored flint, none of which assume significant proportions within the total assemblage.

Weight and Size Correlations of the Chipped-Stone Assemblage

The mean size and weight in a chipped-stone assemblage seems to be trivial data and devoid of cultural meaning. Too many factors seem to control their values and the procedure for recovering the data, especially the mean size, is extremely time consuming. Tipped off by the highly significant increase in nodule size from Terminal Archaic to Late Woodland, we checked to see if this might bear any consequences on the mean size of flint chips derived from the nodules. We devised a simple method of sorting the assemblage into size classes from 3 inches to less than one-fourth of an inch.

The chips were passed in their maximum dimension through a set of successively smaller screens (3", 2", 1.5", 1.25", 1", .75", .5", < .5"). At the end, the number of flint chips retained by the different size meshes were counted, the number per screen size and the figures added up. The mean of these measurements by occupation horizon is shown in Table 8. Dividing these values by the number of measured flint chips we arrive at a relative figure of mean size, which can be compared from occupation horizon to occupation horizon and should come rather close to the true mean size of the assemblages. Our assumption turned out to be correct. We can observe a highly significant increase of mean size from the Terminal Archaic to the Late Woodland assemblage.

This size increase is again mirrored by the increase in mean weight in the Late Woodland assemblage (Table 9) which is even more drastically observed in the Late Woodland features.

TABLE 8

CHIPPED STONE ASSEMBLAGE

Size Correlations (Nonfeature)

	Late Woodland	Terminal Archaic
N	5284	5871
S (size) . . .	3226"	2985"
X̄	.61"	.50"

TABLE 9

WEIGHT AND SIZE CORRELATIONS OF THE CHIPPED-STONE ASSEMBLAGE

A. Weight Distribution by Time Horizon - Nonfeature (In Grams)

	Plow Zone and Disturbed Provenience			Late Woodland Provenience			Terminal Archaic Provenience		
	N	Wt.	X̄	N	Wt.	X̄	N	Wt.	X̄
10 X 10A . .	22,110	1,434.5	...	2,557	2,042.6	...	532	343.2	...
400 E 480 . .	1,356	1,042.8	...	545	474.5	...	356	214.2	...
490 E 490 . .	1,230	827.3	...	186	164.6	...	316	176.5	...
395 E 510 . .	3,449	2,655.8	...	854	621.6	...	1,779	1,296.0	...
365 E 480 . .	4,223	2,414.7	...	1,142	902.5	...	2,888	1,586.7	...
Total . . .	12,368	8,375.1	.68	5,284	4,205.8	.79	5,871	3,616.6	.62

B. Weight Distribution by Time Horizon - Feature (In Grams)

	Number	Weight	X̄
Late Woodland	679	764.7	1.12
Terminal Archaic II . . .	2021	1,444.6	0.71
Terminal Archaic I . . .	140	89.3	0.63
Total	2840	2,298.6	...

TABLE 10

MEAN NODULE SIZE, FLINT CHIP SIZE, AND FLINT CHIP WEIGHT AT THE BUTTERFIELD SITE

	Terminal Archaic		Late Woodland	
	X̄	Per Cent	X̄	Per Cent*
Nodule size (inches)	2.12"	100	2.82"	133
Flint chip size (inches) . . .	0.50"	100	0.61"	122
Flint chip weight (grams). .	0.62g	100	0.79g	120

*Of Terminal Archaic parameters.

Table 10 shows us clearly that the mean weight and size of flint chips increase significantly with the increased nodule size. The uniform recovery during the whole excavation and close control over the stratigraphy, and the size of the sample make it impossible that the observed increase could be due to sampling error or geologic activity such as settling of the lighter flint chips. It would be interesting to know if this size increase is a site-specific cultural factor, or if it can be generally observed in Terminal Archaic and Late Woodland assemblages. Although Fitting (n.d.) observes at the Schultz site a consistent decrease in mean size of flint chips from Early through Late Woodland, the mean weight of the Late Woodland chipped stone is practically identical to our figure (.798g.). Much more work will have to be done, however, before we can employ our site-specific observation for cross-cultural comparisons.

Types of Debitage

No patent method has yet been outlined for the cultural analysis of debitage applicable to any prehistoric site regardless of time and space. In this sense our model is not going to differ from anything that has been published so far. Many industry-specific methods of analysis have recently been presented, proving that every industry has its own character, and the model which is used in the analysis of one industry will not be of much help in the analysis of another assemblage. Several analytical procedures were tested by trial and error before a specific model could be derived for the Butterfield site. Many of the recently published models had to be rejected because the number of descriptive categories was too large and the categories themselves too closely defined to account for the range of variation in the morphology of flint chips, as observed at the Butterfield site. I am particularly suspect of models that manage to assign a closely defined place within the chipping process leading from nodule to artifact to every flint chip discovered on the site, without stating how much subjective judgment went into each flint chip's assignment to a specific category and without defining where the border between categories X and Y was drawn.

Thus we noticed that there was no criterion to differentiate flakes of bifacial retouch from those struck from acute-angled convex cores such as in Plate I*b*. Chips from tool use, resharpening, marginal retouch, and preparation of the striking platform have the same morphology. Again, a block fracture flake (Fitting, DiVisscher, and Wahla, 1966) might look identical to a broken blank, a core fragment, or to a large core-derived flake, the striking platform of which was broken off.

Observed Categories of Debitage

Four criteria should determine the utility of any descriptive model of debitage: (1) the model should be economical to facilitate analysis and interpretation of large assemblages; (2) every flint chip should find its place within the descriptive model; (3) there should be no overlap between descriptive categories; and (4) the categories should have cultural significance in order to permit the interpretation of a cultural assemblage.

These considerations led to the breakdown of the Butterfield assemblage into four categories, which in turn are subdivided each into two subcategories. This model, of course, is site specific and does not boast general utility, although since it is objective, it permits duplication.

Debitage of Category A consists of chert fragments derived from natural agencies such as heat-fracturing and frost-cracking. It also includes fragments of nodules that have been shattered by hard hammer blows, and flakes lacking a striking platform which cannot be assigned to classes B and C. Debitage of this category is marked by the lack of a striking platform and bulb of percussion, and by its amorphous shape making distinction between inner and outer face impossible.

Category B is defined as flakes struck from cores. They are characterized by an angle of around 90 degrees between striking platform and inner face. The striking platform, if preserved, is usually prepared with a few faceting blows. They are, in general, thicker than class C flakes. Comparative thickness measurements of 200 flakes of class B and 200 flakes of class C (with striking platforms) yielded a bimodal thickness distribution on the basis of which we were able to attribute flint chips without striking platforms to either one of these classes (Table 11).

In category C the angle between the outer face and the striking platform is highly acute; the flakes are thin, and their striking platform is usually prepared. The bulb of percussion is absent in most of the flakes of the C category. Fitting's term "flakes of bifacial retouch," has been adopted for this category, although it should be pointed out that the term might also include flakes from highly acute-angled convex cores. Flakes without striking platform are assigned to this class if they fit its thickness range as outlined below.

PLATE I

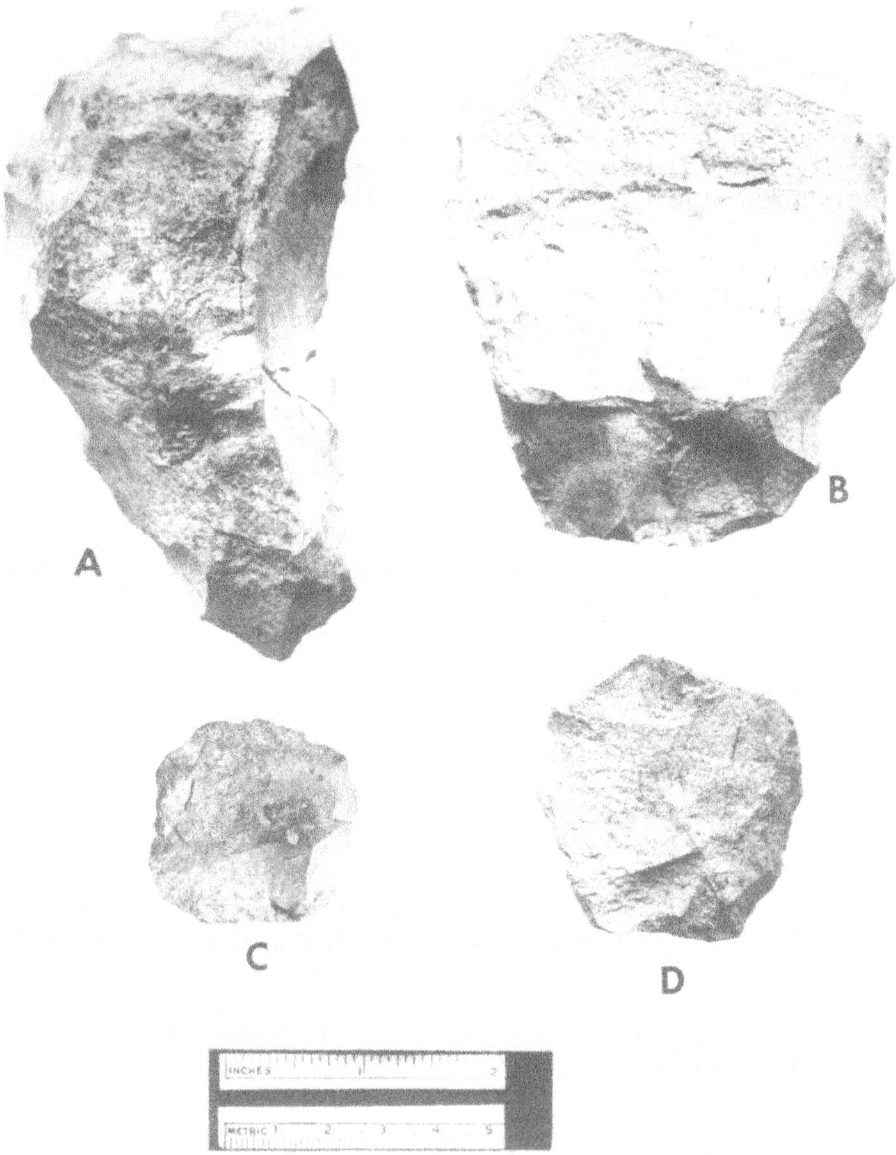

Planoconvex cores: *a, b,* true planoconvex cores. Face exposed is opposite striking platform; *c, d,* planoconvex core nuclei.

TABLE 11

CATEGORY B *vs.* CATEGORY C FLAKES

(N = 200 Each)

Category B: . . .	Angle at striking platform 70° - 90° Thickness (maximum) 0.2 - 1.5 Mean thickness 0.545
Category C: . . .	Angle at striking platform 60° Thickness (maximum) 0.15 - 0.7 Mean thickness 0.323

The last category includes all flakes of less than 0.5 cm. maximum extension. It consists of use, marginal retouch, resharpening chips, and those derived from the preparation of striking platforms. In addition, each of the categories was broken down into flakes with and without cortex.

The Cultural Significance of the Categories

Fitting (Fitting, DiVisscher, and Wahla, 1966) has demonstrated that most of his amorphous flakes were due to heat-fracturing. We might expect, however, that our category A flakes, slightly differently defined, are derived from both cultural and natural causes. Thus, cultural causes would include heat-fracturing and core shattering, while among the natural agencies contributing to this category we would expect frost-cracking and accidental breakage. Only a thorough analysis of the debitage at a given locus can provide an answer to the definite cause.

Category B will help us to define cache-pits and workshop areas, where the nodules were broken down to produce blank flakes. They could either serve as tools such as blades or secondary decortication flakes, or could be retained until they might be needed for the production of a tool.

Category C flakes are the result of bifacial retouch. As a consequence we might expect a high percentage of C flakes at loci where bifacial tools were manufactured.

The last category is expected to reach high percentage within specific assemblages where the tools were actually used, since this activity produces the use chips and resharpening chips that make up this category.

The presence or absence of cortex serves as an indicator as to the degree nodules were utilized on the site (instead of imported blanks), and of how far at any given locus at the site the workshop activity was removed from the nodule stage.

Since, however, we would expect all four categories to be present at any locus within the site, the interpretation of the debitage has to be correlated with other factors such as proximity of features, artifacts, or fauna. Only then will we be able to arrive at meaningful predictions of the specific activity performed at a given locus at the site.

The Vertical Distribution of Debitage

Analysis by cultural horizon suggests that no marked changes occurred in the composition of the debitage through time (Table 12). Thus, we should not expect any marked differences in workshop technology in our horizons. The relatively constant percentage of class A debitage in our horizons indicates just that on first sight. The observed mean weight of these flakes should be a function of their ages, the Terminal Archaic ones being lighter since they were subject to the natural forces causing block fracturing much longer. Accepting this assumption, however, we can no longer conclude that this category constituted the same percentage in the Late Woodland and Terminal Archaic assemblage at the time of deposition. The total weight of Category A should remain constant, while numerically it should increase markedly in time. Since the opposite is true, we have to conclude that the percentage of these flakes at time of deposition was much lower in the Terminal Archaic horizon than in the overlying assemblage Because many of these flakes are produced by the shattering of nodules, we can assume less reliance on nodules at starting points of tool production on the site in Terminal Archaic time than during later occupations.

This hypothesis finds support in the low percentage of category B debitage in the lower horizon. The relatively high total and mean weight of this category in the Terminal Archaic assemblage is explained by a higher percentage of blank flakes (larger) and fewer waste flakes resulting from striking a core (smaller).

The observed frequency of Class C flakes closely agrees with our expectations; no matter if the tool production on the site began with the preparation of cores from a nodule or with bifacial retouch on the blank, the same number of flakes of bifacial retouch would result. The higher mean weight of these flakes in the Late Woodland horizon is a corollary of the larger size of the utilized nodules.

Finally, we observe a marked decrease in the frequency of debitage of category D in time. This is the more remarkable

TABLE 12

VERTICAL DISTRIBUTION OF DEBITAGE BY TYPES - NONFEATURE
(Weights in Grams)

Category		All Flakes				Flakes With Cortex				Weight[3]	Weight[4]
		No.	Per Cent	Wt.	Per Cent	No.	Per Cent[1]	Wt.	Per Cent[2]		
Plow zone	A.	790	6.31	1,847.1	22.05	85	10.74	383.3	20.07	2.33	4.50
	B.	927	7.48	2,036.9	24.33	67	7.22	287.5	14.11	2.19	4.29
	C.	6,409	51.77	3,826.3	45.68	112	1.73	231.3	6.30	0.59	2.06
	D.	4,252	34.44	665.6	7.94	. . .	. . .	. . .	. . .	0.15	. . .
	Total . .	12,378	100.00	8,375.1	100.00	264	3.24	902.1	11.70	0.61	3.41
Late Woodland	A.	518	9.81	1,074.2	25.56	139	26.83	557.7	53.25	2.06	4.01
	B.	475	8.99	1,130.0	26.87	108	22.73	455.6	40.31	2.37	4.21
	C.	2,982	56.51	1,808.2	42.04	107	3.58	139.6	7.72	0.60	1.30
	D.	1,309	24.69	192.8	5.53	. . .	. . .	. . .	. . .	0.14	. . .
	Total . .	5,284	100.00	4,205.2	100.00	354	8.90	1,152.9	28.03	0.61	3.25
Terminal Archaic	A.	470	8.00	897.4	24.81	161	34.25	314.7	35.07	1.47	1.95
	B.	376	6.40	913.2	25.25	94	27.12	323.5	35.41	2.42	3.44
	C.	3,295	56.12	1,546.6	42.76	136	4.12	162.7	10.52	0.47	1.19
	D.	1,730	29.48	259.4	7.18	. . .	. . .	. . .	. . .	0.14	. . .
	Total . .	5,871	100.00	3,616.6	100.00	391	9.44	800.9	23.85	0.51	2.04

Note.—[1]Percentage of cortex flakes by number within total number of category; [2]percentage within total figure for category; [3]mean weight, all flakes within category; [4]mean weight, cortex flakes within category.

since the larger mean size of Late Woodland flakes would suggest an increase in category D rather than a decrease. Three hypotheses might be formulated to account for this phenomeon: (1) tool use tended to be less concentrated on the site during Late Woodland occupation; (2) different activities performed during the Late Woodland occupation led to a decrease in this category; and (3) different retouch techniques were employed during the later occupation.

The analysis of the flakes retaining part of the nodular cortex supports our conclusions. Since cortex is structurally the weakest part of a nodule, we would expect cortex flakes to increase in amount and decrease in mean weight (total weight remaining constant) as time since deposition passes, due to the weight of overlying deposits and the actions of frost and moisture. In categories A and B the mean weight of flakes with cortex increases considerably while their share by number within these categories decreases from Terminal Archaic to Late Woodland time. The total weight percentage of these flakes within category A and B, however, increases as much as 20 per cent at the same time, lending additional support to our hypothesis that the Terminal Archaic occupants favored imported blanks rather than nuclei as raw material for tool production on the site. These blanks must have been cruder during Terminal Archaic times than during the later occupations, since cortex flakes in category C of the Terminal Archaic assemblages reach a significantly higher weight percentage than in the overlying horizon.

Vertical Distribution of Debitage in the Features

The observed percentages of our categories in the two assemblages agree well with our expectations (Table 13). We observe the most marked changes in the weight percentages of categories B and D. Category B increases its share of the total weight by more than 50 per cent in the Late Woodland horizon implying an increased reliance on imported nodules as opposed to the imported blanks in the Terminal Archaic horizon. Category D, on the other hand, decreases in its weight percentages by 75 per cent in the Late Woodland assemblages, a trend which was previously observed in lower magnitude in the nonfeature assemblages. Thus, we cannot explain this difference by a shift of activities producing category D flakes, such as marginal retouch, resharpening, and use-chipping, from the features to other areas of the site. Since we know that in both assemblages the tools themselves were manufactured on the site and since we do not

TABLE 13

VERTICAL DISTRIBUTION OF DEBITAGE IN THE FEATURES

By Types

Category		All Flakes				Flakes With Cortex Only				Weight[3]	Weight[4]
		No.	Per Cent	Wt.	Per Cent	No.	Per Cent[1]	Wt.	Per Cent[2]		
Terminal Archaic	A.	200	9.25	451.4	29.62	53	26.73	220.7	48.18	2.25	4.15
	B.	203	9.40	398.9	26.18	36	17.89	127.8	32.03	1.96	3.55
	C.	1,066	49.33	559.1	36.68	47	4.41	50.9	9.11	0.52	1.08
	D.	692	32.02	114.5	7.52	. . .	. . .	. . .	. . .	0.16	. . .
	Total	2,161	100.00	1,523.9	100.00	136	6.33	399.4	26.22	0.70	2.86
Late Woodland	A.	54	7.93	193.5	25.30	17	32.30	116.6	60.29	3.58	6.86
	B.	80	11.85	301.6	39.44	25	31.95	131.6	43.63	3.78	5.36
	C.	442	65.08	255.2	33.37	21	4.69	30.0	11.75	0.57	1.43
	D.	103	15.14	14.4	1.89	. . .	. . .	. . .	. . .	0.13	. . .
	Total . .	679	100.00	764.7	100.00	63	9.27	278.2	36.37	1.12	4.41

Note.—[1]Percentage of cortex flakes by number with total number of category; [2]percentage within total figure for category; [3]mean weight, all flakes within category; [4]mean weight, cortex flakes within category.

observe any difference in marginal retouch technique (cf. tool analysis), two alternative explanations are open to us: (1) the amount of marginal retouch chips remained constant, but due to different activities performed on the site, more use and resharpening chips were produced on the site; or (2) the amount of use and resharpening chips remained constant, but different tools were produced at the site, resulting in the observed differences in category D. The tool analysis will help us decide between the two alternatives. Two more factors support our nodule versus blank hypothesis in the feature assemblages: (a) simplifying our four category models to two categories--the first made up of chips produced by chipping a nodule down to get blanks (including former categories A and B) and the second consisting of chips produced by modifying a blank into a tool (Category C and D), we see that the weight percentage of the former category is about 10 per cent higher in the Late Woodland horizon implying decreased reliance on blanks; and (b) the flakes with cortex have a much higher frequency in the Late Woodland horizon than in the underlying assemblage, implying increased reliance on imported nodules.

Conclusions

On the basis of our debitage analysis, we can conclude that we are dealing with two distinct assemblages. In the Terminal Archaic assemblage we noted a heavy reliance on small nodules and blanks as first stage of tool manufacture on the site. During Late Woodland times, the occupants utilized mainly large nodules for this purpose. The raw material consists almost entirely of Bayport chert due to the proximity of the source area. Exotic raw material was imported to the site in the form of blanks and decreases in importance during Late Woodland times. Apart from the shift from blanks to nodules, no technological evolution was observed on the site. Finally, the analysis of the debitage suggests the use of different tools on the site in the two horizons as a function of different activities performed on the site. The horizontal distribution of debitage will be discussed in the context of the horizontal distribution of cultural material.

A. Chipped-stone Tools

Introduction

A total of 215 flint artifacts and 21 cores were recovered during our excavation (Table 14). This sounds like an impressive sample worthy of statistical examination. However, once the artifacts and cores from the plow-disturbed horizons, the utilized flakes, and the tool fragments are removed from the sample, the remaining tools--spread out over five excavation units and belonging to two time horizons--do not seem to constitute a statistically reliable sample. Therefore, I decided to determine the functional aspects of the tools before beginning to analyze the stylistic features. This would enable me to incorporate into my sample unaltered flakes and fragments that could not be put into a pigeonhole on the basis of their morphology alone. After the functional categories had been defined and its members were identified, I could apply the description and analysis of the tool sample in terms of larger and more meaningful categories.

The following method of functional analysis was employed. The supposed working edge of a tool, a fragment of a tool, or a flake was covered with a solution of silver nitrate in ether to bring out fine surface irregularities in sharper contrast. Then, the edge was analyzed under a high power microscope for traces of use, such as use striae, use polish, or minute marginal use retouch. The traces, if present, could be interpreted in terms of the activity performed with the tool.

This method enabled me to select those unretouched flakes that had actually been used from those whose "utilized-flake" appearance was merely due to natural causes. Good results were obtained on tools that had been utilized for a short time only, so that use traces could be distinctly recognized. This category includes most of the utilized flakes and fragments which constitute that part of the assemblage that normally would be the most difficult to assign to functional categories on the basis of their morphology alone. No problem was encountered when a tool was utilized for a long period of time for the same activity. Borderline cases, showing signs of use as side scraper and knife were assigned to one category on the basis of dominant morphology and use striae. This group, however, represents less than 5 per cent of all tools. Possibly, this method is biased against utilized flakes of poor quality chert, but since this raw material constitutes only a small percentage of the intentionally retouched tools, the distortion introduced by this bias should be minimal.

Table 14, following, represents the outcome of this analysis. The tool categories are analyzed in terms of their subgroups, characteristic features, vertical distribution, and ecological importance. Reference to known "types" has been avoided whenever possible since the site is in an area in which the chronological significance of most well-known types has not yet been established.

TABLE 14

VERTICAL DISTRIBUTION OF FUNCTIONAL CATEGORIES

	Plow Zone	Late Woodland	Terminal Archaic	Total
Cores	15	1	5	21
Side-scrapers	21	21	12	54
End-scrapers	15	12	4	31
Projectile points	36	11	29	76
Blades	8	...	5	13
Knives	13	7	8	28
Drills	6	1	6	13
Total	114	53	69	236

This tool analysis should be a first step toward developing the distribution of these types in time and space. None of the extensive surface collections from the area of the site have been included in the analysis, since the sand ridge from which they stem covers a large area containing many different occupations. Their analysis at this point would add confusion instead of evidence. Only additional excavations in the area of the site could help to tie these surface collections into a stratigraphically-founded chronology.

Chipped-stone Tool Categories

Cores

Twenty-one cores were recognized in the chipped-stone assemblage at the Butterfield site. Unfortunately, only six of these were discovered *in situ*, the remainder deriving from the plow zone and historic features. The cores could be separated into three groups, all of which are reported from sites of a similar range in Michigan (Table 15).

TABLE 15

CORE CATEGORIES - VERTICAL DISTRIBUTION

	Plow Zone	Late Woodland	Terminal Archaic	Total
Amorphous cores	8	...	1	9
Plano-convex cores	3	...	4	7
Bipolar cores	4	1	...	5
Total	15	1	5	21
Per cent of tool kit	...	1.89	7.24	...

Amorphous cores (Fitting, 1965:53-5), also described as block cores (Binford and Papworth, 1963:83), owe their shape to the utilization of flake scars on the core as striking platforms for the removal of succeeding flakes (Fitting, n.d.). In our assemblage, they were found to be of small dimensions and displaying only one area of flake removal. Variations in shape and size are so large, that a further breakdown of this core category into subgroups might be expected with a larger sample.

Seven plano-convex cores and fragments could be identified. This category, as usually described, seems to define only the discarded nuclei of such cores, rather than the cores themselves. Support for this hypothesis is provided by the large-sized flakes derived from plano-convex cores, which greatly exceed the size of the nuclei found on the site. A good example of a true plano-convex core is provided in Plate I, *a-b*. It suggests that this core category is produced by splitting the nodule in the middle and removing the undesirable cortex. Then flakes are removed around the edges, using the flat face of the nodule as striking platform until the stage of the commonly described plano-convex core, alias nucleus, is obtained. Since its size prohibits removal of additional flakes, it is discarded, bearing little similarity in size and shape to its original dimensions (Plate I, *c, d*).

Five "bioplar cores" are present in the sample. A microscopic analysis of these suggested that they have not been utilized as tools, although this might have been the aim of their manufacturer.

A chi-square test performed on the frequency of cores as opposed to all other flint tools from the site does not lend support to the hypothesis that the change in frequency from Terminal Archaic to Late Woodland was due to factors other than chance ($p = < .9$). Therefore, no conclusions should be drawn about the frequency of cores in different horizons. It might be suspected that the high frequency of cores in the Terminal Archaic assemblage is due to sampling error only, on the basis of the conflicting evidence from the debitage, which is less likely to be influenced by this error. An alternative explanation might be that during the Terminal Archaic occupation workshop activities were performed around the hearth, while the Late Woodland occupants tried to keep them away from their immediate occupation area.

Scraping Tools

Side scraping Tools

The fifty-three side scraping tools can be described in just about as many tool categories suggesting that they were artifacts made on the spot whenever needed, and that stylistics did not carry much weight during the manufacturing process. Functional differentiation within this category is practically impossible. Therefore, the best way to deal with side scraping tools seems to be *Bordes' Typology* (1961), subdividing the scrapers on the basis of the position and shape of the working edge. This is the only typology allowing us to include in my analysis the large amount of utilized flakes.

Single side scrapers.--The most frequently found category of side-scraping tools consists of single scrapers (Table 16), ranging from the most superficially utilized flake--barely recognizable as such by use striae--to finely flaked scraping tools for long term use.

TABLE 16

SIDE SCRAPERS: VERTICAL DISTRIBUTION

	Single Side Scrapers		Double Side Scrapers		Others		Total	
		Per Cent		Per Cent		Per Cent		Per Cent
Plow zone.......	15	*	3	*	3	.....	21	.....
Late Woodland....	14	26.4	7	13.2	...	.....	21	39.6
Terminal Archaic..	10	14.7	2	2.9	...	.....	12	17.6
Total.......	39	.....	12	.....	3	.....	54	.....

*Percentage within total tool assemblage of this horizon.

The single scrapers were subdivided for further analysis on the basis of the shape of their working edge, the position of the working edge, and the type of flake utilized. Table 17 shows the vertical distribution of single scrapers for these features.

TABLE 17

1. VERTICAL DISTRIBUTION OF SINGLE SCRAPERS: UTILIZED FLAKES *vs.* SCRAPING TOOLS

Horizon	Scraping Tool	Utilized Flake	Total
Plow zone.........	8	7	15
Late Woodland......	8	6	14
Terminal Archaic....	1	9	10
Total.........	17	22	39

TABLE 17 (Cont'd.)

2. VERTICAL DISTRIBUTION OF SINGLE SCRAPERS BY TYPE

a. Type of Flake

Horizon	Blade	Flake	Decortication Flake
Plow zone.	...	13	2
Late Woodland.	2	7	5
Terminal Archaic.	...	8	2
Total	2	28	9

b. Kind of Working Edge

Horizon	Straight and Convex	Concave	Spokeshave	Derticulate
Plow zone.	13	2	...	...
Late Woodland.	13	...	...	1
Terminal Archaic. . .	8	1	1	...
Total	34	3	1	1

c. Position of Working Edge

Horizon	Outer Face	Inner Face	Bifacial
Plow zone.	9	4	2
Late Woodland.	8	3	3
Terminal Archaic.	9	...	1
Total	26	7	6

3. COMPOSITE SINGLE SIDE SCRAPERS

Horizon	With Knife Element	With End Scraper Element	Total
Plow zone.	1	1	2
Late Woodland.	3	1	4
Terminal Archaic	...	...	...
Total	4	2	6

4. SIDE SCRAPERS: MEASUREMENTS

Horizon	Working Edge		Length		Width		Thickness	
	$\bar{X}$	Range	$\bar{X}$	Range	$\bar{X}$	Range	$\bar{X}$	Range
Plow zone.	2.79	1.4-6.7	3.51	1.8-6.9	2.54	1.1-4.0	0.70	0.4-1.1
Late Woodland. . . .	3.75	1.7-5.5	4.29	1.9-5.8	2.86	1.4-3.7	1.10	0.4-2.6
Terminal Archaic. .	2.62	1.6-5.1	3.30	1.7-5.2	2.47	1.1-4.9	0.82	0.4-1.3

Single side scrapers, although found in all horizons, are of some value for technical differentiations of the Late Woodland and Terminal Archaic horizons. They reach their highest concentration during the Late Woodland horizon. At the same time, the amount of tools (purposely retouched) versus utilized flakes (unretouched flakes showing use striae and use retouch) reaches its peak, implying that more time and effort went into scraper production, and side scrapers were considered a more important part of the tool assemblage. A similar conclusion can be drawn from the types of flakes utilized. While during the Terminal Archaic occupation of the site, any amorphous flake (80 per cent) was considered suitable for use as a scraper. The percentage of this flake category drops to 50 per cent in the overlying horizon. A subdivision of the scrapers on the basis of working edge shape did not turn out to provide much insight into the analyzed industries. It was impossible to set up metrical characteristics by which convex and straight scrapers could be separated, since the degree of curvature formed a complete range between the two descriptive criteria, convex and straight. It is suspected here that a similar range would ordinarily exist between straight and concave scrapers, the differentiation here being merely due to sampling error (failing to find the intermediate shapes). The other two types of working edge form such a minority that not much weight can be attached to them.

If the small sample can be trusted, the vertical distribution of the different working edge positions (Table 17, 2*c*) points out the same thing as Table 17, 1 and 2*a*. During Late Woodland times more attention was paid to the characteristics of individual flakes, so that the most advantageous face of the artifact was retouched (outer *vs*. inner face), and utilized flakes were used more than once (bifacial scraping striae). Compared to this the Terminal Archaic single scrapers were made for short use after which they were discarded. If the observed "composite tools" are of any significance within the sample (Table 17, 3), they only underline the conclusions drawn on the basis of the other criteria, namely that during Terminal Archaic times scrapers served a "no deposit-no return" function on the site, while during Late Woodland occupation flakes were more carefully selected for single scraper manufacture; more time went into their production, and they were used for a longer time, including occasional reuse as knife and end scraper.

The data in Table 17, 4, showing that Late Woodland scrapers are in general sturdier than their Terminal Archaic counterparts, are presented as additional support of these conclusions.

TABLE 18

DOUBLE AND POLYHEDRAL SCRAPERS

Descriptive Data
(All measurements in centimeters)

UMMA No.		Provenience	Type	Type of Flake	Working Edge I			Working Edge II			L	W	T
					Shape	Position	Length	Shape	Position	Length			
70652	U	Pl 10X10A	Convergent	Flake	Concave	Outer F.	Frag.	Convex	Outer F.	Frag.	. . .	. . .	0.5
70697	U	Pl 490E490	Polyhedral	Flake	. . .	Outer F.	. . .	. . .	. . .	. . .	4.4ø	. . .	1.6
70720	U	Pl 395E510	Polyhedral	Flake	. . .	Outer F.	. . .	. . .	. . .	. . .	3.4ø	. . .	1.3
No. 7	T	Pl 10X10A	Polyhedral	Flake	. . .	Outer F.	. . .	. . .	. . .	. . .	2.3ø	. . .	0.6
70740	T	Pl 365E480	Double	Flake	Straight	Outer F.	2.6	Concave	Outer F.	2.6	1.8	1.9	0.8
70742	T	Pl 365E480	Double	Flake	Convex	Outer F.	2.4	Convex	Outer F.	2.0	2.3	3.3	0.8
70767	U	LW 10X10A	Double	Flake	Straight	Bifacial	Frag.	Straight	Bifacial	Frag.	. . .	. . .	0.7
70674	U	LW 10X10A	Double	Flake	Convex	Outer F.	3.2	Convex	Outer F.	2.8	4.6	2.6	0.6
70727	U	LW 395E510	Double	Flake	Concave	Outer F.	3.7	Straight	Outer F.	3.8	3.8	2.0	0.8
No. 16	T	LW 10X10A	Double	Flake	Straight	Outer F.	2.5	Straight	Outer F.	2.3	2.5	1.7	0.4
70663	T	LW 10X10A	Double	Flake	Convex	Inner F.	Frag.	Convex	Inner F.	Frag.	. . .	. . .	. . .
No. 38	T	LW 10X10A	Double	Decortication Flake	Straight	Bifacial	3.8	Straight	Outer F.	3.8	4.0	3.7	1.2
No. 262	T	LW 395E510	Double	Blade	Straight	Outer F.	2.8	Irregular	Inner F.	3.0	4.9	1.9	0.5
70774	U	TA 365E480	Double	Flake	Straight	Outer F.	2.5	Straight	Inner F.	2.7	3.5	2.6	0.7
70765	T	TA 365E480	Double	Flake	Concave	Outer F.	1.6	Concave	Outer F.	1.3	3.5	2.6	0.8

Note.—T = tool; U = utilized flake; ø = diameter; Pl = Plow zone; LW = Late Woodland; TA = Terminal Archaic.

Multiple side scrapers.--As can be seen in Table 18 there are as many different multiple-side scraper types as there are multiple side scrapers. The small size of the sample, however, warranted only a superficial subdivision into double side scrapers (i.e., scraping tools with two parallel working edges), convergent side scrapers (with two converging working edges), and polyhedral side scrapers (tools with scraper retouch on several sides). Again, we notice the incidence of these scraper types in the Late Woodland (Table 19). Since descriptive data are given in Table 18, the descriptions do not have to be repeated here. The only remarkable tool of this assemblage is UMMA 70765 (Plate II, Fig. 1*a*), a double spokeshave, which together with the single Terminal Archaic spokeshave (Plate II, Fig. 1*b*) might point to some bone-working activity during this occupation on the site. Binford and Binford (1966) assign the same function to concave scrapers. How ever, as pointed out above, concave scrapers might only be accidental variants of the general convex and straight scraper categories. Therefore, unless supported by empirical data, not too much specialization should be assigned to such unspecialized tools

End scrapers (Plate II, Fig. 2; Plate III, Plate IV)—What was said about the side scrapers above seems to apply as well to the sample of 31 end scrapers from the Butterfield site. End scrapers reac importance within the tool kit only during the Late Woodland occupation (Plate IV), while the Terminal Archaic tools of this category

TABLE 19

DOUBLE AND POLYHEDRAL SCRAPERS - VERTICAL DISTRIBUTION

	Double	Polyhedral	Total
Plow Zone.	3 (1)	3 (2)	6 (3)
Late Woodland.	7 (3)	. . .	7 (3)
Terminal Archaic.	2 (1)	. . .	2 (1)
Total	12 (5)	3 (2)	15 (7)

TABLE 20

END SCRAPERS - VERTICAL DISTRIBUTION

Horizon	Total	Per Cent Within Assemblage	Number of Finished Tools		Utilize Flakes
			Unbroken	Fragments	
Plow zone.	15	. . .	2	6	7
Late Woodland. . . .	12	22.6	2	3	7
Terminal Archaic. .	4	5.8	2	. . .	2
Total	31	. . .	6	9	16

PLATE II

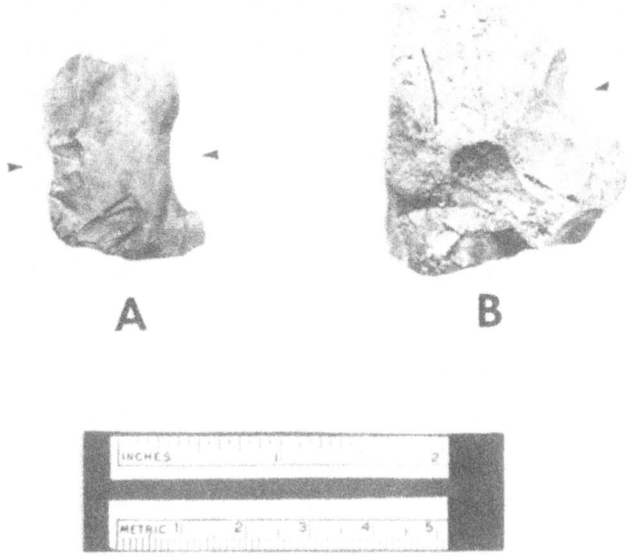

Fig. 1. Spokeshaves: *a*, double spokeshave; *b*, single spokeshave. Arrows denote working edges.

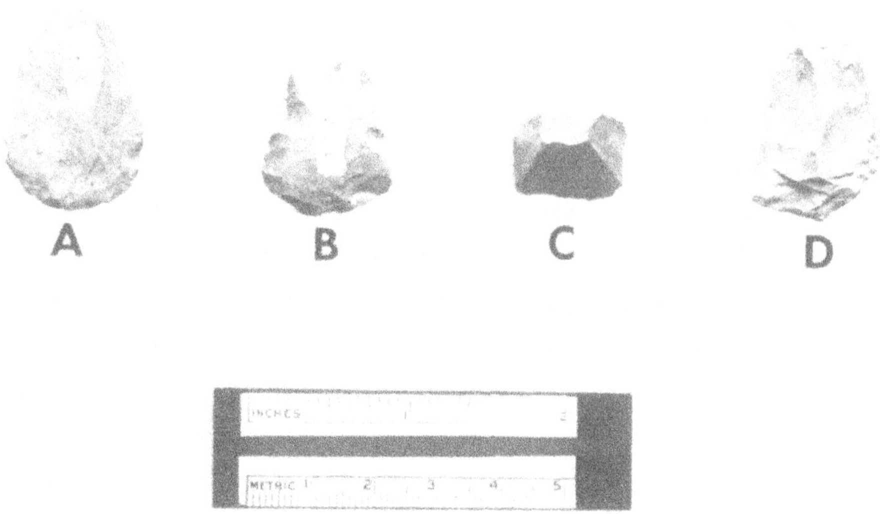

Fig. 2. Terminal Archaic end scrapers.

PLATE III

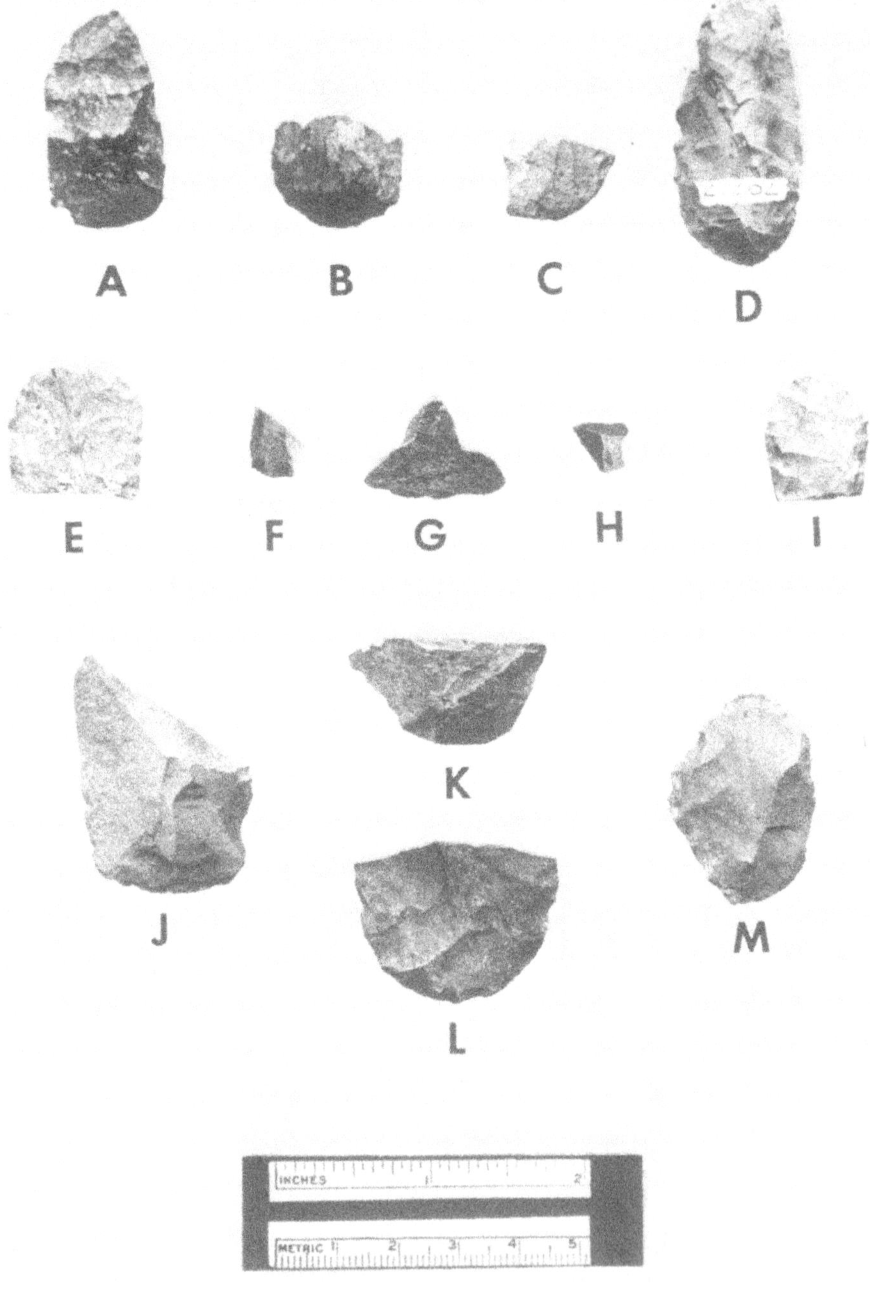

End scrapers from the plow zone.

PLATE IV

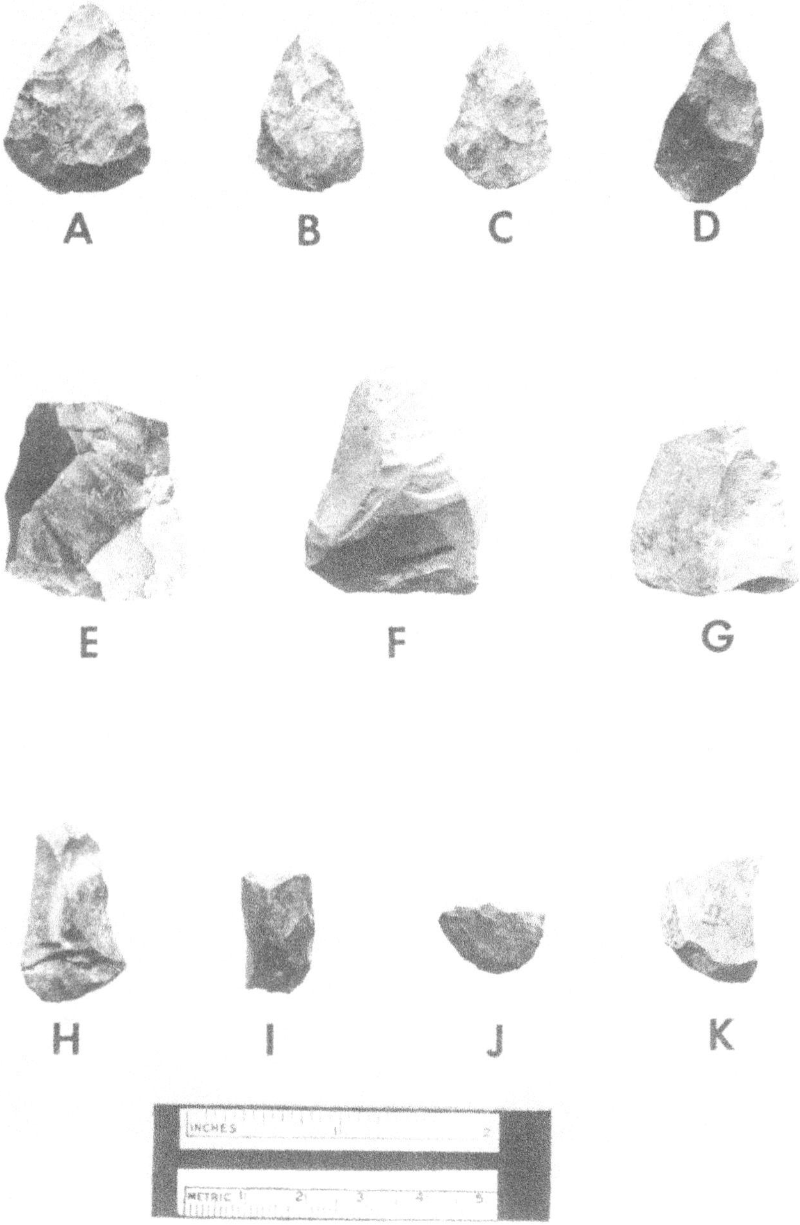

End scrapers from the Late Woodland horizon.

TABLE 21

ATTRIBUTE LIST OF END SCRAPERS

(All measurements in centimeters)

UMMA No.	Horizon and Unit	Description	Shape of Working Edge	Retouch		Metrical Data		
				Outer Face	Inner Face	L	W	T
70651	Pl 10X10A	Utilized flake, amorphous, fragment	Irregular	Flat	Steep, irregular	2.4	3.7	0.6
70677	Pl 10X10A	Utilized flake, amorphous	Convex	Flat	...	...	...	...
70677	Pl 10X10A	Utilized flake, amorphous	Convex	Steep	...	2.5	1.7	0.5
70681	Pl 400E480	Utilized flake on blank	Convex	Flat	Flat	2.5	1.9	0.9
70700	Pl 490E490	Utilized flake, amorphous, fragment	Irregular	Stepped, flat	Flat	4.4	2.9	1.0
70739	Pl 365E480	Utilized flake, amorphous	Convex	Steep, fine	...	2.6	2.2	0.5
70740	Pl 365E480	Utilized flake, fragment	Convex	...	Flat, irregular	...	0.6	...
70693	Pl 400E480	Thumbnail, tool, fragment	Convex	Very steep	...	2.4	2.3	0.6
70715	Pl 395E510	Flakescraper, tool, fragment	Convex	Flat	Flat	2.8	3.5	0.7
70717	Pl 395E510	Thumbnail?, tool	Convex	Very steep	Flat	5.0	2.2	1.7
70718	Pl 395E510	Tool, thumbnail	Convex	Flat	Flat	2.2	1.9	0.6
70740	Pl 365E480	2 fragments, tool	...	Very steep	...	...	...	0.6
70747	Pl 365E480	Stemmed end scraper	Convex	Steep, irregular	...	1.8	2.5	0.8
70749	Pl 365E480	Thumbnail, fragment	Convex	Very steep	...	1.9	2.3	0.8
70753	Pl 365E480	Thumbnail, fragment	Convex	Flat	...	...	2.1	0.6
70658	LW 10X10A	Utilized tabular flake, quartzite	Irregular	Flat	...	3.0	3.0	0.9

70658	LW 10X10A	Utilized tabular flake, fragment	Irregular	Flat, irregular	...	2.1	1.9	0.6
70662	LW 10X10A	Utilized polyhedral flake	Irregular	Steep, irregular	...	3.4	3.3	1.4
70686	LW 400E480	Utilized flake, prismoidal	Convex	Steep	Steep	3.2	1.8	0.8
70704	LW 490E490	Utilized polyhedral flake	Straight	Irregular, flat	Irregular, flat	4.3	3.0	1.3
70706	LW 490E490	Utilized flake, fragment	Subconvex	Steep	Flat	...	...	0.9
70707	LW 490E490	Utilized flake, prismoidal	Subconcave	...	Stepped	...	2.4ø	...
70681	LW 400E480	Trianguloid tool	Convex	Very steep	...	2.6	1.9	0.7
70682	LW 400E480	Trianguloid tool, fragment	Convex	Very steep	Steep	3.2	1.8	1.0
70708	LW 490E490	Trianguloid tool	Convex	Very steep	Flat	3.2	2.5	0.9
70722	LW 395E510	Tool fragment	Convex	Very steep	...	1.3	1.9	0.4
70722	LW 395E510	Tool fragment	Convex	Very steep	...	...	2.2	...
70730	TA 395E510	Ovoid tool (flake)	Convex	Steep	Flat	2.8	2.1	0.6
70734	TA 395E510	Utilized flake, fragment	Straight	Fine, steep	...	...	1.2	0.8
70760	TA 365E480	Utilized flake	Irregular	Flat	...	2.8	2.4	0.8
70759	TA 365E480	Flake tool, ovoid	Convex	Very flat	Flat	3.4	2.2	0.5

Note.—Pl = Plow zone; LW = Late Woodland; TA = Terminal Archaic; ø = diameter.

remain low in number, atypical in their morphology, and non-homogenous as a population (Plate II, Fig. 2). Table 20 shows the vertical distribution of this tool category. From this table it should become clear that not much of a typology can be developed from this sample. Table 21 substantiates this by providing us with a strongly diversified attribute catalogue for the end scrapers from the site. Nevertheless, some generalized categories could be singled out, and their vertical distribution is shown in Table 22. The first of these, the flake scrapers, show the largest differentiation in shape, size and technical attributes. It includes all the unretouched flakes which have been utilized as end scrapers, as well as generalized retouched flakes which served the same purpose. A further subdivision of this category did not seem rewarding on the basis of the limited sample. The next category comprises the ovoid, triangular, and thumbnail end scrapers, all of which represent finished tools. For the manufacture of these, flakes of a certain size and shape had to be selected and much specialized work went into their production. The final "group," consisting only of one item, is characterized as a hafted scraper. Table 22 shows that the end scrapers during the Terminal Archaic occupation were rather generalized tools

TABLE 22

END SCRAPERS - VERTICAL DISTRIBUTION BY CATEGORY

Horizon	Total	Flake Scrapers	Ovoid, Trianguloid and Thumbnail Scrapers	Hafted Scrapers
Plow zone	15	8	6	1
Late Woodland	12	7	5	. . .
Terminal Archaic. . .	4	. . .	4	. . .
Total	31	15	15	1

TABLE 23

PROJECTILE POINTS - VERTICAL DISTRIBUTION

Horizon	Complete Specimen	Frag-ments	Blanks	Total	Per Cent of Assemblage
Plow zone	11	21	4	36	31.57
Late Woodland	4	6	1	11	20.37
Terminal Archaic. . .	6	18	5	29	41.43
Total	21	45	10	76	31.31

and not much time went into their manufacture. Very likely they were utilized only a few times and then discarded. During the Late Woodland occupation of the site, special flakes were selected, better adapted to the function of an end scraper, and with careful retouch prepared into a tool which could withstand long-term use. The high percentage of the category of endscraping tools *vs.* flakes utilized as end scrapers among the plow zone artifacts (Plate III), should again indicate that a large part of these tools is derived from the Late Woodland horizons of the site. The end scrapers, therefore, are additional evidence that different activities were performed on the site by the Late Woodland and Terminal Archaic inhabitants.

Projectile Points

The sample of 76 projectile points from the excavations is proof of the dense concentration of cultural material at the Butterfield site. The utility of the sample, however, is severely limited, since only 55 per cent of the recovered points derive from undisturbed horizons (Table 23). If the unidentifiable fragments are subtracted from the remaining 55 per cent, the sample decreases to 18 identifiable projectile points from undisturbed horizons (Tables 23 and 24)--a population too small for statistical interpretation. In addition, the observed range of variation is so large, that any attempt at classification beyond the description of single tools seems to lack any basis. Nevertheless, eight general categories were singled out and are described below. Any reference to type names has been avoided, since the exact chronological sequence of these types remains to be worked out for this area.

Thirteen points within the sample of 39 identifiable specimens were characterized by their small size, a general trianguloid

TABLE 24

PROJECTILE POINTS - IDENTIFIABLE SPECIMENS

Horizon	Complete Specimen	Identifiable Fragments			Total
		Distal	Medial	Basal	
Plow zone.......	11	...	1	7	19
Late Woodland....	4	...	2	2	8
Terminal Archaic..	6	...	1	5	12
Total.......	21	0	4	14	39

shape, and extremely poor workmanship compared to the other categories (Plate V, *a-m*). Only three of these have been corner-notched for hafting; but apparently all three broke during this process, incidating that their small size together with poor workmanship prohibited the hafting of these points. Five others are marginally retouched only on the outer face, while the inner face carries only superficial face retouch. Most of the 13 points (8) have straight bases, although concave (1) and convex bases (2) occur. The blades range from contracting ovate to straight, the former being more frequent (8). The metrical data are given below:

	Length	Width	Thickness
N.	7	12	13
$\bar{X}$.	2.52	1.74	0.50
Range. .	2.1-3.4	1.3-2.0	0.4-0.7

Next in frequency are large-sized side-notched points (Plate VI, *a-g*). All of these are bifacially retouched on the margins and considerable skill went into their production. The bases of these points are straight to subconvex, and the blades are of parallel-to-contracting-ovate outline. The angles of juncture in the base element between base and notch and between notch and blade element, are in general obtuse circular, all points of juncture usually falling on one line (blade to base). Points which have been less utilized are wider, since continued use of this point category apparently decreased them considerably in width. No lateral or basal grinding could be recognized. The metrical data are summarized below:

	Length	Width	Thickness	Minimum Stem Ø	Base to Min. S. Ø	Basal Width	Notch Length
N . . .	2	5	5	5	7	5	7
$\bar{X}$ . . .	5.0	2.4	0.7	1.64	0.77	2.06	0.58
Range	4.7-5.3	1.9-2.8	0.5-0.9	1.4-2.1	0.5-1.1	1.5-2.3	0.2-0.9

Six small corner-notched points could be grouped into a single category (Plate VI, *i-n*). All are characterized by steep bifacial marginal retouch on all edges, and usually show signs of lateral grinding along the blade and in the haft element, while the base containing the former striking platform has been bifacially thinned. The base is either straight or subconvex and becomes more convex only in those points that have been extensively

PLATE V

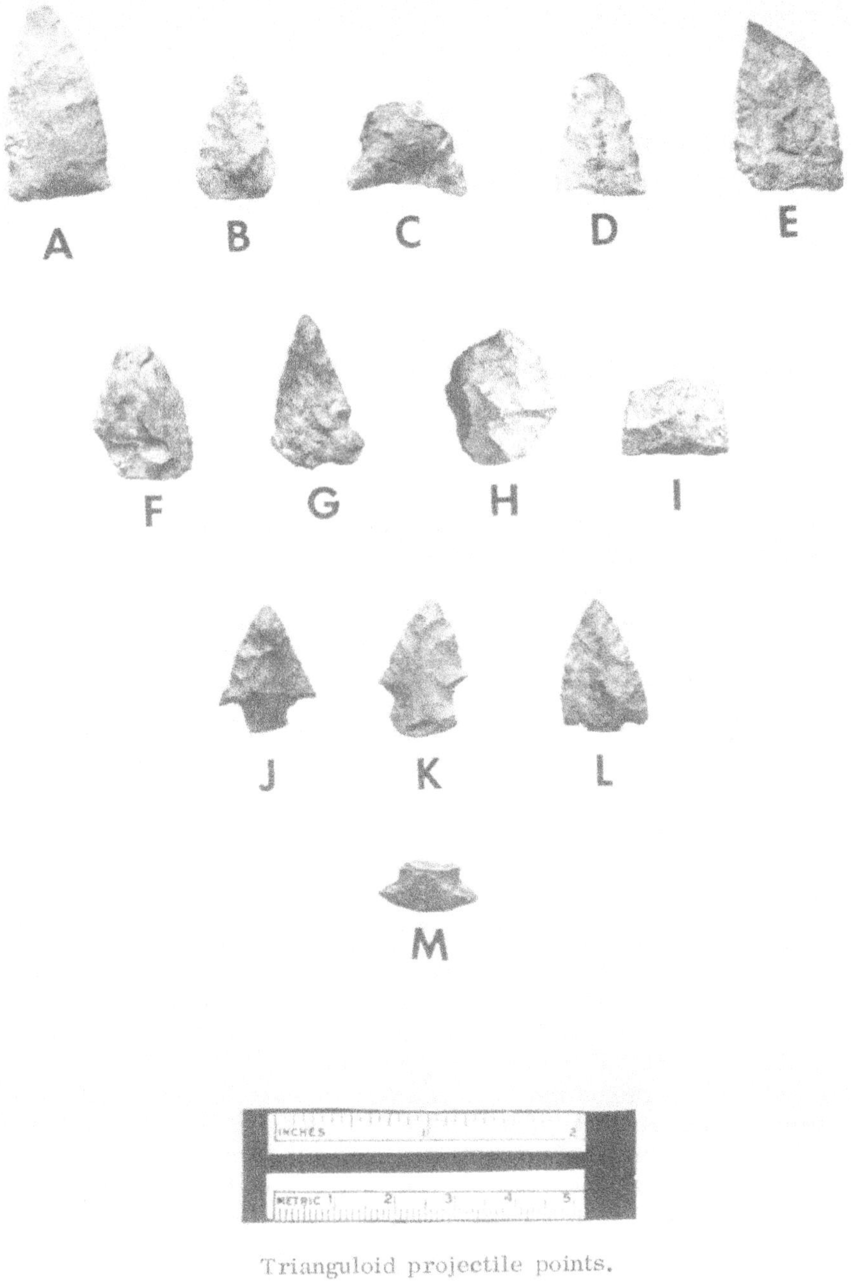

Trianguloid projectile points.

resharpened. The base and the haft element form an acute angle at their point of juncture, the position of which is basal. The corner notch is formed by one continuous concavity lacking intermittent points of juncture. An obtuse or right angle is formed at the point of juncture between the haft and blade element. The shape of the blade is contracting ovate to straight. The following metrical data were obtained from the sample:

	Length	Width	Thickness	Minimum Stem Ø	Base to Min. S. Ø	Basal Width	Notch Length
N. . . .	4	6	6	6	6	6	6
X̄. . . .	3.42	2.08	0.71	1.13	0.86	1.41	1.02
Range.	2.0–4.6	1.8–2.5	0.6–0.8	1.1–1.2	0.7–1.0	1.3–1.6	0.7–1.4

A highly nonhomogeneous group of 4 points has been classified as large corner-notched points (Plate VI, *o-r*). Their larger size, however, is not the only criterion on the basis of which they have been separated from the preceding category. They are marked by poor workmanship and absence of lateral grinding. The notch is of smaller size than on the preceding corner-notche point type, and the minimum stem diameter is larger, making it appear as though the corner-notching were only a superficial alteration of a basically trianguloid to ovoid point. The metrical attributes were the following:

	Blade Length	Width	Thickness	Minimum Stem Ø	Base to Min. S. Ø	Basal Width	Notch Lengtl
N. . . .	4	4	4	4	1	1	1
X̄. . . .	3.37	2.27	0.7	1.5	0.03	1.5	0.4
Range.	2.9–3.9	1.9–2.5	0.6–0.9	1.4–2.0	. . .	. . .	. . .

It is surprising that the next category, large trianguloid cache blades (Plate VII, *a-b*), is only represented by two specimens from the excavation units. This type is the most frequent category in Walter Schmidt's surface collection from the site. The reason for the low frequency of this type of blade in the excavation units might be: *a*) sampling error; or *b*) a cache-pit was plowed up, so that this category showed up in such unnatura numbers in the surface collections. These cache blades are characterized by straight bases which have undergone considerable bifacial thinning, and long parallel-ovate blades. The origina outer and inner faces have been almost completely obscured by the removal of wide thin flakes, while the margins are bifacially

PLATE VI

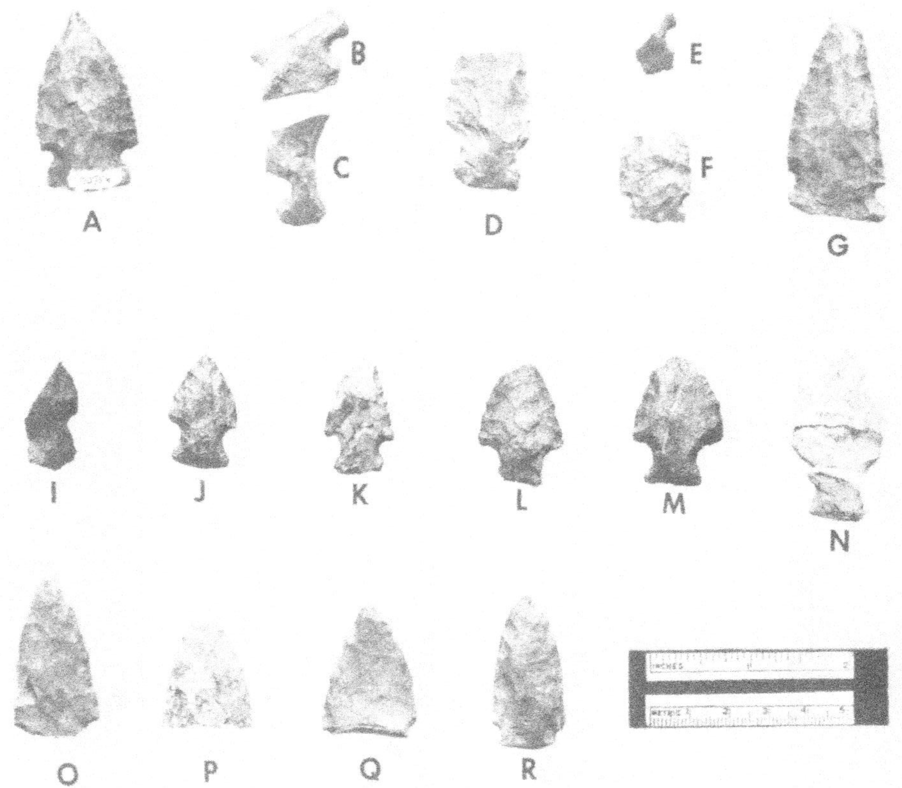

Projectile points: *a–g*, large-sized side-notched points; *i–n*, small corner-notched points; *o–r*, large corner-notched points.

Length	Width	Thickness
5.2	2.3	0.7
5.2	2.2	0.8

retouched by the removal of very small short and thin flakes. The two representatives of this point type have such similar metrical and other features, that they seem to derive from the same core. The sixty-eight points of this category in the surface collections from this site by Walter Schmidt have exactly the same mean as the measurements obtained in our collections. The homogeneity of this category might support our hypothesis that a cache pit with these points was plowed up on the site. Under a binocular microscope, the edges revealed no signs of use.

The four stemmed points from the excavations belong to two categories: a narrow contracting-stemmed one, and a large-sized straight or expanding-stemmed group. The former (Plate VII, *f,g*) has been described by Ritchie (1961) and defined as Lamoka points for the New York area. In Michigan these points are known as Dustin points and a large sample of these from the Schmidt site, 50 miles to the south of our site has recently been described in detail (Harrison, 1966). The two points from the Butterfield site are marked by a strong median ridge, a rhomboid to trianguloid cross section and little irregular marginal retouch. The blade edges are obtained largely by steep facial retouch. The base and stem element has been retouched on one of the specimens, while on the other this section has been left untouched. Evidence for grinding might be present in the shoulder area, although this might have been produced by hafting these points.

Length	Width	Thickness	Minimum Stem Ø	Base to Min. S. Ø	Basal Width
4.0	1.7	0.7	0.9	0.8	1.2
3.7	2.0	0.8	1.0	0.9	1.2

The two large-stemmed points (Plate VII, *h, i*) unfortunately are only fragments, so that it is impossible to decide whether they actually belong in the same category or whether their bases turned out similarly by accident. The bases of both points are straight, but the points of juncture on the two points are accentuated by different angles. One specimen shows right angles

PLATE VII

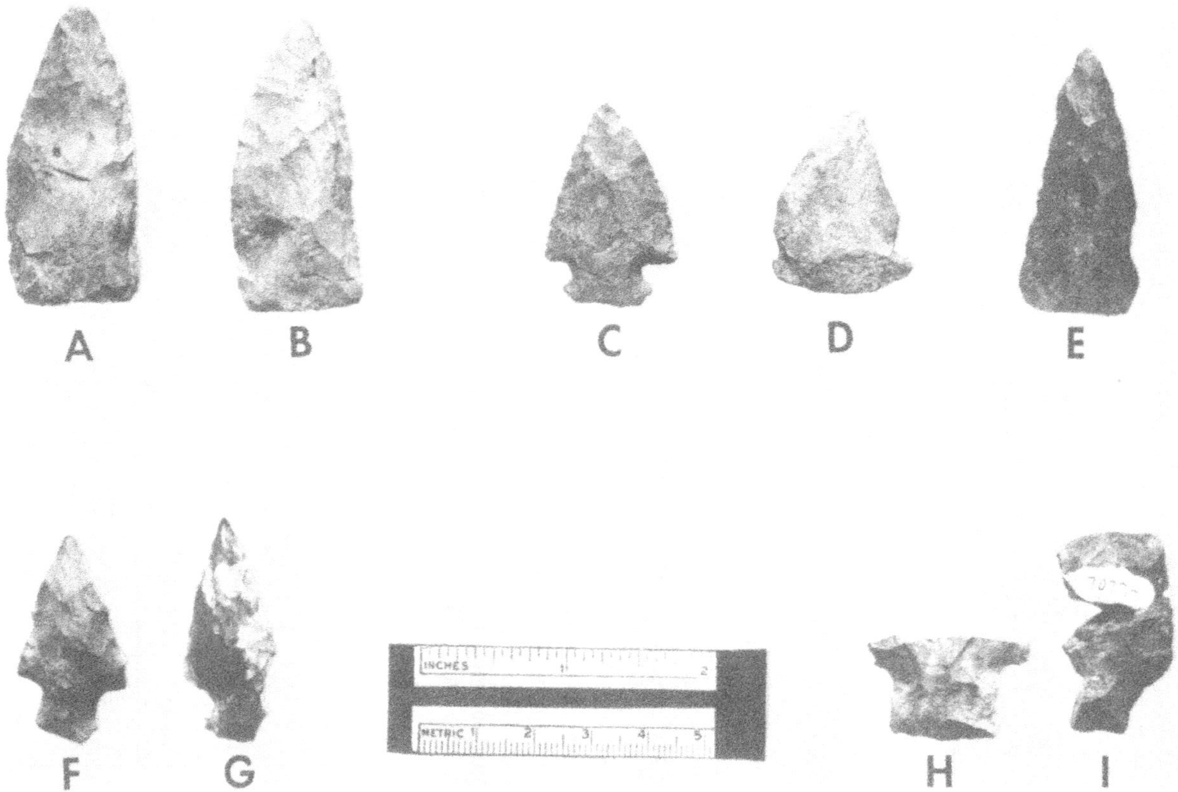

Projectile points: *a,b*, large trianguloid cash blades; *f,g*, Dustin-Lamoka points; *h,i*, large-stemmed points; *c–e*, miscellaneous points.

exclusively at all points of juncture, while the other one has obtuse angles of juncture. The stem of the former is straight, and of the latter expanding. Both fragments have a plano-convex medial cross section.

Width	Basal Width	Thickness	Minimum Stem ∅	Base-Shoulder
2.8	1.9	1.0	1.9	1.5
...	...	0.8	...	1.3

Finally, three points are included in the miscellaneous category. The first of these is a small corner-notched point (Plate VII, *c*) distinct from both previously discussed in size, shape, and workmanship. The base is subconcave, and an acute angle is formed with the haft element at the point of juncture. The points of juncture within the haft element accentuate obtuse angles, while the angle formed between the blades and the shoulder element is acute. The blades are of contracting ovate shape. The point carries fine marginal and facial retouch on both faces.

The next point (Plate VII, *e*) might be included in the large corner-notched variety described earlier, constituting an intermediate stage in manufacture between the blank and the final tool. The base had not yet been prepared and the point had not yet been side-notched. It seems that the point had not been finished because the flake removed for side-notching cut too deeply into the point.

The third point in this group (Plate VII, *d*), finally, shows poor workmanship. It has been worked on a naturally pointed rigid flake. Lacking facial retouch, the marginal retouch--although regular--is restricted to the inner face. Superficial side-notching has been obtained by irregular stepped retouch on the outer face. The metrical data on the last three points are given below.

UMMA No.	Length	Width	Thickness	Minimum Stem ∅	Base to Min. S. ∅	Basal Width	Notch Length
70678	3.5	2.4	0.6	1.3	0.6	1.6	0.9
70785	4.6	2.2	0.9	...	...	2.0	...
70743	3.3	2.3	0.6	2.1	0.7	2.5	0.5

Projectile Point Blanks.—The 10 items defined as projectile point blanks were identified as such on the basis of two criteria:

a) absence of use striae, and *b*) shape and proportions approaching those of finished points. Although the posibility remains that some of these were not intended to be prepared into projectile points, there is no other category of pointed tools present within the assemblage into which they might have been worked; so the assumption that these items actually represent point blanks gains credibility.

The blanks from the Butterfield site seem to fall into four broad categories. The first group (4 specimens) (Plate VIII, *a-d*) is of ovoid shape and seems to represent the blank type for the small corner-notched points. It is characterized by the same all-round bifacial marginal retouch; shows rudimentary signs of lateral grinding on the margins, and is of the same size proportions as its associated point category. Since all of these blanks are made with the same raw material (a slightly opaque whitish-grey and smooth chert), and this material is not represented by large decortication flakes in the debitage of the site, and since they all represent the same stage of manufacture (prenotching), it is suspected that they were imported as such to the site. The metrical data are summarized below:

	Length	Width	Thickness
N	4	4	4
$\bar{X}$	4.4	2.53	1.05
Range. . .	4.0-4.7	2.2-2.7	0.8-1.2

Four other blanks (Plate VIII, *e-h*) were made of local Bayport Chert. The general characteristics of this category are: 1) straight base, 2) parallel ovate blade, 3) irregular bifacial and marginal retouch, and 4) medium size. It is impossible to deduce from their morphology which projectile point type was to be manufactured from them. Most of them seem to have been discarded due to some accident in the manufacturing process or when the poor nature of the raw material became clear. Their metrical features seem to be in internal agreement:

	Length	Width	Thickness
N	4	4	4
$\bar{X}$	4.25	2.70	1.10
Range. . .	4.1-4.5	2.3-3.1	0.8-1.4

Two other blanks are single representatives of their categories. The first of these is long narrow leaf-shaped blank (Plate

PLATE VIII

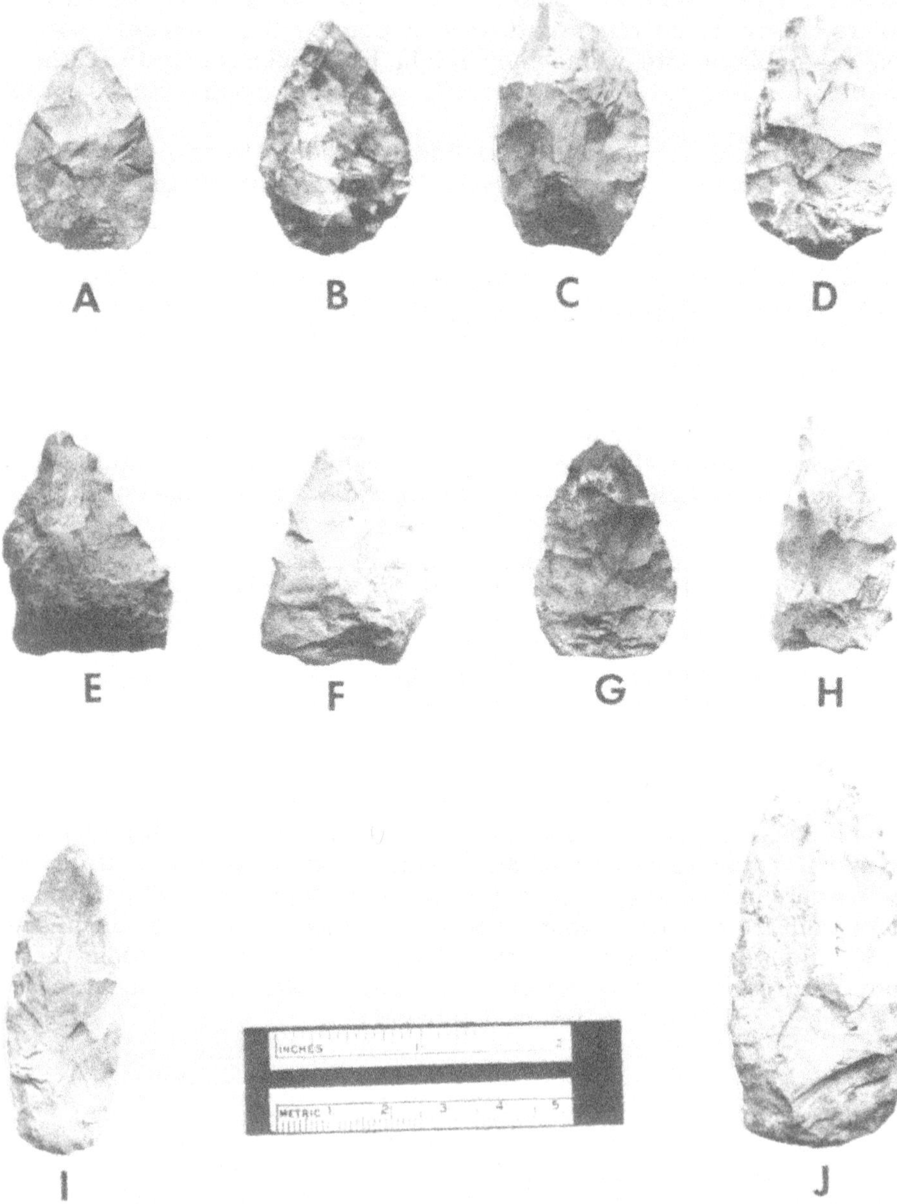

Projectile point blanks: *a–d*, ovoid blanks for small corner-notched points; *e–h*, straight-based parallel ovate blanks; *i*, leaf-shaped blank; *j*, rough blank.

VIII, *i*) with irregular retouch on both faces and all around the margins; the second is a large thick blank (Plate VIII, *j*) on a ridged flake with very rudimentary facial retouch, showing traces of marginal retouch only by some scars on the outer face at the base and on the inner face along one side.

UMMA No.	Length	Width	Thickness
70705	5.6	2.0	0.8
70729	7.1	3.2	1.5

Vertical Distribution of Projectile Point Categories.—Even though the possibility of sampling error is great in such a small sample, some general conclusions can be drawn about the chronological significance of the observed distribution of projectile points. The validity of the conclusions can be checked against the evidence from sites nearby, and against other evidence from the site itself. The most obvious feature of the assemblage, of course, is the high percentage of projectile points within the Terminal Archaic assemblage (Table 23), going hand in hand with a high number of fragments within the assemblage (Table 25). This implies that: 1) the activities performed by the Terminal Archaic occupants were more specialized, and 2) that projectile points were more intensely used during this period of occupation. These hypotheses are supported by the fact that during the Terminal Archaic occupation, the projectile points were manufactured on carefully selected flakes, and much time and effort went into the tool production, evidenced by the far better workmanship displayed by the Terminal Archaic occupation. The Late Woodland occupants of the site did not consider projectile points important parts of the tool kit. Most of the specimens could be produced instantly, the raw material did not have to be carefully selected and the points were very likely discarded after short use.

TABLE 25

PROJECTILE POINTS - VERTICAL DISTRIBUTION OF FRAGMENTS

Horizon	Number of fragments	Percentage of fragments within projectile point assemblage
Plow zone.	21	58.3
Late Woodland.	6	54.5
Terminal Archaic. . .	18	62.0

TABLE 26

VERTICAL DISTRIBUTION OF PROJECTILE POINT CATEGORIES

	Plow Zone	Late Woodland	Terminal Archaic	Total
Small trianguloid points	9	4	. . .	13
Large side-notched points . . .	3	. . .	4	7
Small corner-notched points. .	3	. . .	. . .	4
Large corner-notched points .	1	3	. . .	4
Dustin-Lamoka points	. . .	. . .	2	2
Large-stemmed points.	. . .	1	1	2
Large cash blades	1	. . .	1	2
Miscellaneous	1	. . .	2	3
Blanks:				
Ovoid blanks	2	1	1	4
Trianguloid blanks	2	. . .	2	4
Miscellaneous	. . .	. . .	2	2
Total	22	9	18	49

Several of the observed categories seem to be of chronological significance (Table 26). This, however, should not tempt the reader to draw conclusions about the general chronological and spatial significance of these categories in this area, since: *a*) the observed distribution might be a site-specific phenomenon, and *b*) it might be biased by sampling error. Much more work has to be done in this area, especially on sites with more complete stratigraphic sequences before any general inferences are possible.

The Terminal Archaic assemblage on the site is characterized by large side-notched and small corner-notched points. The small corner-notched point seems to have been manufactured on blanks imported to the site from elsewhere. The two Dustin-Lamoka points, because of their exotic raw material, lead to the same conclusion. Possibly they were picked up from the Dustin site across the river and reused by the later occupants, since the material of which they were made is found frequently on this site. Large cache blades, equivalent although not identical to the Terminal Archaic Pomranky points in parts of the Saginaw valley area, are frequently found in the plow disturbed area of the site and seem to have their stratigraphic source in the Terminal Archaic horizon. The chronological significance of the various other categories present in this assemblage cannot be safely evaluated on a one point per category basis. The high frequency of projectile point blanks leads to the same conclusion as that derived from the debitage, namely that tool manufacture on the site during the Terminal Archaic occupation began with the blank stage, instead of nodules as during the later occupation.

Two elements characterize the Late Woodland projectile point assemblage: small trianguloid points and large corner-notched points. This is not at all surprising, since similar observations have been made on all other sites of the same time horizon in the area and in other parts of Michigan. Thus, Walter Schmidt has collected a large number of trianguloid points from other Late Woodland sites along the Kawkawlin and Pinconning rivers. Small triangular points appear in Late Woodland context at the Schultz site (Fitting, n.d.). Corner-notched points are found throughout Michigan in the Middle and Late Woodland strata of excavated sites, such as at the Bussinger site in Saginaw County (Halsey, personal communication), where they represent the dominant projectile point type. Blanks are rare in the Late Woodland horizon. It has been impossible to incorporate the large sample of projectile points collected by Walter Schmidt from the general area of the site into our consideration since it apparently includes several occupations that are not represented in the stratigraphic sequence of our excavation, and only extensive test excavations covering the whole area of the sand ridge can provide a stratigraphic tie for this beautiful surface collection.

Blades

The blades found at the Butterfield site can be divided into two groups; backed blades and simple blades. The latter category, consisting of eight fragments from the plow-disturbed area is marked by two straight parallel to slightly contracting edges (Plate IX, *d-j*). In lateral cross section they appear as triangular or trapezoidal, since the outer face is characterized by one or two marked ridges, while the inner face is nearly perfectly plain. Due to their small thickness and size proportions, they are extremely fragile, so that none of the specimens of this category survived use unbroken.

The backed group, consisting of three blades (Plate IX, *a-c*) from the Terminal Archaic occupation, are more break-resistant, so that all three specimens are complete. They constitute merely a special type of simple blade with the added characteristic that one of the sides consists of a cortex or a nodule breakage plane. By coincidence, two of these blades fit into each other (Plate IX, *a*, *b*; Plate X), providing a valuable insight into the process of blade manufacture (Figure 2).

PLATE IX

Blades: *a–c,* backed, double ridged blades (*a* and *b* fit into each other); *d–j,* simple blades and blade fragments.

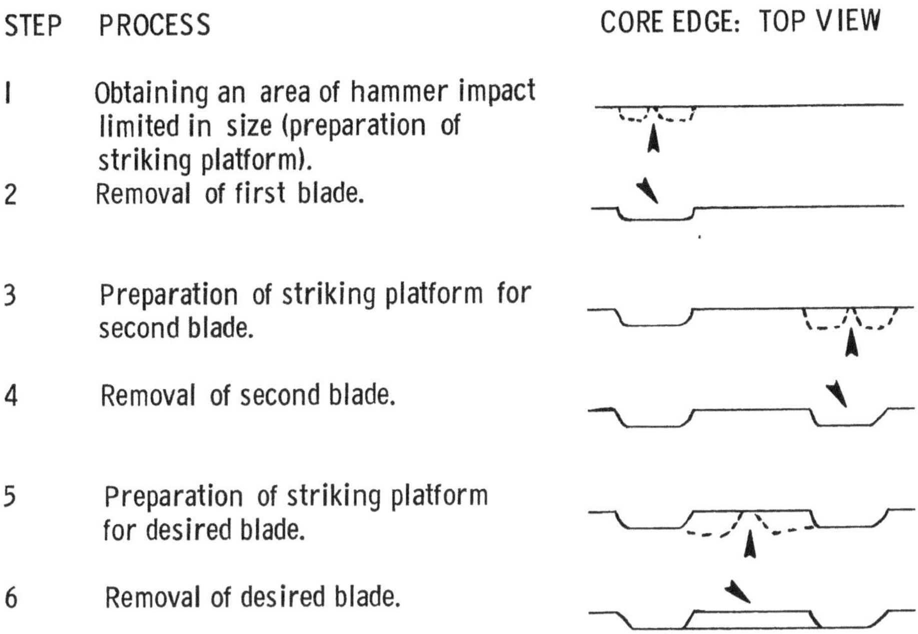

FIG. 2. The production of ridged blades at the Butterfield site - model.

The blades at the Butterfield site were obtained from plano-convex cores that would allow the removal of long flakes. After a striking platform has been prepared by limiting the possible area of impact by the removal of tiny spalls to the right and left of the intended point of percussion (Plate X), probably of the same size and shape as marginal pressure-retouch spalls, a first blade is removed. The point of percussion for the successive blade to be removed from the core is so chosen that it is only half a blade's width apart from the point of percussion of the first removed blade along the edge of the core. The point of percussion is prepared in the same way by limiting the area of the hammer impact. If the blade is then removed, its shape is predetermined: on one side the size of the blade is predetermined by the scar left by the preceding blade, or on both sides by removing another blade on the other side, prior to obtaining the desired blade. This also accounts for the rigid outer face of the blades, produced by the outer face of the core and the flake scars of the neighboring blades. Very likely, the absence of blades from the Late Woodland horizon is explained by sampling error.

PLATE X

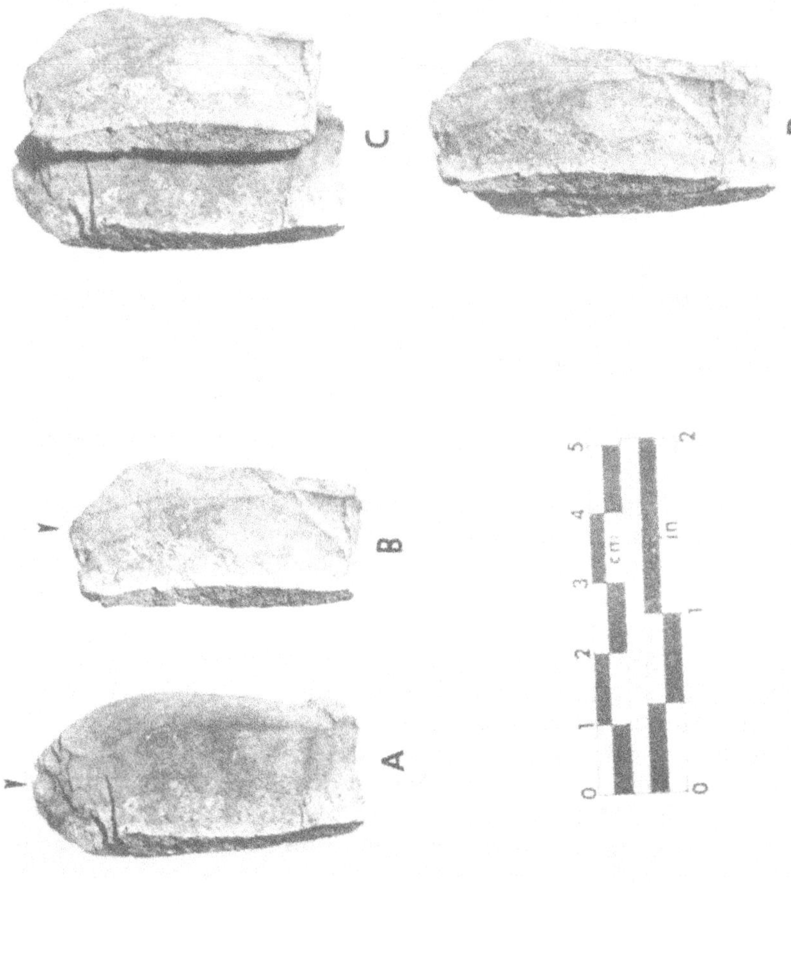

Insight into blade manufacture: *a*, *b*, double-ridged blades. *c*, *d*, fit each other.

BLADES - SUMMARY OF METRICAL DATA

	Length	Width	Thickness
N.	3	13	13
$\bar{X}$.	4.2	1.69	0.43
Range.	3.8-4.6	0.9-2.3	0.3-0.5

Knives

A short look at Table 27 should convince the reader of the nonhomogeneity of the population. More than 50 per cent of the knife assemblage consists of utilized flakes, recognizable in their knife function only on the basis of use striae. With the four unbroken tool specimens we cannot very well construct a tool typology. Nevertheless, some general inferences can be drawn from the vertical distribution of the sample. While the percentage of knives within the tool kit seems to be the same in the Late Woodland and Terminal Archaic horizons (Table 28), we note a steep size differential between the two assemblages (Table 29). While the Terminal Archaic knives are large, heavy cutting tools (Plate

TABLE 27

KNIVES - TOOLS, TOOL FRAGMENTS, UTILIZED FLAKES; VERTICAL DISTRIBUTION

Horizon	Tools - Complete Specimens	Tool Fragments	Utilized Flakes
Plow zone.	2	3	8
Late Woodland.	1	2	4
Terminal Archaic.	1	4	3
Total	4	9	15

TABLE 28

KNIVES - VERTICAL DISTRIBUTION

Horizon	Total	Percentage of Assemblage
Plow zone.	13	. . .
Late Woodland.	7	13.2
Terminal Archaic.	8	11.6
Total	28	. . .

TABLE 29

KNIVES - SUMMARY OF METRICAL DATA

(In Centimeters)

Horizon	Length			Width			Thickness			Length of Working Edge		
	N	$\bar{X}$	Range	N	$\bar{X}$	Range	N	$\bar{X}$	Range	N	$\bar{X}$	Range
Plow zone.	9	3.4	2.1-5.6	9	2.56	1.3-3.5	10	0.84	0.6-1.5	9	3.12	1.2-5.2
Late Woodland. . . .	5	3.8	2.3-4.3	6	2.00	1.1-3.0	7	0.68	0.4-0.9	6	3.40	1.4-4.1
Terminal Archaic. .	4	5.1	2.8-8.1	7	3.74	2.5-4.9	8	1.15	0.5-2.9	4	3.77	2.4-4.8

TABLE 30

DESCRIPTIVE ATTRIBUTES OF KNIFE-PERFORATORS

(Metrical Data in Centimeters)

UMMA No.	Horizon	Length	Width	Thickness	Length of Knife Edge(s)	Perforator Formed by	Shape of Knife Edge(s)
70653	P. Z.	3.3	1.9	0.6	3.3; 3.3	2 knife edges	Convex, Concave
70653	P. Z.	4.1	2.9	1.5	4.2; 1.5	2 knife edges	Convex, Concave
70656	L. W.	3.1	1.4	0.6	3.1; 0.6	2 knife edges	Convex, Straight
70688	L. W.	4.3	1.7	0.7	4.3; 4.3	2 knife edges	Convex, Straight
70711	P. Z.	2.3	1.3	0.6	1.3	Knife breakage plane	Convex
70755	L. W.	. . .	2.8	0.9	5.6	Knife breakage plane	Convex

	Length	Width	Thickness	Dominant Edge
N.	5	6	6	6
$\bar{X}$.	3.42	2.00	0.81	3.63
Range. . . .	2.3-4.3	1.3-4.0	0.6-1.5	1.3-5.6

XI, *c*, *d*, *k*), their Late Woodland counterparts are slender blades and thin flakes. Possibly, this size decrease can be attributed to different tasks performed with the knives during the two occupations: heavy knives were required for activities such as skinning, meat-cutting, and carving bones; thin flake and blade knives could be utilized during the collection and preparation of vegetable foods, as well as for the manufacture of clothing.

Two categories could be singled out of the knife sample. The first of these consists of large, straight-based knives (Plate XI, *a-b*). The knife blades are of expanding-ovate shape. Both faces have been thinned by the removal of long flat flakes, while the margins (base and sides) have been treated by very regular pressure retouch. In their total morphology, these two specimens are identical to what has been defined on other occasions in the literature as Paleo-Indian knives. Since no Paleo-Indian sites have yet been reported from the area and are not expected on the basis of the low elevation, we have to reject the possibility that these knives were picked up elsewhere and utilized on the site, and consider them to be genuine Terminal Archaic tools.

UMMA No.	Length	Width	Thickness
70673	. . .	3.8	0.8
70660	. . .	3.9	0.7

The other category can be defined as a composite tool: knife-perforator (Table 30). Six of these specimens (Plate XI, *e-j*) could be singled out from the assemblage, all in the Late Woodland horizon or in the plow-disturbed zone. The combination of these two components lends credibility to our prediction above that the Late Woodland knives were utilized for clothing work. While the shape differences are marked within the category, the size range is small. In five of six cases the knife edge has been obtained by bifacial retouch. The perforator point is formed either by another knife edge, or by a former breakage plane or striking platform. The descriptive attributes of the six specimens are shown in Table 30.

Drills

With the exception of two specimens, all thirteen drills recovered during the excavation are fragments (Table 31). Such might be expected since their structure makes them extremely vulnerable to accidental fracture. Unfortunately five of the

PLATE XI

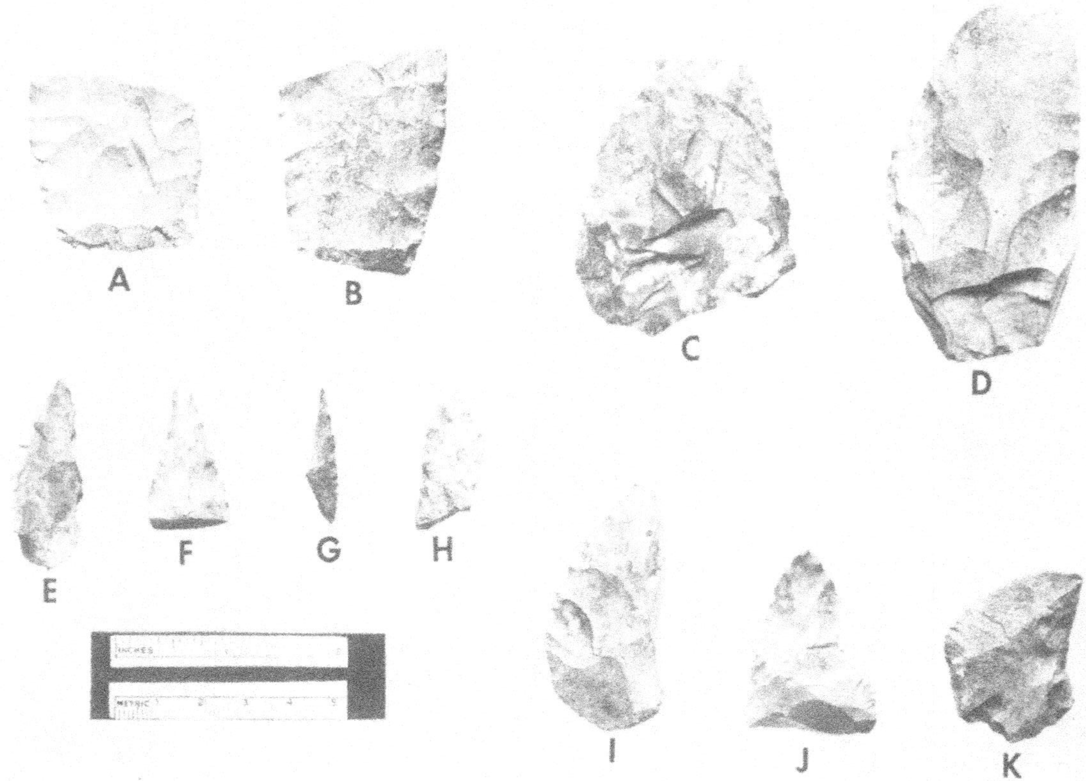

Knives: *a*, *b*, large straight-based knives; *c*, *d*, heavy terminal Archaic knives; *e*, *k*, knife perforators.

TABLE 31

DRILL CATEGORIES

A. VERTICAL DISTRIBUTION

	Plow Zone	Late Woodland	Terminal Archaic	Total
Tip fragments	2	. . .	3	5
Expanding base drills	1	. . .	3	4
Contracting base drills . . .	. . .	1	. . .	1
Hafted drills.	1	. . .	. . .	1
Drill-endscrapers	1	. . .	. . .	1
Drill blank	1	. . .	. . .	1
Total	6	1	6	13
Per cent of tool kit . .	5.81	1.89	8.69	. . .

B. METRICAL ATTRIBUTES

(In Centimeters)

	Length			Width Base			Width Stem			Thickness		
	N	$\overline{X}$	Range	N	$\overline{X}$	Range	N	$\overline{X}$	Range	N	$\overline{X}$	Range
Tip fragments	...	. . .	. . .	...	. . .	. . .	4	0.97	0.7-1.2	5	0.66	0.5-1.2
Expanding base drills	2	. . .	4.9; 6.0	4	1.93	1.8-2.0	4	1.13	0.8-1.4	4	0.80	0.5-1.2
Contracting base drills	...	. . .	. . .	1	0.9	. . .	1	1.4	. . .	1	0.9	. . .
Hafted drills	1	3.6	. . .	1	1.5	. . .	1	1.5	. . .	1	0.7	. . .
Drill endscraper	1	2.1	. . .	1	0.6	. . .	1	0.6	. . .	1	0.6	. . .
Drill blank	...	. . .		1	2.1	. . .	1	2.1	. . .	1	1.3	. . .

fragments are unidentifiable drill tips. Although not much differentiation seems to be present in the sample, it can be subdivided nevertheless on the basis of base shape, since eight of the drills preserve at least part of their base element.

A first category is characterized by an expanding base. Only one of the four specimens in this group of four drills retains the whole base, which is convex (Plate XII, *a-d;* Table 31). In another drill (Plate XII, *e*) the sides contract toward the proximal extremity, the base itself being subconvex. This tool is made of a brownish glassy exotic flint that does not have representatives in the debitage from the site. The third category, again represented by only one member, is a hafted drill of Lamoka-like proportions, carrying shallow side notches above the convex base (Plate XII, *f*). Very likely this drill is a former Lamoka point, which through resharpening became useless in its point function and was utilized as a drill, as proven by the use striae on the working edge. Another drill has some noteworthy characteristics (Plate XII, *g*). Its point has been worn down completely by extensive use, so that its lateral cross section approaches a circle. Use striae are so marked that they are visible without magnification. The direction of drilling was clockwise. The depth of the use striae indicates that stone was the object to be drilled. In addition to the drill, the small object's base has been worked into an endscraper by steep marginal retouch and marginal grinding. Again the use polish on the retouch face is visible without magnification. Proof that drills by no means have to originate from the resharpening of projectile points is provided by a drill blank of heavy proportion (Plate XII, *h*). The Indian craftsman had to discard it since his attempt to notch the blank was premature, producing a gaping hole in the side which made further work impossible.

It is impossible to deduce any inference in the chronological significance of the drill categories from such a small sample. Suffice it to say that drills did not represent any significant part of the tool assemblage during the Late Woodland occupation, and that very likely most of the drills discovered in the plow-disturbed horizons are derived from the Terminal Archaic occupation. The high frequency of fractures (Plate XII, *i-m*) in this assemblage, as well as the extremely worn-down composite drill-endscraper, suggest that during this occupation drills formed an important part of the tool kit and were extensively used. The only drill from a Late Woodland horizon, although a fragment, lacks any sign of use. The vertical distribution of the drill categories and their metrical data are summarized in Table 31.

PLATE XII

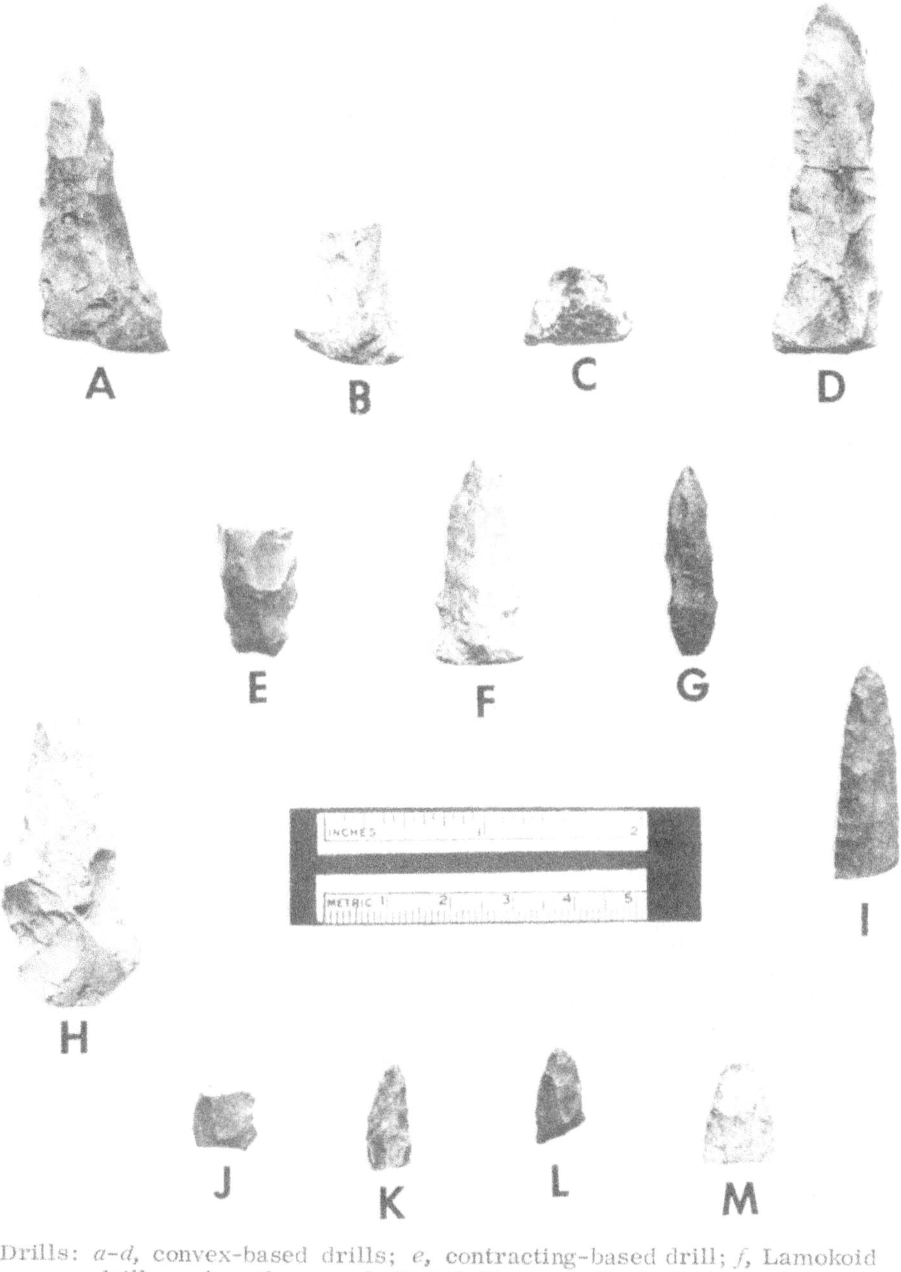

Drills: *a-d*, convex-based drills; *e*, contracting-based drill; *f*, Lamokoid drill; *g*, heavily worn hafted drill; *h*, drill blank; *i-m*, drill fragments.

Conclusions and Ecological Inferences

Without the help of pottery and the geological features of the site, it becomes obvious from the analysis of the chipped stone that we are dealing with two assemblages, distinct in time and function. The Terminal Archaic assemblage, in general, is marked by good workmanship and a large degree of homogeneity within types. The assemblage is characterized by a high percentage of projectile points, backed blades, and heavy knives. Such tools clearly suggest that the inhabitants of the site during this time period were preoccupied with the hunting of large game. The tools had to be prepared carefully if they were to prove successful. This explains the large number of blanks, of tools manufactured on imported exotic chert, the good workmanship, and the high homogeneity of the sample. The fact that the site was occupied rather than visited on occasion by wandering hunters is evidenced by the large amount of debitage on the site accumulated during the Terminal Archaic occupation. Game was apparently not killed in the immediate neighborhood of the site, but skinned before the meat was taken to the base camp; this can be deduced from the absence of scraping and skinning tools from the site. That meat was brought to the site can be inferred from the large number of projectile point fragments in the tool assemblage, implying possibly that they were returned to the site with the meat from the kill they effected. On the basis of the tool assemblage it would seem, therefore, that the Terminal Archaic people on the site had an economy centered on hunting, and that the site was a base camp for longer hunting trips.

The Late Woodland tool assemblage leads to completely different conclusions. It is characterized by a high percentage of scraping tools, by light and thin knives, by perforators, and by a low percentage of projectile points. Most of the tools were made on the spot by picking up the next best flake, and good workmanship seemed to be without adaptive advantage. Such a tool kit is only useful in an economy that is based on a hospitable environment and centered on vegetable foods and the processing of rich resources. A likely time for such specialized activities might be late fall.

IV

POTTERY

Introduction

A ceramic sample of 6501 body sherds and 77 rim sherds was recovered from the excavation units (Table 32). Considering the small excavated area and the shallow Late Woodland horizon, these numbers might impress the reader. Yet, as with other artifact categories from the site, the numbers lose their importance once unidentifiable fragments are removed from the sample. Thus, we retain only 1224 body sherds and 58 rim sherds after fragments that are unidentifiable in terms of their physical and descriptive features are removed (Table 32). The 58 rim sherds yield a minimum vessel count of 24. It follows that the number of rims per vessel is disturbingly low (Table 33).

Since more than 40 per cent of the sample by weight consists of sherds of less than 0.6 grams mean weight, we have to conclude that post-depositional conditions were unfavorable for the preservation of pottery. After deposition, the potsherds were

TABLE 32

CERAMIC SAMPLE

Body Sherds	Amount	Per Cent	Weight	Per Cent	Mean Weight
Sherdlets (0.5cm Ø).	3708	57.03	820.6g	19.53	0.22g
Unidentifiable sherds . . .	1569	24.10	1042.1g	24.81	0.66g
Identified sherds	1224	18.87	2337.4g	55.66	1.90g
Total body sherds . . .	6501	100.00	4200.1g	100.00	0.64g

Rim Sherds	Amount	
Unidentifiable	19	
Identified	58	Total Ceramic Sample
Total rim sherds	77	6578 Sherds

TABLE 33

NUMBER OF RIM SHERDS PER VESSEL

Number of Sherds	Number of Vessels	Percentage
1	13	54.17
2	5	20.83
3	2	8.33
4	1	4.17
More than 4	3	12.50
Total	24	100.00

covered with windblown sand, which in turn contributed to the ongoing processes of soil formation. The resulting intense chemical exchange of the forest soil deprived us of much of our sample.

General Features of the Sample

If we compare the Butterfield ceramic assemblages with pottery samples from contemporaneous sites in Michigan, such as Spring Creek, Schultz, Juntunen, and others, we immediately note some of the site-specific features of our assemblage: 1) the sample shows a high degree of homogeneity for such physical characteristics as paste, temper, hardness and breaking characteristics, color, and methods of manufacture; 2) the same relative homogeneity is displayed in such descriptive attributes as decorative techniques, surface finish, and vessel form; and 3) the over-all manufacturing craftsmanship at the Butterfield site is sloppy and uninventive compared to contemporaneous sites.

The first point is going to enable us to discuss the physical attributes mentioned summarily. The second observation will help us to isolate types within our assemblage, while the last characteristic might possibly be of ecological importance.

Paste

The pottery clay was very likely obtained on the site itself, or nearby, where silty clay is readily available below the surface. On the site this material constitutes the horizons immediately underlying the Terminal Archaic occupation levels. This silty clay displays extremely variable microfacies, changing color and composition vertically on an inch-by-inch scale, and horizontally within every foot. Therefore, an analysis of the pottery clay beyond microscopic analysis does not seem to be rewarding.

More refined methods of paste analysis would attribute three different pots to three different raw material sources, if the clay were obtained at slightly different locations from the same source on the site. A small admixture of fine quartz sand in the fine grain size category (<0.25 mm Ø), was naturally present within the silty clay paste. This constituent was below 10 per cent by volume in all analyzed sherds.

Temper

The tempering material utilized by the Butterfield potters consisted of crushed granitic rock, most commonly granitic quartz with orthoclase, biotite, and hornblende. The size range of this material is large compared to other sites, beginning with fine grained particles below 0.25 mm. in diameter and reaching .8 cm. in diameter. A size cluster, determined on 100 particles of crushed rock, was established at around 2.5 mm. This size range is independent of the ceramic categories, and it often happened that the size range within a single sherd approached the size range observed within the sample. In the analyzed pastes, the temper made up between zero to 40 per cent of the volume; no generalizations about percentages in a given ceramic category could be derived. The tempering material is readily available on the site in the form of fire-cracked granitic rock, and in the general area as weathered granitic pebbles exposed on fields.

Hardness

The hardness determined on Moh's scale fell in all cases between 2 and 3. This, however, is an empty statement since the same range can be obtained from a single sherd. The fact that the hardness of the Butterfield ceramics is quite low in general, and can be recognized without Moh's scale by applying fingernail pressure on a fresh break, or by simply dropping a sherd and listening to the sound.

Color

The observed color of the Butterfield ceramics ranges from gray buff to a dark reddish brown. Color readings clustered around 2.5 YR 6/6 on the Munsell chart. This measurement turned out to be utterly useless since the same color variation as the one pertaining to the whole sample could be observed on a single sherd. This is not surprising since ceramic color is not so much a function of paste, temper, or firing conditions as of discoloration due to the use of the pottery and post-depositional factors such as soil, color, and humidity.

Manufacture

The pottery assemblage on the Butterfield site was manufactured uniformly by working thin sheets of clay together. This can be deduced by microscopic analysis of the laminated paste structure in fresh breaks. Negative evidence is supplied by the complete absence of coil breaks in the sample. Unfortunately, the laminated structure of the pottery contributed much to the post depositional destruction of the ceramics.

Surface Finish

The analysis of bodysherds for the mode of surface finish posed a great analytical problem. Since the mean weight of the 1224 body sherds is so low, it was often impossible to determine whether they were cord-marked or textile-impressed, or plain- or effectively-smoothed. Several safeguards were employed to limit analytical bias: 1) small sherds were correlated with large sherds that left no question about the kind of surface treatment; 2) proveniences that required much sherd-to-sherd subjective judgment were resorted at time intervals, and if no agreement between the counts resulted, borderline cases were added to the indeterminate category. We do not expect that the remaining error is larger than a few points in any direction.

Four methods of surface treatment were recognized: A) sherds without surface treatment beyond smoothing; B) cord-marking; C) cord-wrapped stick-impressing; D) textile-impressing (Table 34). Textile-impressing turned out to be most commonly employed (46.3 per cent), followed by cord-marking, smoothing, and cord-wrapped core techniques. Among the latter three methods subsequent smoothing was found on 11 per cent of the cord-marked sherds and cord-wrapped stick sherds, and only 0.7 per cent of the textile-impressed sherds. This, however, might be due to analytical error, since it is practically impossible to distinguish a smoothed-over textile from cord-marking and cord-wrapped stick-impressing. If all the smoothed-over sherds in the latter three categories were combined, they would constitute 5.6 per cent of this total, which seems to be a more useful figure.

Among the plain sherds 7.0 per cent showed subsequent brushing of the exterior surface. No interior surfaces underwent

TABLE 34

SURFACE FINISH ON RIM SHERDS

	Number of Vessels	Plate Number
Cord-marked	8	XIII, *a–c*; XII, *a–e*
Cord-marked smoothed	3	XV, *a–c*
Textile-impressed	3	XIV, *b–d*
Textile-impressed smoothed	1	XIV, *a*
Cord-wrapped stick-impressed . .	2	XVI, *a, b*
Total	17	. . .

surface treatment beyond brushing. The high percentage of textile-impressing is surprising; thus, at the Riviere au Vase site 7 per cent of the sherds showed this treatment (Fitting, 1965), only 1 per cent of the Spring Creek assemblage could be placed into this category (Fitting, this volume), and it also ranks low on comparative horizons at the Schultz site. In this feature, the square-lipped types are subdivided into those thickening at the lip (B1) and those with parallel rim walls (B2). The former group consists of two vessels (11.6 per cent, Figure 3, Plate XVII, *a,b*), while group B2 is made up of 2 subgroups: B2*a* contains vessels with angular articulation at the interior rim-lip juncture only (N=3, 17.4 per cent, Figure 3, Plate XV *b-d*); B2*b* rims are characterized by two angular articulations (interior and exterior rim-lip juncture) and this category contains six vessels (34.8 per cent, Plate XV *a*, XIV *a-e*, Figure 3). None of the rims is collared.

Three main types of exterior surface finish were singled out from the sample of 17 vessels: cord-marking, textile-impressing, and cord-wrapped stick-impressing. The former two modes of surface treatment have unobscured and smoothed variants. None of the vessel interiors shows any sign of surface treatment beyond smoothing. Table 35 shows the breakdown of the assemblage for vessels with this attribute. The distribution of surface finish follows that observed among the body sherds. It is surprising, however, that plain sherds are absent among the vessel rims, and that cord-marked sherds are much more common among rim sherds than among the body sherds. The former might be explained by assigning the plain body sherds present in the sample to the basal part of an unknown vessel, while the low percentage of textile impressed rim sherds must be due to sampling error.

Within the classes of surface finish, the various utilized tools

TABLE 35

SURFACE TREATMENT: BODY SHERDS

Method	No.	Per-centage	Brushed	Per-centage Within Group	Smoothed	Per-centage Within Group
Plain	268	21.9	19	7.09	...	...
Cord-marked	286	23.4	...	...	32	11.19
Textile-impressed	567	46.3	...	...	4	0.70
Cord-wrapped stick-impressed	103	8.4	...	...	12	11.65
Total	1224	100.0	19	1.55	48	3.92

can be fairly well identified. Thus, textile-impressed vessels have either been finished by impressions with a textile-wrapped paddle or by direct application of a textile to the vessel walls. In the first case, the paddel seems to have been about 3 cm. long and 1.5 cm. wide. The width of a single element within the textile does not exceed 1.5 mm., with approximately ten fibers per square centimeter. In the case of direct textile application, the mesh and cord size was somewhat larger with less than eight fibers per square centimeter, each fiber being about 2 mm. thick. Impressions of this kind are somewhat deeper, and have been applied while the clay was still soft so that subsequent handling of the vessel obscured many individual impressions. The textile-wrapped paddle impressions, on the other hand, tend to have been obscured by overlap. The textile in both instances is loosely woven, with over and under weave at right angles. Similar observations have been made on the Valley Sweets ceramics, Saginaw County (Brose, 1966).

Cord-marking was produced with cords of 1.5-3 mm. diameter, the impressions of which if not obscured by subsequent smoothing are from 0.5 to 1.5 mm. deep. Among this group, cord-wrapped paddle impressions are recognizable by more parallel core impressions, a higher density of cords per cm. (4-5), and by clearly distinguishable individual cord impressions. Single cord impressions have been smoothed over in general, the individual cords are thicker (~3 mm.), and the density of impressions per square centimeter is lower (2-3). As at the Valley Sweets site, the cords have been manufactured from thin bast fibers (less than 0.1 mm. in diameter).

Cord-wrapped stick impressions were obtained by wrapping thin cords (1 mm. or less in diameter) tightly around a thin fish bone. Up to 12 cords per centimeter were counted, although 7 cords per square centimeter was the mode. It was impossible to determine the exact dimensions of this tool since the individual stick impressions were overlapping.

In terms of decorating motifs, the Butterfield potters were rather uninventive. Except for the lip, decoration was restricted to linear tool impressions and fingernail impressions, usually vertical to the lip, and grouped horizontally around the rim. Four of the vessels are undecorated. Fingernail impressions on the rims were obtained by impressing the thumbnail at an angle oblique to the rim and withdrawing it perpendicular to it, thus producing a crescent-shaped impression. If on the lip, the nail was withdrawn the same way it was impressed, so that something like an incision resulted. Flint blades were most likely responsible for the tool impressions. For deep punctates and rectangular notches, a breakage plane was pressed into the plastic clay, while linear features were obtained by using the blade of the same tool. If cord-wrapped sticks were utilized for decoration, their impressions were characterized by an extreme density of cords per centimeter, in some cases exceeding twelve. Only occasionally do we find punctates produced with broken bird bones; they seem to have been added only as an afterthought.

Little variation is exhibited by the metrical features of the assemblage. Only for the rim diameter could any clustering by classes be observed (see below). The thickness of body sherds stayed within a range from 0.3 to 1.3 cm. with a clear cluster at 0.75 thickness (one sigma standard deviation = .191 cm., N = 1224).

Microvessels show a larger variability and display more inventiveness on the part of the potter. Thus, we find a few vessels with plain surface finish, punctates of various sorts and even dentate stamping. The appearance of these sherds lends itself to two possible hypotheses: (1) these microvessels were the personal belongings of children who were free to let their fancy play on them; or (2) they were the personal treasure of the potters themselves, not used for vegetable or meat storage, nor for cooking. The workmanship on these vessels is as careless as that on the large pots in assemblage, although the tempering material seems to have been more carefully prepared for the small vessels, the mean grain size not exceeding 1 mm. in diameter. The "microrim fragments" of these sherds are shown in Plate XVII, *c-j*.

On the basis of their attribute clusters, fifteen of the large vessels were assigned to already established pottery types: Wayne

PLATE XIII

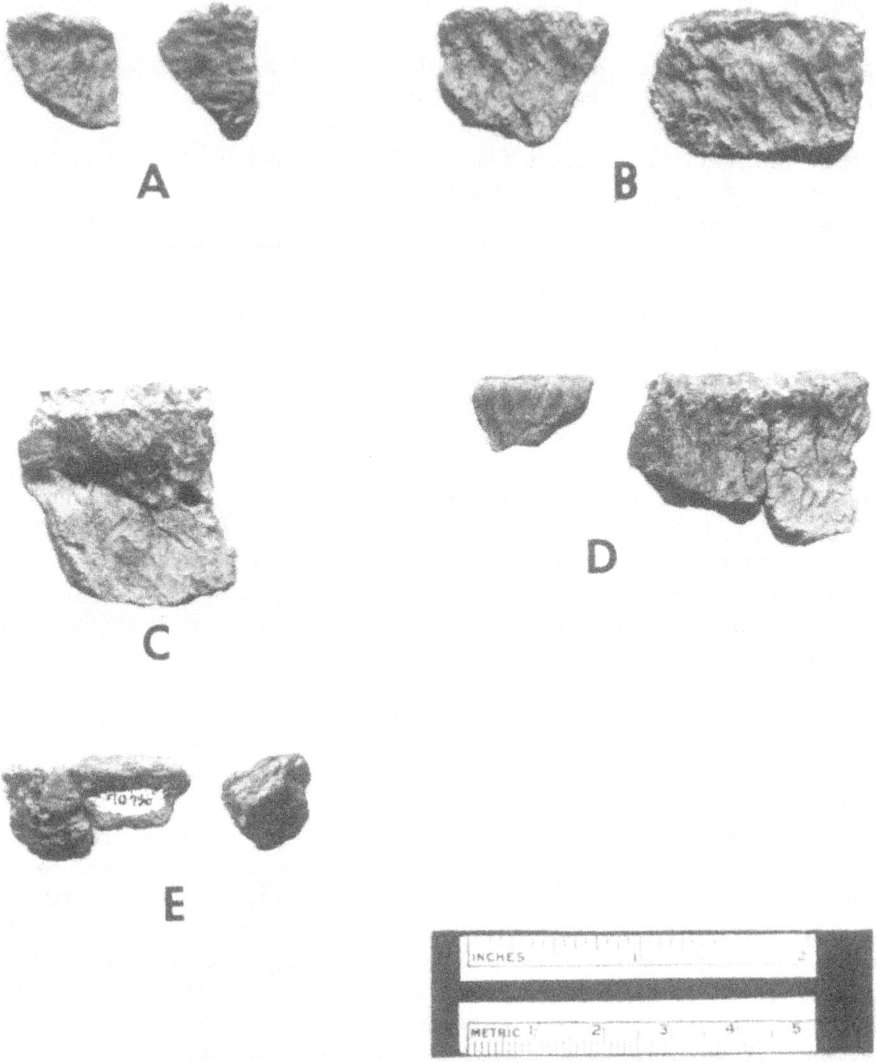

Wayne Cord-marked ceramics: Wayne Cord-marked Variant I.

and Mackinac ware. Wayne Cord-marked (Fitting, 1965) is represented by its variants Nos. 1 and 2 (Fitting, this volume). The five vessels of the variant No. 1 in the Butterfield ceramic assemblage are of small size (rim diameter 12 cm.). Their rims thicken outward toward the lip with a thickness differential of 0.2-0.3 mm. between body and lip thickness. The interior rim is slightly excurvate at the lip, and the body is out-curving. The lips are slightly outward-sloping. The surface finish was obtained by vertical cord-marking with a cord-wrapped paddle on the exterior, with approximately four parallel cord impressions to the centimeter. This cord-marking is unobscured by subsequent smoothing over, and with individual cords still clearly recognizable it reaches directly up to the lip juncture. The interior rim surface is unfinished. All five vessels show lip decoration (Plate XIII, *a-e*). In two cases (Plate XIII, *a, b*) the lip has been notched by tool impressions (XIII, *a*) or fingernail impressions (XIII, *b*) at a 75 degree angle to the vessel wall. Notching is replaced by cord-wrapped stick impressions of the same direction in two other vessels (Plate XIII, *c, d*). In one of these (XIII, *d*), the impressions are crosscut in the middle of the lip by a single line of continuous cord-wrapped stick impressions produced by a different cord-wrapped stick. The lip surface of the fifth vessel (Plate XIII, *e*) finally shows two parallel lines of single cord impressions (0.15 cm. deep and wide) parallel to the vessel walls. None of these vessels show any decoration on the exterior rim or lip. In one instance only, the interior lip has been decorated by short vertical cord-wrapped stick impressions (XIII, *e*), while the rim interior shows the same design in three cases (Plate XIII, *c-e*).

Three of the vessels (Plate XIV, *c-e*) were identified as Variant No. 2 of the Wayne Cord-marked ware (Fitting, this volume). They are the smallest vessels in the assemblage, aside from the microvessels, their rim diameter ranging from 7.5 to 9 cm. In profile their rims become thinner toward the lip, where they turn slightly inward. The body, as far as can be deduced from the fragments, seems to be straight or incurving--the thickness being around 0.5 cm. As with Variant No. 1, the surface finish consists of vertical cord-marking extending right up to the lip, which is rounded. Neither the rims nor the lips show any kind of decoration.

Since both the number of cords per centimeter on the surface finish and the thickness of the body sherds form a continuous range, it was impossible to assign any body sherds to these types. In addition, even the general correlation of cord-marked rims to

PLATE XIV

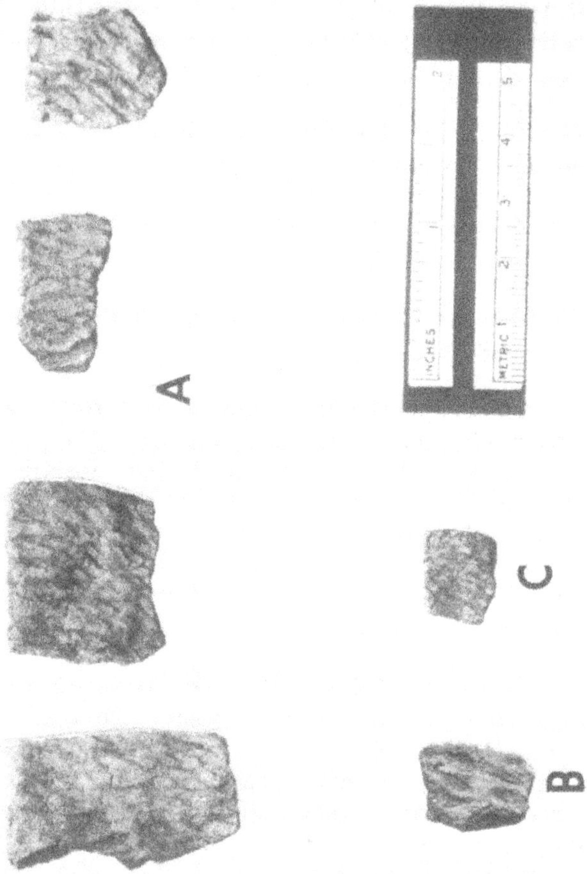

Wayne Cord-marked ceramics: Wayne Cord-marked Variant II.

cord-marked body sherds cannot be established, since the cord-marked rims are not restricted to the Wayne Cord-marked sherds on the site but have also representatives among the Mackinac ware. A single body sherd in this category reaching up into the rim would have been sufficient to correlate the body sherd cord-marked category to the various rims. But apparently neck sherds, as shown by their general scarcity in the sample, are of extremely sensitive structure and did not offer much resistance to the soil's destructive forces.

Although Wayne ware was originally defined in southeastern Michigan, its occurrence on the Butterfield site is not surprising. It seems to be part of an Early Late Woodland ceramic style of wide distribution throughout the southern Lower Peninsula of Michigan. The Butterfield site marks its northernmost representation at a village site along the Lake Huron shore. Further to the north it is only known from spot occurrences, such as at the West Twin Lake burial (Hinsdale, 1930). Fred Dustin (1932) reported a single sherd of Wayne Cord-marked and some Wayne-smoothed sherds (Plate I, *a-b*) from the Butterfield site ceramics which most closely approach those of the Valley Sweets site, in Saginaw County where 47 per cent of the statistically small assemblage fell into this category (Brose, 1966).

The body sherd assemblage has several negative aspects. Thus, despite several weeks of trial and error it was impossible to fit any two sherds together besides those which had disintegrated during or after excavation. Since the sherds are very small, decoration on them is practically absent and physical and metrical features vary within an extremely small range; it proved to be impossible to assign any body sherd with certainty to a given rim. Only categories of sherds could be correlated with categories of rims. Even among these categories, for example the plain body sherds (21.9 per cent of the sample), lack any representation among the rims.

Rim Sherds

The 58 rim sherds in the sample were assigned to a minimum number of 24 vessels. None of these are reconstructable and the information we have does not extend below the necks of the vessels. On the basis of rim diameter, the sample was divided into 2 groups of vessels: those above 7 cm. in diameter, and microvessels of less than 7 cm. in diameter at the rim. Only the 17 large vessels were of help in the classification of the assemblage, because the microvessels were represented only

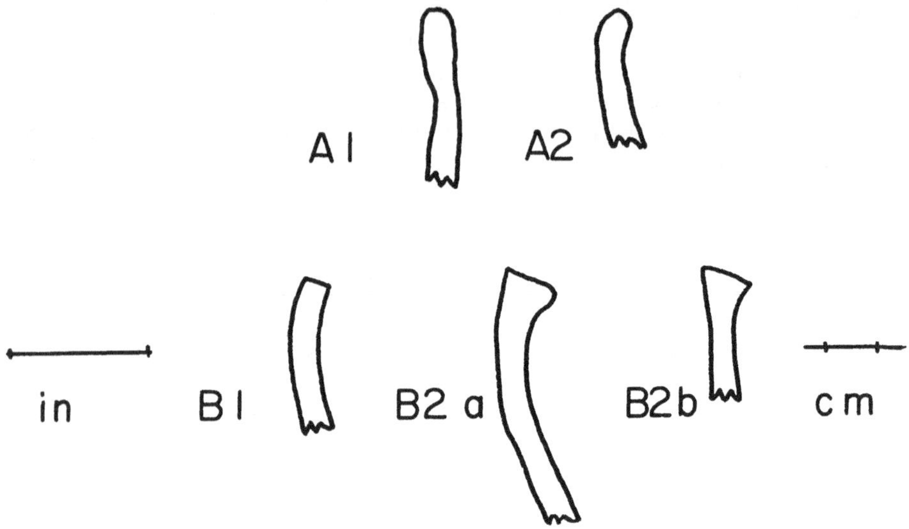

FIG. 3. Rim profiles.

by micro sherds, which rendered them useless in terms of descriptive features.

The large vessels form a homogeneous assemblage. Two main types of rim profile were noted: those with rounded lips (type A) and those with square lips (type B) (Figure 3). Several subtypes were recognized: group A1 rims thin just below the lip, the interior being slightly incurvate and thickening inward (N=5, 29 per cent, Figure 3; Plate XIII, *a-c*; XVI, *b*, *c*); while group A2 has parallel rim walls and thickens outward from the rim at the lip (N=1, 5.8 per cent, Figure 3; Plate XVI, *a*); the Ogemaw County earthworks (Plate I, *c*). The general sloppiness in pottery temper and manufacture displayed by the sample from the Butterfield site, as well as the absence of any decorating inventiveness, might be a function of the position of the site on the northern margins of the distribution of this ceramic type. Further to the south, the closest site where it is of importance to the ceramic assemblage is the Valley Sweets site (Brose 1966) in Saginaw County, and to the west it forms the dominant vessel type at several sites in the Muskegon River valley (Fitting, this volume). Its occurrence on the Butterfield site together with Mackinac ware is the first recorded instance of hybridization between the two styles and should be of importance in evaluating the chronological position of the site and its importance in terms of the Carolinian-Canadian edge area.

Mackinac ware is found on the site contemporaneous with Wayne ware in its 2 variants: Mackinac Undercorated and Mackinac Punctate (McPherron, 1967). The former is represented by 4 vessels (Plate XV, *a-d*). They are of medium size (rim diameter 10 to 14 cm.) and are characterized by a thickened rim at the lip, curving outward; the thickening has been produced by folding the lip over toward the outside, or by simply depressing it by tool notches while still in a soft state. The lip is flat, square (Type B2*a*), and sloping outward, In one case (Plate XV, *c*), the lip is slightly undulating. The exterior surface has been directly impressed with a fairly large mesh textile (cf. above). These impressions extend right up to the lip. Only in one vessel have the impressions been effectively smoothed over (XV, *d*), whereas they are clearly distinguishable in the other three. The exterior has not been decorated at all. Lip decoration, when present, consists of notching by a sharp-edged blade breakage plane (XV, *a*, *c*) at an oblique angle to the vessel walls. The interior of the vessel rims has been impressed on two vessels by vertical fingernail impressions (XV, *a*, *b*), and on a third (XV, *c*) by tool impressions. Vessels similar to the ones described here are shown in McPherron, 1967 (Plate XI, *c-d* of our III, *a* and Plate X, *a* of our III, *d*).

Mackinac Punctate is represented on the Butterfield site by three rather homogeneous vessels (Plate XVI, *a-c*) of large size (rim diameter about 18 to 20 cm.). In profile, their rim is characterized by a rounding and the walls are parallel, either of Type A1 or A2 (A1—XVI, *b*, *c;* A2--XVI, *a*). The body, as far as can be deduced from the fragments, curves out strongly from the rim. The surface has been finished by cord-marking which subsequently has been smoothed over. This surface finish extends up to the lip. The lip was decorated on the surface by thin notches perpendicular to the rim, but the lip exterior and interior carry the same decoration at a slight angle to the vessel wall, perpendicular to the impressions on the other side. The rim exterior has been punctated deeply with a bladelet breakage plane, with individual vertical punctates about 7 cm. long, aligned horizontally along the wall with relatively small interstices (~0.7 cm.). The same punctates, usually produced by the same tool, are found on the interior rim surface. Similar, although more elaborately decorated vessels are illustrated in McPherron, 1967 (Plate XI, *b*, *e-h;* Plate XII).

The major difference between the Juntunen site Mackinac ware and that found at the Butterfield site seems to be the sloppy manufacture of the Butterfield ceramics. Again I would attribute the

PLATE XV

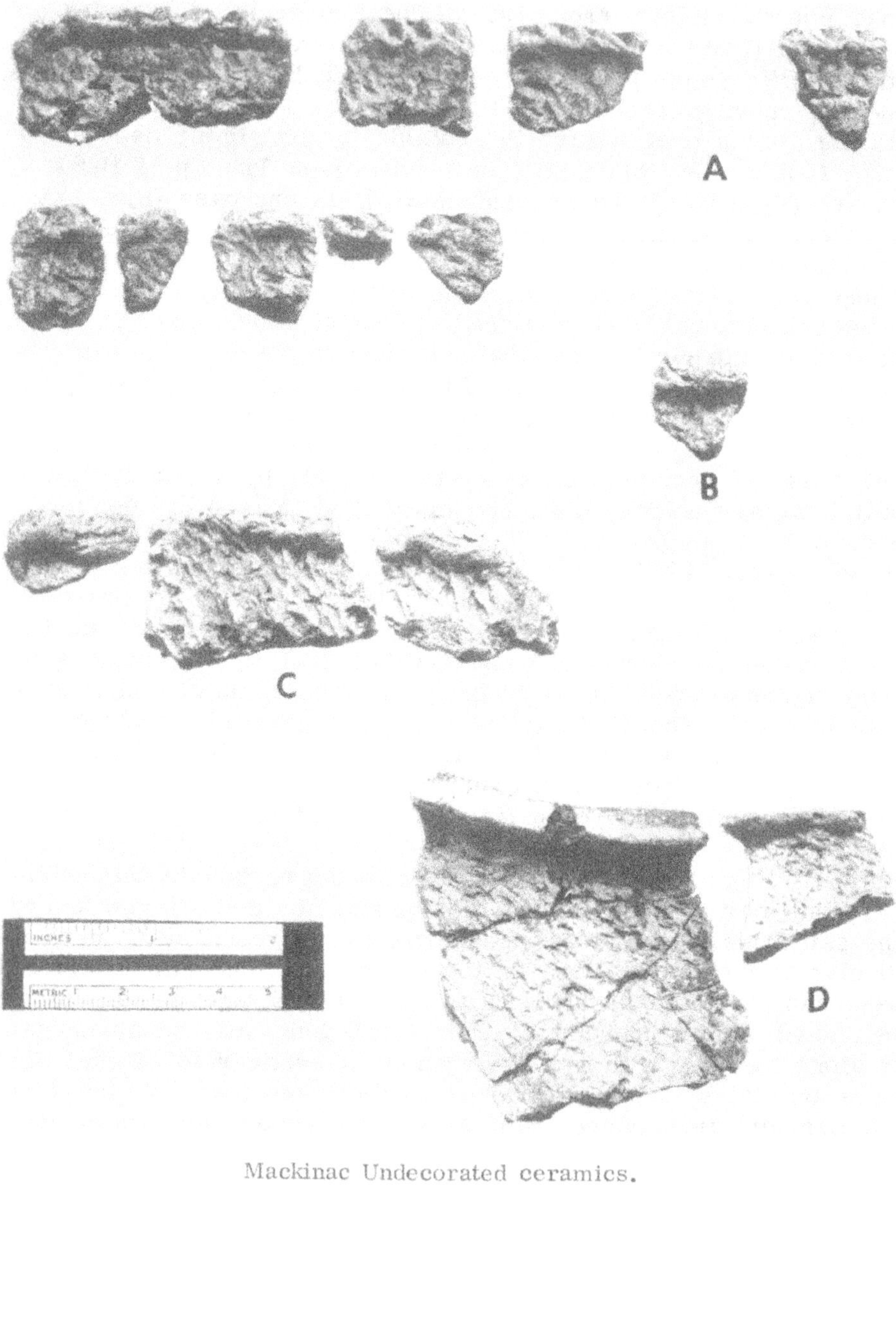

Mackinac Undecorated ceramics.

PLATE XVI

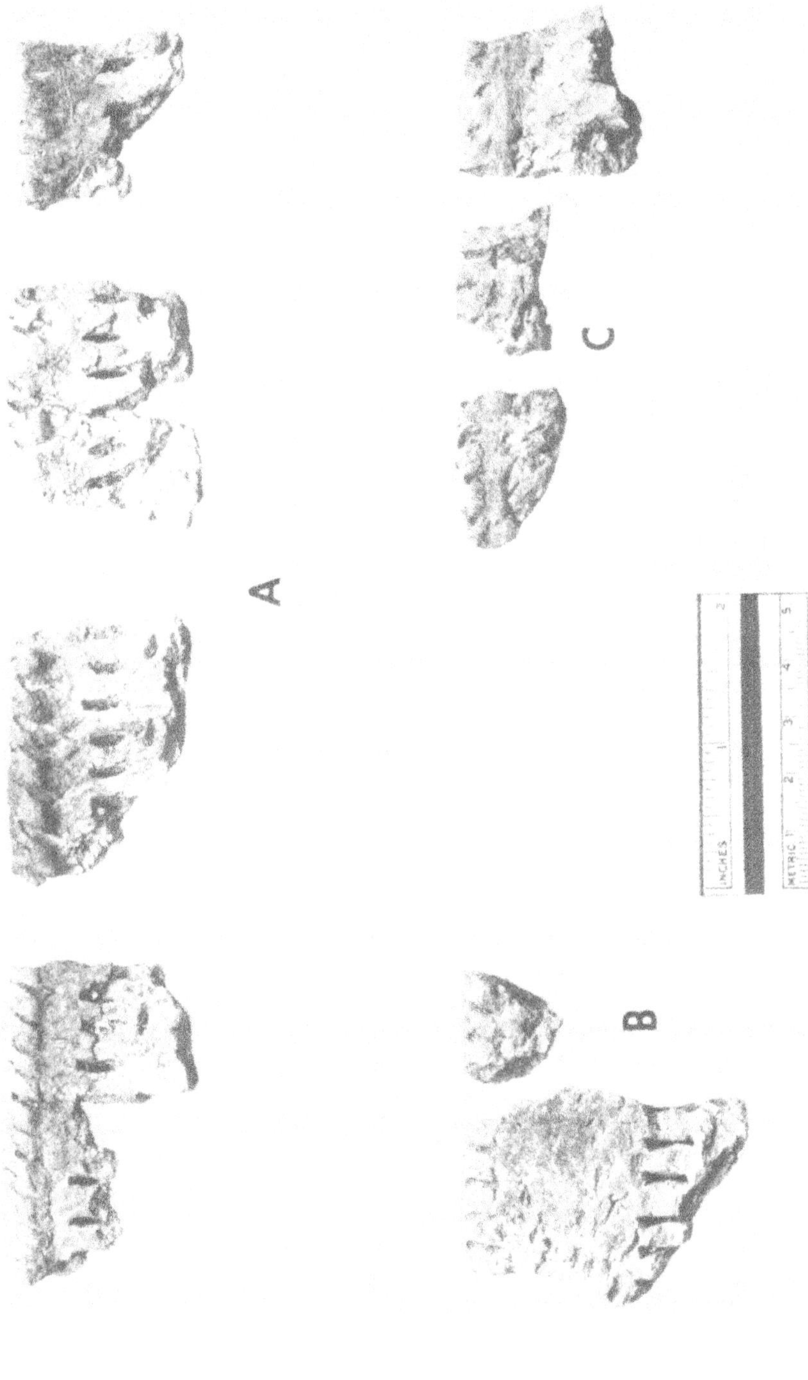

Mackinac Punctate ceramics.

lack of decorative talents on our site to the marginal position of the Butterfield site in terms of this ceramic style. The southernmost occurrence of this pottery type recorded so far, and the one closest to the Butterfield site, is Skegemog Point in the Grand Traverse Bay area, still far away from our site. From the Juntunen site to the west and north, it is the dominant ceramic type at many sites of the same time horizon. It is obvious from its occurrence on the Butterfield site that further research along the Lake Huron shore should produce intermittent sites between Juntunen and Butterfield. The discovery of Wayne and Mackinac ware on the same site and in the same stratigraphic horizon proves what was already expected on the basis of radio-carbon dates and stylistics, namely that the two are contemporaneous and local aspects of the same fairly wide distribution of early Late Woodland ware. The co-occurrence of these regional types on the same site will help us to evaluate the Butterfield site in its culture and geographical context.

Two vessels could not be attributed to any published ceramic type in Michigan. Since these vessels are represented only by one rim sherd each (Plate XVII, *a-b*), it does not seem rewarding to establish a new type on the basis of this sample. The vessels are of small size (rim diameter 10 cm.). In profile, their lips are flat to subrounded and angular at the interior and exterior rim-lip juncture. The rims thicken slightly toward the exterior at the lip, and curve outward from the vessel center. The bodies appear to be outcurving; no information is available on the base. What sets these vessels apart from the other thirteen pots is their castellated rim. The surface was finished by cord-wrappe paddle or cord-wrapped stick impressions reaching up to the rim. The size of the individual cords is much larger than in the case of the Wayne Cord-marked sherds and the individual impressions have usually been obscured by subsequent overlap. The decoration at the lip surface consists of tool impressions or cord-wrapped stick impressions (thin, tightly wrapped) at 90 degree angles to the outside of the vessels, while the interior has been decorated, in one case (Plate XVII, *b*), by a row of vertical punctates produced by tool impressions. The same vessel reveals long parallel cord-wrapped stick impressions at a 60 degree angle to the lip on the exterior rim. The metrical features (lip thickness 0.7, body 0.5, rim diameter 10 cm.) of these vessels, as well as their rim profile, surface finish, and decorative motifs fall well within the range of Wayne Cord-marked ware, but uniformly castellated rims are absent in vessels of this type.

PLATE XVII

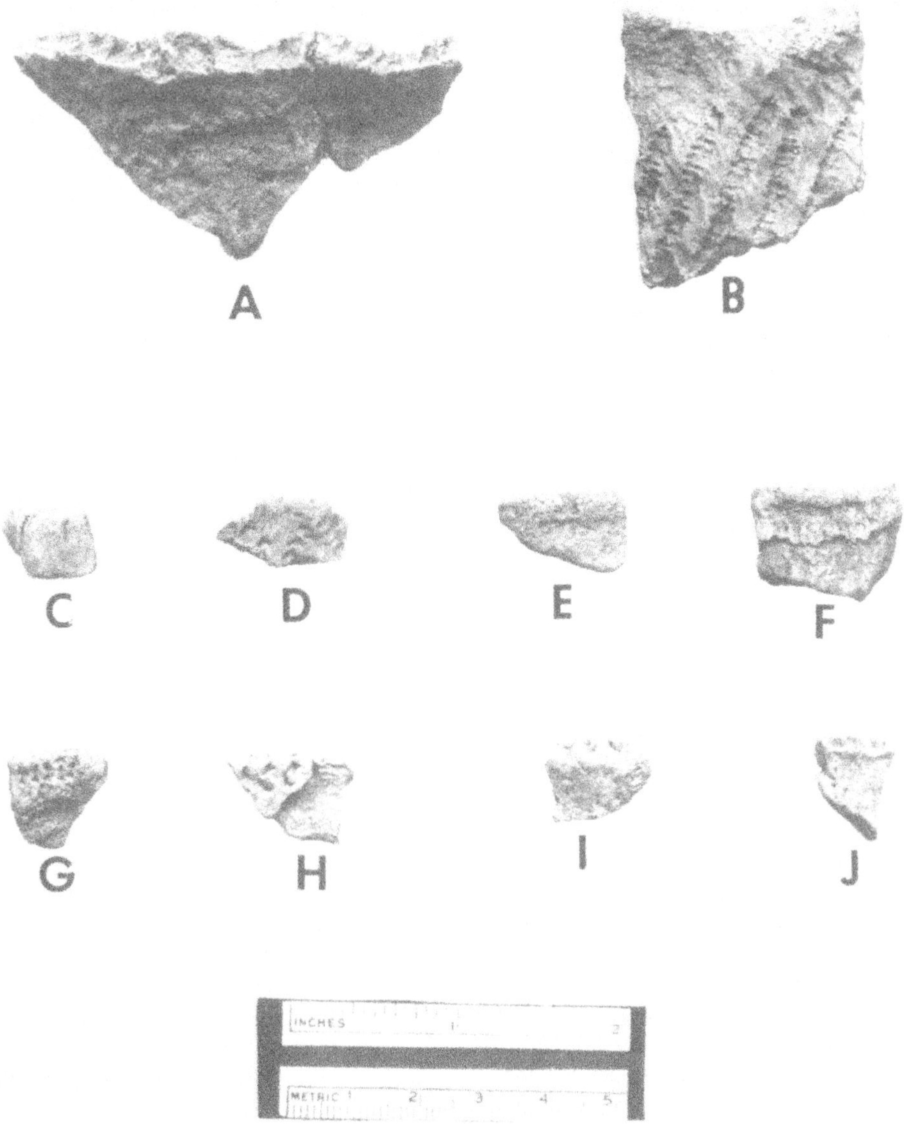

Miscellaneous rim sherds: *a*, *b*, castellated rim sherds (untyped); *c–j*, mini vessels.

The absence of plain body sherds and implications of their absence have been discussed above. On the basis of the four or possibly five ceramic styles represented in the rim sherd assemblage, we might attribute the textile-impressed and textile-impressed smoothed body sherds to Mackinac Undecorated type. The cord-marked sherds can be correlated with Wayne Cord-marked variants, while the cord-marked smoothed sherds can be attributed to the Mackinac Punctate vessels. Lack of percentage consistency between body and rim sherds of a given type indicate that this is only a rough estimate and not one to use correlation. In the case of the textile-impressed body sherds, this might be due to two factors: *a*) both Wayne ware and Mackinac Undecorated were represented on the site by their textile-impressed variants but did not show up in the rim assemblage of our sample due to sampling error, and *b*) the Mackinac Undecorated vessels, because they are larger, are represented in the body sherd assemblage as out of proportion to their actual number. The presence of textile-impressed and cord-marked surface finish on the same ware indicates that not much discrimination was employed between the two kinds of surface finish; this is further substantiated by their similar appearance.

Summary and Conclusion

The Butterfield ceramic assemblage is derived from a stratigraphically well-defined, single-component horizon. Its most striking feature is the co-occurrence of the two ceramic wares: Wayne ware and Mackinac ware. Despite this dichotomy the sample is internally consistent in terms of physical characteristics, metrical features, and decorative attributes--indicating that the vessels were manufactured by local potters and did not represent imported trade goods.

The mere fact of co-occurrence suggests that the Butterfield site was located in the transitional area between the two ceramic styles. This is further substantiated by the site-specific features of the vessels compared to those from the type sites. Thus, Wayne ware pots are, in general, smaller than those reported from Fort Wayne Mound (Halsey, this volume), southeastern Michigan (Fitting, 1965), and western Michigan (Fitting, this volume). On the Butterfield site the vessels show a more sloppy manufacture than do those to the south, and they are more homogeneous. Vessels of Mackinac type are characterized by the same features: less pride in workmanship (sloppy surface finish, little experimenting with decoration) and little attribute variation from vessel to vessel.

While Wayne ware is known from spot occurrences to the north of our site, Mackinac ware is unknown south of it, the closest site yielding this ceramic type being some hundred miles to the north, although further research along the shore of the north of Butterfield should yield additional sites. The distribution of the regional ceramic types in the Lower Peninsula suggests that the Carolinian-Canadian edge constituted an *area*, rather than a linear boundary. Thus cultural hybridization and overlap are to be expected, and diffusion in both directions seems likely. Possibly the transition area eventually can be defined as a separate cultural entity, once more sites have been scientifically evaluated.

The co-occurrence of the two wares on the Butterfield site allows us: *a*) to tie the Early Late Woodland horizon of the Butterfield site to the Michigan chronological sequence, and *b*) to establish the contemporaneity of Mackinac and Wayne wares stratigraphically. Wayne ware has been dated at the Spring Creek site (Fitting, this volume), at West Twin Lake Mound, at Riviere au Vase and at the Fort Wayne Mound (Halsey, this volume); the dates range from 700 to 950 A.D. Mackinac ware carries radiocarbon dates of the same range (McPerron, 1967). Heins Creek ware, the Wisconsin equivalent, is dated at around 700 A.D. (Mason, 1966). Thus, the Early Late Woodland horizon at the Butterfield site ought to be safely assigned to the time period from 700-900 A.D.

V

OTHER ARTIFACTS

Ground Stone

Only four pieces of ground stone turned up during our excavations, all of them ill-defined in terms of their function. Only one of these was found *in situ* in the Late Woodland horizon (Plate XVIII, *d*) while the others stem from the plow-disturbed zone. The first of these, of impure greenish slate, appears to be a gorget that broke after its surfaces had been superficially smoothed (Plate XVIII, *c*). A rectangular slab of quartzy-red sandstone with rounded edges shows heavy battering marks on both surfaces (Plate XVIII, *a*). Since it lacks any sign of battering along the edges it cannot have served as a hammer for chipping, so its function remains uncertain. The remaining two items in this category of artifacts are pieces of ground slate, of bluish color, that were tentatively identified as slate knives (Plate XVIII *b*, *d*), although this cannot be proved since it is impossible to tell use striae from grinding striae on the supposed cutting edge. The metrical data are given below:

Horizon	Stone	UMMA No.	Length	Width	Thick-ness	Plate No.
Plow zone. .	Gorget fragment	70792	(4.9)	(3.5)	1.1	XVII, *c*
Plow zone. .	Battered tool	70789	5.0	3.5	1.5	XVII, *a*
Plow zone. .	Slate knife	70791	6.7	2.3	0.55	XVII, *b*
Late Woodland .	Slate knife	70790	5.2	3.2	0.5	XVII, *d*

The lack of ground stone artifacts from the excavation units of the site is surprising, since Walter Schmidt's surface collections from the general site area contain several large hammers, adzes, celts and gorgets. Even a birdstone was discovered (Schmidt, 1962), and several local amateurs claim to possess adzes from the area. Hopefully further excavations in this region of the state can establish a stratigraphical and chronological sequence, into which these surface collections can be placed.

PLATE XVIII

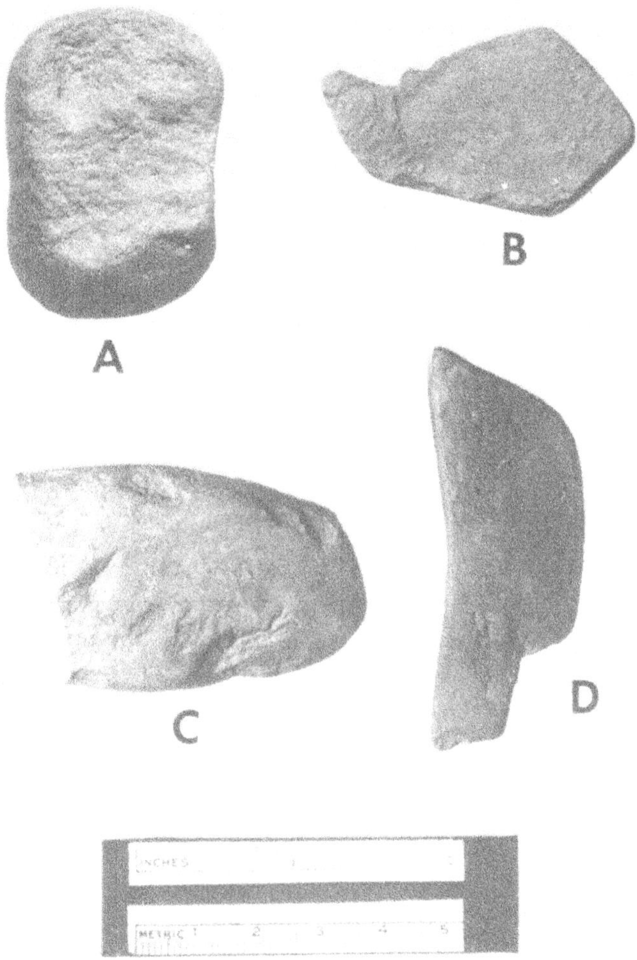

Ground-stone artifacts: *a*, hammer; *c*, broken unfinished gorget; *b*, *d*, slate knives?

Fire-cracked Rocks

Considering the small size of the excavated area, 77,111 fire-cracked rocks weighing a total of more than 1200 lbs. seems to be an extremely high number. The rock material consists mainly of coarse-grained diorite, granite, and sandstone transported to the area from nearby riverbeds or from the lake shore. During use, the heat of the fire caused it to spall. Table 36 shows the vertical distribution of the sample. The low number of fire-cracked rocks in the Late Woodland horizon seems to be an indication that stone boiling was not as extensively employed during this period of occupation. No significant differences were noted in the material utilized between the two assemblages. In both cases the fire-cracked rocks indicate that occupation of the site was dense, intense, and repetitive, as inferred from the small mean size of the rocks. Unfortunately, fire-cracked rocks have received little attention as artifacts and ecological keys in literature.

TABLE 36

DISTRIBUTION OF FIRE-CRACKED ROCKS

Horizon	N	Weight	Percentage N	Percentage Wt.
Plow zone.	35,349	559.7	45.4	43.2
Late Woodland	12,894	242.8	18.1	18.7
Terminal Archaic. . .	28,868	491.8	36.5	38.1
Total	77,111	1295.2	100.0	100.0

Historic Material

The plow zone yielded a total of 41 historic items, consisting of squared and round nails, corrugated metal, glass, a round musket ball, and a leather strap and rivet. None of this material is of chronological significance beyond suggesting a provenience around the turn of the century (Brose, personal communication). Walter Schmidt suggested an Indian trading post might have been in the general site area, and many local residents are proud of their historic pipe bowls and stems from the area. The excavation did not yield anything in support of such an early trading post and a thorough analysis of the literature in the Michigan Historical Collections and the Clements Memorial Library failed to turn up supporting evidence. The main trading activity in the area took place in Saginaw and possibly at the Indian Mission on the Kawkawlin River. The historic artifacts on the site stem either from these sources or from bartering that took place with early settlers in Pinconning after 1860.

Faunal Remains

The faunal remains from the site were sorted by the author and identified as to species, whenever possible, by Randy Rosenblatz. Seven hundred fourteen and six tenths grams of animal bone were recovered from the site consisting of 2354 bone fragments. This means that the mean weight per bone fragment is less than 1/3 of a gram. Only three individuals of *Odocoileus virginianus* (whitetailed deer) could be singled out in the assemblage, two of these in Late Woodland context, the other one in the Terminal Archaic horizon. In addition, the Terminal Archaic horizon yielded a carnivore tooth. Beaver, although frequent in the plow disturbed zone was not recognized among the bones from the stratified horizons.

The remainder of the sample was sorted out by the author into reptile, fish, and mammal bone (Table 37). No bird or reptile bone could be singled out, and the fish bone made up only 1.02 per cent of the total bone fragments. It is interesting to note, however, that fish bone is virtually absent in the Late Woodland horizon while it constitutes 2.44 per cent of the Terminal Archaic faunal remains. Also, it should be pointed out that calcined bone constitutes 31.5 per cent of the Late Woodland unidentified bone, and amounts to 91.1 per cent in the Terminal Archaic assemblage. Mollusk remains are entirely absent from the site.

This sample, of course, does not provide much insight into the ecology of the people who occupied the site. The reasons for the poor condition of the faunal remains from the site are twofold: strong rodent activity, and high soil pH. Nevertheless, we

TABLE 37

VERTICAL DISTRIBUTION OF UNIDENTIFIED FAUNAL MATERIAL

Horizon	Number of Bone Fragments	Weight	Mean Weight	Fish Bone No.	Per Cent	Calcined Bone No.	Per Cent
Late Woodland....	1372	444.8	0.32	1	0.07	432	31.41
Terminal Archaic..	982	269.8	0.27	23	2.44	898	91.14
Total	2354	714.6	0.30	24	1.02	1330	56.92

can infer that hunting formed one of the occupations of the inhabitants, and that fishing was practiced to any extent only by the Terminal Archaic occupants of the site. This is astonishing if the proximity of the Pinconning River is taken into account. The absence of fish remains from the site during this period might imply that people had more readily available food sources such as hunting, collecting, and agriculture. Fitting (this volume) comes to the same conclusion about the Spring Creek site, where fish bone is absent and hunting was limited to a few select species of the regional fauna.

Plant Remains

Plant remains survived postdepositional decay only if they had been charred. This means that our sample is limited to charred wood, seeds and nuts. The following procedure of analysis was employed: all undisturbed provenience units were sorted for remains of charred nuts, seeds, and fruit. The result was negative. Walnuts and acorn seeds were only present in plow disturbed horizons, a statement which does not help us since they might have been deposited there by natural agencies. The charcoal from the features was sorted by the author into types with the help of a high power microscope. Fel Brunett of the Ethnobotany Division of the Museum of Anthropology undertook the laborious task of identifying these types as to species (Table 38).

A quick look at this table should convince the reader that: *a*) a large variety of wood was utilized by the occupants of the Butterfield site, and *b*) there is no recognizable difference between the wood utilized by the Late Woodland and Terminal Archaic occupants. We can also deduce from the observed species that during both occupations a mixed deciduous forest was close to the site that could yield such a variety of species. The mere presence of these species on the site in the charcoal remains suggests that the occupants did not burn over the forest before they inhabited the site, otherwise the number of species would have to be restricted. Any additional hypotheses on the sample should be avoided, since the observed distribution is subject to sampling error and might bear no direct correlation with the immediate environment at the site (Fel Brunett, personal communication).

TABLE 38

Species	Feature Number																		No.
	1	2	3	4	5	6	7	10	13	14	15	16	18	19	24	25	27	28	
Acer sp.												X		X					2
Betula sp.												X							1
Carya sp.	X	X			X		X		X	X		X	X	X	X	X	X		12
Carya lacimiosa		X				X			X										3
C. ovata	X					X	X			X		X	X						6
Celtis occidentalis						X			X		X								3
Fagus grandifolia											X								1
Fraxinus alba														X					1
F. americana						X		X											2
Juglans nigra										X				X					2
Ostrya virginiana										X		X							2
Picea sp.	X	X	X	X	X	X	X	X	X	X		X					X	X	13
Pinus strobus	X	X	X	X	X	X	X		X	X	X	X	X	X	X			X	15
Populus hemuloides	X	X																	2
Quercus alba	X						X		X	X	X	X	X		X				8
Q. bicolor	X								X		X	X		X	X				6
Q. rubra	X	X				X				X		X		X					6
Ulmus americanus											X								1
Platinus occidentalis	X	X	X	X		X	X			X		X							8
Number of Species	9	7	3	3	3	8	6	2	7	9	6	11	4	7	4	1	2	2	

Summary and Conclusions

Four hundred and fifty square feet of excavated area, spread out over a site that follows the sand ridge for at least a mile, is certainly not a sufficient sample from which to derive general conclusions about the cultural sequence in the Northeastern Carolinian-Canadian transition area. Nevertheless, a few hypotheses can be supported by our small sample

Part of these are based on the horizontal distribution of the sample. During the Terminal Archaic occupation on the site, the intensity of occupation judged in terms of feature density of cultural material increased successively, and reached its peak in the period represented by the occupation floor in and on the paleosoil (IIA_3). During the first Terminal Archaic occupation of level III the site was probably only a few feet above the lake shore. The density of cultural material indicates that this was not sufficient to attract more than occasional visits to the site. In addition, the surrounding area must have consisted largely of barren sand ridges or lake bottom sediments covered with pioneer plants. Slowly a climax forest began to develop on the higher sand ridges, and a swamp and marsh environment developed in the lowlands around the site from the continuing recession of the shore line. This environment must have been ideal for a Terminal Archaic economy, permitting fishing, hunting, and gathering. It was at this time that most of the Terminal Archaic assemblage was deposited on the site (within and on top of IIA_1). The archaeological assemblage indicates that large game was killed and skinned in the surrounding areas and brought back to the site. The flint tool assemblage suggests preoccupation with large game hunting, although ecological data indicate that fishing constituted part of the food of the population. The tool kit, consisting of projectile points of good workmanship, heavy knives, and backed blades, typologically and functionally is similar to contemporaneous assemblages to the north and south of the site. Thus, no ecological boundary should have existed during this time. In other words, the edge did not form a barrier for the penetration of the Terminal Archaic culture northwards along the shore and into the Central Plains.

Following the peak of the Terminal Archaic occupation the still receding shoreline must have decreased the appeal of the area for occupation, possibly due to a drying up of swamps and marshes surrounding the site. In addition, Early Woodland culture began to make inroads into the Saginaw Valley. The marginal areas such as the lake shore and the Central Plains were unable to support agriculture at this early stage of development. Gradually the area around the site, and to the north, was deserted by its inhabitants, and Saginaw became the focus of an agricultural Woodland people. This explains our occupational hiatus at the end of the Terminal Archaic occupation.

The edge continued to act as a barrier against northward population expansion until the early Late Woodland period when either a more developed agriculture or population pressure in the Saginaw Valley led to renewed occupation of the area. During this period we find the site extensively occupied. Although direct ecological evidence is absent from the site, the stone tool assemblage consisting of scrapers, light blades, and thin knives suggests at least that vegetable food formed the basis of the local economy. Fishing was not required to supplement the diet. At this time the function of the edge must have changed from population boundary to cultural boundary as evidenced by the overlap of northern and southern pottery types on the site. It is not clear at the present time which ecological factors controlled this cultural boundary.

To summarize, the archaeological record of the Butterfield site suggests that during the Terminal Archaic times the edge did not form a barrier to northward population expansion as long as ideal conditions for a hunting, fishing, and gathering economy existed along the lake shore and around inland lakes. The diffusion of agriculture into the Saginaw Valley did not continue northward because preconditions for an Early Woodland adaptation did not exist in the Central Plains and along the lake shore. Finally, in Late Woodland times the area became the core of transition between northern and southern cultural styles, for as of yet unknown ecological reasons.

REFERENCES

Binford, Lewis R., and Sally R. Binford

1966 A Preliminary Analysis of Functional Variability in the Mousterian of Levallois Facies. American Anthropologist, Vol. 68, No. 2, Pt. 2, pp. 238-95. Menasha.

Binford, Lewis R., and Mark L. Papworth

1963 The Eastport Site, Antrim County, Michigan. *In:* Miscellaneous Studies in Typology and Classification, University of Michigan, Museum of Anthropology, Anthropological Papers No. 19, pp. 71-123. Ann Arbor.

Brose, David S.

1966 The Valley Sweets Site, 20 SA 24, Saginaw County, Michigan. The Michigan Archaeologist, Vol. 12, No. 1, pp. 1-21. Ann Arbor.

Dustin, Fred

1932 Indian Earthworks in Ogemaw County, Michigan. Cranbrook Institute of Science, Scientific Publication No. 1. Bloomfield Hills.

Fitting, James E.

1965 Late Woodland Cultures in Southeastern Michigan. University of Michigan Museum of Anthropology, Anthropological Papers No. 24. Ann Arbor.

n.d. Lithic Industries of the Schultz Site. Ms. on file at the University of Michigan Museum of Anthropology. Ann Arbor.

Fitting, James E., Jerry de Visscher, and Edward J. Wahla

1966 The Paleo-Indian Occupation of the Holcombe Beach. University of Michigan Museum of Anthropology, Anthropological Papers No. 27. Ann Arbor.

Griffin, James B.

1961 Post-glacial Ecology and Culture Changes in the Great Lakes Area of North America. University of Michigan Institute of Science and Technology, Great Lakes Research Division, Publication No. 7, pp. 147-55. Ann Arbor.

1966 Late Quaternary Prehistory in the Northeastern Woodlands. *In:* The Quaternary of the United States, H. E. Wright and David G. Frey, eds., pp. 655-68. Princeton.

Harrison, Sidney

1966 The Schmidt Site (20 SA 192), Saginaw County, Michigan. The Michigan Archaeologist, Vol. 12, No. 2, pp. 49-70. Ann Arbor.

Hinsdale, Wilbert B.

1930 Reports of Archaeological Field Work in the Summer of 1928 in Montmorency, Newaygo, and Lake Counties, Michigan. Papers of the Michigan Academy of Science, Arts, and Letters, Vol. 12 (1929 Meeting), pp. 127-35. Ann Arbor.

Leverett, Frank, and F. B. Taylor
1915 Pleistocene of Indiana and Michigan and the History of the Great Lakes. U. S. G. S. Monograph 53. Washington, D.C.

McPherron, Alan L.
1967 The Juntunen Site and the Late Woodland Prehistory of the Upper Great Lakes Area. University of Michigan Museum of Anthropology, Anthropological Papers No. 30. Ann Arbor.

Mason, Ronald J.
1966 Two Stratified Sites on the Door Peninsula. *Ibid.*, No. 26. Ann Arbor.

Ritchie, William A.
1961 A Typology and Nomenclature for New York Projectile Points. New York State Museum and Science Service Bulletin No. 384. Albany.

Schmidt, Walter L.
1962 Birdstones of the Saginaw Bay Area. The Michigan Archaeologist, Vol. 8, No. 1, pp. 63-69. Ann Arbor.

Wright, Gary A.
1966 Eastern Edge Survey: 1965 Season. *Ibid.*, Vol. 12, No. 4, pp. 151-68. Ann Arbor.

www.ingramcontent.com/pod-product-compliance
Lightning Source LLC
LaVergne TN
LVHW050020250826
846302LV00008B/36
* 9 7 8 1 9 4 9 0 9 8 1 5 0 *